Spreadsheet Modeling in Corporate Finance

To accompany *Financial Management Theory and Practice* by Brigham, Gapenski, and Ehrhardt
and *Intermediate Financial Management* by Brigham, Gapenski, and Daves

CRAIG W. HOLDEN
Richard G. Brinkman Faculty Fellow and Associate Professor
Kelley School of Business
Indiana University

Prentice Hall, Upper Saddle River, New Jersey 07458

To Kathryn, you're the inspiration,
and to Diana and Jimmy, with joy and pride.
Craig

Editor-in-Chief: PJ Boardman
Executive Editor: Mickey Cox
Managing Editor: Gladys Soto
Assistant Editor: Beth Romph
Media Project Manager: Torie Anderson
Manager, Print Production: Christy Mahon
Editorial Assistant: Kevin Hancock
Production Editors: Carol Zaino and Wanda Rockwell
Manufacturer: Von Hoffmann Graphics

ISBN 0-13-049905-6

10 9 8 7 6 5 4 3

CONTENTS

Preface

Preface

For nearly 20 years, since the emergence of PCs, Lotus 1-2-3, and Microsoft Excel in the 1980's, spreadsheet models have been the dominant vehicles for finance professionals in the business world to implement their financial knowledge. Yet even today, most Corporate Finance textbooks rely on calculators as the primary tool and have little (if any) coverage of how to build spreadsheet models. This book fills that gap. It teaches students how to build financial models in Excel. It provides step-by-step instructions so that students can build models themselves (active learning), rather than handing students canned "templates" (passive learning). It progresses from simple examples to practical, real-world applications. It spans nearly all quantitative models in corporate finance.

Why I Wrote This Book

My goal is simply to *change finance education from being calculator based to being spreadsheet modeling based*. This change will better prepare students for the 21st century business world. This change will increase student satisfaction in the classroom by allowing more practical, real-world applications and by enabling a more hands on, active learning approach.

There are many features which distinguish this book from anything else on the market:

- **Teach By Example.** I believe that the best way to learn spreadsheet modeling is by working through examples and completing a lot of problems. This book fully develops this hands-on, active learning approach. Active learning is a well-established way to increase student learning and student satisfaction with the course / instructor. When students build financial models themselves, they really "get it." As I tell my students, "If you build it, you will learn."

- **Supplement For All Popular Corporate Finance Textbooks.** This book is a supplement to be combined with a primary textbook. This means that you can keep using whatever textbook you like best. You don't have to switch. It also means that you can take an incremental approach to incorporating spreadsheet modeling. You can start modestly and build up from there. Alternative notation versions are available that match the notation of all popular corporate finance textbooks.

- **Plain Vanilla Excel.** Other books on the market emphasize teaching students programming using Visual Basic for Applications (VBA) or using macros. By contrast, this book does everything in plain vanilla Excel. Although programming is liked by a minority of students, it is seriously disliked by the majority. Plain vanilla Excel has the advantage of being a very intuitive, user-friendly environment that is accessible to all. It is fully capable of handling a wide range of applications, including quite sophisticated ones. Further, your students already know the basics of Excel and nothing more is assumed. Students are assumed to be able to enter formulas in a cell and to copy formulas from one cell to another. All other features of Excel (graphing, built-in functions, Solver, etc.) are explained as they are used.

- **Build From Simple Examples To Practical, Real-World Applications.** The general approach is to start with a simple example and build up to a practical, real-world application. In many chapters, the previous spreadsheet model is carried forward to the next more complex model. For example, the chapter on binomial option pricing carries forward spreadsheet models as follows: (a.) single-period model with replicating portfolio, (b.) eight-period model with replicating portfolio, (c.) eight-period model with risk-neutral probabilities, (d.) full-scale, fifty-period model with volatilities estimated from real returns data. Whenever possible, this book builds up to full-scale, practical applications using real data. Students are excited to learn practical applications that they can actually use in their future jobs. Employers are excited to hire students with spreadsheet modeling skills, who can be more productive faster.

- **A Change In Content Too.** Spreadsheet modeling is not merely a new medium, but an opportunity to cover some unique content items which require computer support to be feasible. For example, the full-scale, real data spreadsheet model in Corporate Financial Planning uses three years of historical 10K data on Nike, Inc. (including every line of their income statement, balance sheet, and cash flow statement), constructs a complete financial system (including linked financial ratios), and projects these financial statements three years into the future. The spreadsheet model in Life-Cycle Financial Planning includes a detailed treatment of federal and state tax schedules, social Security taxes and benefits, etc., which permit the realistic exploration savings, retirement, and investments choices over a lifetime. The spreadsheet model in US Yield Curve Dynamics shows you 30 years of monthly US yield curve history in just a few minutes. The spreadsheet model in Three Valuation Techniques demonstrates the equivalence of the Adjusted Present Value, Flows To Equity, and the Weighted-Average Cost of Capital methods, not just in the perpetuity case covered by most textbooks, but for a fully general two-stage project with an arbitrary set of cash flows over an explicit forecast horizon, followed by a infinite horizon perpetuity. As a practical matter, all of these sophisticated applications require spreadsheet modeling.

Conventions Used In This Book

This book uses a number of conventions.

- **Time Goes Across The Columns And Variables Go Down The Rows.** When something happens over time, I let each column represent a period of time. For example in capital budgeting, year 0 is in column B, year 1 is in column C, year 2 is in column D, etc. Each row represents a different variable, which is usually a labeled in column A. This manner of organizing spreadsheets is so common because it is how financial statements are organized.

- **Color Coding.** A standard color scheme is used to clarify the structure of the spreadsheet models. The printed book uses: (1) light gray shading for input values, (2) no shading (i.e. white) for throughput formulas, and (3) dark gray shading for final results ("the bottom line"). The accompanying electronic version of the book (a PDF file) uses: (1) yellow shading for input values, (2) no shading (i.e. white) for throughput formulas, and (3) green shading for final results ("the bottom line"). A few spreadsheets include choice variables. Choice variables use medium gray shading in the printed book and blue shading in the electronic version.

- **The Time Line Technique.** The most natural technique for discounting cash flows in a spreadsheet model is the time line technique, where each column corresponds to a period of time (as an example see the figure below).

	A	B	C	D	E	F	G
1	**NET PRESENT VALUE**		General Discount Rate				
2	(in thousands of $)						
3							
4	**Inputs**						
5	Period	0	1	2	3	4	5
6	Current Investment	$100.00					
7	Future Cash Flows		$21.00	$34.00	$40.00	$33.00	$17.00
8	Discount Rate		8.0%	7.6%	7.3%	7.0%	7.0%
9							
10	**Net Present Value using a Time Line**						
11	Period	0	1	2	3	4	5
12	Cumulative Discount Factor	0.0%	8.0%	16.2%	24.7%	33.4%	42.8%
13	Cash Flows	($100.00)	$21.00	$34.00	$40.00	$33.00	$17.00
14	Present Value of Each Cash Flow	($100.00)	$19.44	$29.26	$32.08	$24.73	$11.91
15	Net Present Value	$17.42					

The time line technique handles the general case of the discount rate changing over time just as easily as the special case of a constant discount rate. Typically one *does* have some information about the time pattern of the riskfree rate from the term structure of interest rates. Even just adding a constant risk premium, yields a time pattern of discount rates. There is no reason to throw this information away, when it is just as easy to incorporate it into a spreadsheet. I use the time line technique and the general case of changing discount rates throughout the capital budgeting spreadsheet models.

- **Explicit Inflation Rate.** A standard error in capital budgeting is to treat the cash flow projections and discount rate determination as if they came from separate planets with no relationship to each other. If the implicit inflation rate in the cash flow projection differs from the implicit inflation rate in the discount rate, then the analysis is inconsistent. The simple fix is to explicitly forecast the inflation rate and use this forecast in both the cash flow projection and the discount rate determination. The capital budgeting spreadsheet models teach this good modeling practice.

- **Dynamic Charts.** Dynamic charts allow you to see such things as a "movie" of the Term Structure of Interest Rates moves over time or an "animated graph" of how increasing the volatility of an underlying stock increases the value of an option. Dynamic charts are a combination of an up/down arrow (a "spinner") to rapidly change an input and a chart to rapidly display the changing output. I invented dynamic charts back in 1995 and I have included many examples of this useful educational tool throughout this book.

Craig's Challenge

I challenge the readers of this book to dramatically improve your finance education by personally constructing all 53 spreadsheet models in all 20 chapters of this book. This will take you about 27 to 53 hours depending on your current spreadsheet skills. Let me assure you that it will be an excellent investment. You will:
- gain a practical understanding of the core concepts of Corporate Finance,
- develop hands-on, spreadsheet modeling skills, and
- build an entire suite of finance applications, which you fully understand.

When you complete this challenge, I invite you to send an e-mail to me at **cholden@indiana.edu** to share the good news. Please tell me your name, school, (prospective) graduation year, and which spreadsheet modeling book you completed. I will add you to a web-based honor roll at:

http://www.spreadsheetmodeling.com/honor-roll.htm

We can celebrate together!

The Spreadsheet Modeling Series

This book is part a series of book/CDs on **Spreadsheet Modeling** by Craig W. Holden, published by Prentice Hall. The series includes:

- **Spreadsheet Modeling in Corporate Finance,**
- **Spreadsheet Modeling in the Fundamentals of Corporate Finance,**
- **Spreadsheet Modeling in Investments,** and
- **Spreadsheet Modeling in the Fundamentals of Investments.**

Each book teaches value-added skills in constructing financial models in Excel. Complete information about the **Spreadsheet Modeling** series is available at my web site:

http://www.spreadsheetmodeling.com

Most of the **Spreadsheet Modeling** book/CDs can be purchased any time at:

http://www.amazon.com

The Spreadsheet Modeling Community

You can access the worldwide spreadsheet modeling community by clicking on **Community (Free Enhancements)** at my web site **http://www.spreadsheetmodeling.com**. You will find free additions, extensions, and problems that professors and practitioners from around the world have made available for you. I will post annual updates of the U.S. yield curve database and occasional new spreadsheet models. If you would like to make available your own addition, extension, or problem to the worldwide finance community, just e-mail it to me at **cholden@indiana.edu** and I will post it on my web site. Your worldwide finance colleagues thank you.

If you have any suggestions or corrections, please e-mail them to me at **cholden@indiana.edu**. I will consider your suggestions and will implement any corrections in future editions.

Suggestions for Faculty Members

There is no single best way to use **Spreadsheet Modeling in Corporate Finance**. There are as many different techniques as there are different styles and philosophies of teaching. You need to discover what works best for you. Let me highlight several possibilities:

1. **Out-of-class individual projects with help.** This is a technique that I have used and it works well. I require completion of several short spreadsheet modeling projects of every individual student in the class. To provide help, I schedule special "help lab" sessions in a computer lab during which time myself and my graduate assistant are available to answer questions while students do each assignment in about an hour. Typically about half the questions are spreadsheet questions and half are finance questions. I have always graded such projects, but an alternative approach would be to treat them as ungraded homework.

2. **Out-of-class individual projects without help.** Another technique is to assign spreadsheet modeling projects for individual students to do on their own out of class. One instructor assigns seven spreadsheet modeling projects at the beginning of the semester and has individual students turn in all seven completed spreadsheet models for grading at the end of the semester. At the end of each chapter are numerous "Skill-Building Problems" and more challenging "Skill-Enhancing Problems" that can be assigned with or without help. Faculty members can download the completed spreadsheet models at **http://www.prenhall.com/holden**. See your local Prentice Hall representative to gain access.

3. **Out-of-class group projects.** A technique that I have used for the last seven years is to require students to do big spreadsheet modeling projects in groups. I assign students to groups based on a survey of students, where they self-rate their own Excel skills on a scale from 1 to 10. This allows me to create a mix of Excel skill levels in each group. Thus, group members can help each other. I have students write a report to a hypothetical boss, which intuitively explains their method of analysis, key assumptions, and key results.

4. **In-class reinforcement of key concepts.** This is the direction I have moved in recent years. The class session is scheduled in a computer lab or equivalently students are required to bring their (required) laptop computers to a technology classroom, which has a data jack and a power outlet at every student station. I explain a key concept in words and equations. Then I turn to a 10-15 minute segment in which I provide students with a spreadsheet that is partially complete (say, 80% complete) and have them finish the last few lines of the spreadsheet. This provides real-time, hands-on reinforcement of a key concept. This technique can be done often throughout the semester. At the end of each chapter are numerous "Live In-class Problems" that can be implemented this way. Faculty members can download the partially complete spreadsheets at **http://www.prenhall.com/holden**. See your local Prentice Hall representative to gain access.

5. **In-class demonstration of spreadsheet modeling.** The instructor can perform an in-class demonstration of how to build spreadsheet models. Typically, only a small portion of the total spreadsheet model would be demonstrated.

6. **In-class demonstration of key relationships using Dynamic Charts.** The instructor can dynamically illustrate comparative statics or dynamic properties over time using dynamic charts. For example, one dynamic chart illustrates 30 years of U.S. term structure dynamics. Another dynamic chart provides an "animated" illustration of the sensitivity of bond prices to changes in the coupon rate, yield-to-maturity, number of payments / year, and face value.

I'm sure I haven't exhausted the list of potential teaching techniques. Feel free to send an e-mail to **cholden@indiana.edu** to let me know novel ways in which you use this book / CD.

Alternative Notation Versions

One nice thing about spreadsheets is that you can use long descriptive labels to describe most variables and their corresponding formulas. However, some finance formulas are complex enough that they really require mathematical notation. When this happens, I provide alternative notation versions that match the notation of all popular corporate finance textbooks. The spreadsheet below shows the symbols that are used in all notation versions. I have selected the notation to fill in any gaps.

SYMBOL LIST	Bodie-Merton	Brealey	Brigham	Gitman	Keown	Ross	Van Horne
All Corporate Finance Versions							
Bonds							
Annual Coupon Rate	CR	CR	CR	CR	CR	CR	CR
Yield To Maturity (Annualized)	y	y	k_d	y	k_b	y	r.
Number of Payments / Period	NOP	NOP	NOP	NOP	NOP	NOP	NOP
Number of Periods to Maturity	n	N	N	n	T	T	n
Face Value	FV	M	M	M	M	F	M
Discount Rate / Period	I	r.	DR	k_d	DR	r.	DR
Coupon Payment	PMT	C.	INT	I	I	C.	C.
Bond Price	PV	PV	V_B	B_0	V_b	PV	P
Forward Rate from T-1 to T	f_n	f_n	$FR_{T-1,T}$	f_n	$f_{T-1,T}$	f_n	$_n r_1$
Capital Structure							
Value of the Firm	V	V	V	V	V	V	V
Debt	D	D	D	D	D	B	B
Equity	E	E	E	E	E	S	S
Face Value of Debt	B	B	B	B	B	D	D
Black-Scholes Option Pricing							
Stock Price	S	P	P	S	S	S	V_s
Exercise Price	E	EX	X	E	E	E	E
Riskfree Rate	r	r	k_{RF}	r	r	r	r
Volatility	σ	σ	σ	σ	σ	σ	σ
Time To Maturity	T	t	t	T	T	t	t
d_1	d_1	d_1	d_1	d_1	d_1	d_1	d_1
d_2	d_2	d_2	d_2	d_2	d_2	d_2	d_2
$N(d_1)$	$N(d_1)$	$N(d_1)$	$N(d_1)$	$N(d_1)$	$N(d_1)$	$N(d_1)$	$N(d_1)$
$N(d_2)$	$N(d_2)$	$N(d_2)$	$N(d_2)$	$N(d_2)$	$N(d_2)$	$N(d_2)$	$N(d_2)$
Call Price	C	C	V	C	C	C	V_o
Put Price	P	Put	Put	P	P	P	V_p
Dividend Yield	d	d	d	d	d	d	d

Acknowledgements

I thank Mickey Cox, P.J. Boardman, Maureen Riopelle, and Paul Donnelly of Prentice Hall for their vision, innovativeness, and encouragement of **Spreadsheet Modeling in Corporate Finance**. I thank Cheryl Clayton, Josh McClary, Bill Minic, Melanie Olsen, and Lauren Tarino of Prentice Hall for many useful contributions. I thank Professors Steve Rich (Baylor University), Tim Smaby (Penn State University), and Charles Trzcinka (Indiana University) for providing detailed and thoughtful comments. I thank my Graduate Assistant Wannie Park and many individual students for providing helpful comments. I thank my family, Kathryn, Diana, and Jimmy, for their love and support.

About The Author

CRAIG W. HOLDEN

 Craig Holden is the Richard G. Brinkman Faculty Fellow and Associate Professor of Finance at the Kelley School of Business at Indiana University. His M.B.A. and Ph.D. are from the Anderson School at UCLA. He is the winner of multiple schoolwide teaching awards and multiple schoolwide research awards. He has written a book/CD series on **Spreadsheet Modeling** in finance, which is published by Prentice Hall. His research on security trading and market making ("market microstructure") has been published in leading academic journals. He has chaired nine dissertations, served on the program committee of the *Western Finance Association* for three years, and served as an associate editor of the *Journal of Financial Markets* for four years. He has chaired a department committee for eight years and chaired various schoolwide committees for seven years. He has lead several major curriculum innovations in the finance department. For more details, Craig's home page is at **www.kelley.iu.edu/cholden**.

PART 1 TIME VALUE OF MONEY

1 Single Cash Flow

1.1 Present Value

Problem. A single cash flow of $1,000.00 will be received in 5 periods. For this cash flow, the appropriate discount rate / period is 6.0%. What is the present value of this single cash flow?

Solution Strategy. We will calculate the present value of this single cash flow in three equivalent ways. First, we will calculate the present value using a time line, where each column corresponds to a period of calendar time. Second, we use a formula for the present value. Third, we use Excel's **PV** function for the present value.

FIGURE 1.1 Spreadsheet for Single Cash Flow - Present Value.

	A	B	C	D	E	F	G
1	SINGLE CASH FLOW	Present Value					
2							
3	Inputs						
4	Single Cash Flow	$1,000.00					
5	Discount Rate / Period	6.0%					
6	Number of Periods	5					
7							
8	Present Value using a Time Line						
9	Period	0	1	2	3	4	5
10	Cash Flows	$0.00	$0.00	$0.00	$0.00	$0.00	$1,000.00
11	Present Value of Each Cash Flow	$0.00	$0.00	$0.00	$0.00	$0.00	$747.26
12	Present Value	$747.26					
13							
14	Present Value using the Formula						
15	Present Value	$747.26					
16							
17	Present Value using the PV Function						
18	Present Value	$747.26					

How To Build Your Own Spreadsheet Model.

1. **Inputs.** Enter the inputs in the range **B4:B6**.

2. **Present Value using a Time Line.** Create a time line from period 0 to period 5. Enter the single cash flow in period 5. Calculate the present value of each cash flow and sum the present values as follows.

   o **Period.** Enter **0, 1, 2, ..., 5.** in the range **B9:G9**.

   o **Cash Flows.** Enter **$0.00** in cell **B10** and copy it to the range **C10:F10**. Enter **=B4** in cell **G10**.

   o **Present Value of Each Cash Flow** = (Cash Flow) / ((1 + Discount Rate/Period) ^ Period). Enter **=B10/((1+$B$5)^B9)** in cell **B11** and copy it across. The $ signs in **$B$5** lock the column as **B** and the row as **5** when copying.

1

- o **Present Value** = Sum over all periods of the Present Value of Each Cash Flow. Enter **=SUM(B11:G11)** in cell **B12**.

3. **Present Value using the Formula.** For a single cash flow, the formula is Present Value = (Cash Flow) / ((1 + Discount Rate/Period) ^ Period). Enter **=B4/((1+B5)^B6)** in cell **B15**.

4. **Present Value using the PV Function.** The Excel **PV** function can be used to calculate the present value of a single cash flow, the present value of an annuity, or the present value of a bond. For a single cash flow, the format is =-PV(Discount Rate / Period, Number of Periods, 0, Single Cash Flow). Enter **=-PV(B5,B6,0,B4)** in cell **B18**.

The Present Value of this Single Cash Flow is $747.26. Notice you get the same answer all three ways: using the time line, using the formula, or using the PV function!

1.2 Future Value

Problem. A single cash flow of $747.25 is available now (in period 0). For this cash flow, the appropriate discount rate / period is 6.0%. What is the period 5 future value of this single cash flow?

Solution Strategy. We will calculate the future value of the single cash flow in three equivalent ways. First, we will calculate the future value using a time line, where each column corresponds to a period of calendar time. Second, we use a formula for the future value. Third, we use Excel's **FV** function for the future value.

FIGURE 1.2 Spreadsheet for Single Cash Flow - Future Value.

	A	B	C	D	E	F	G
1	SINGLE CASH FLOW Future Value						
2							
3	Inputs						
4	Single Cash Flow	$747.26					
5	Discount Rate / Period	6.0%					
6	Number of Periods	5					
7							
8	Future Value using a Time Line						
9	Period	0	1	2	3	4	5
10	Cash Flows	$747.26	$0.00	$0.00	$0.00	$0.00	$0.00
11	Future Value of Each Cash Flow	$1,000.00	$0.00	$0.00	$0.00	$0.00	$0.00
12	Future Value						$1,000.00
13							
14	Future Value using the Formula						
15	Future Value	$1,000.00					
16							
17	Future Value using the PV Function						
18	Future Value	$1,000.00					

How To Build Your Own Spreadsheet Model.

1. **Inputs.** Enter the inputs in the range B4:B6.

2. **Future Value using a Time Line.** Create a time line from period 0 to period 5. Enter the single cash flow in period 0. Calculate the period 5 future value of each cash flow and sum the future values as follows.

- o **Period.** Enter **0, 1, 2, …, 5.** in the range **B9:G9**.

- o **Cash Flows.** Enter **=B4** in cell **B10**. Enter **$0.00** in cell **C10** and copy it across.

- o **Future Value of Each Cash Flow** = (Cash Flow) * (1 + Discount Rate/Period)^((Number of Periods) - (Current Period)). Enter **=B10*(1+$B$5)^($B$6-B9)** in cell **B11** and copy it across. The exponent **($B$6-B9)** causes the period 0 cash flow to be compounded 5 times into the future, the period 1 cash flow to be compounded 4 times into the future, the period 2 cash flow to be compounded 3 times into the future, etc. The $ signs in **$B$5** and **$B$6** lock the column and the row when copying.

- o **Future Value** = Sum over all periods of the Future Value of Each Cash Flow. Enter **=SUM(B11:G11)** in cell **B12**.

3. **Future Value using the Formula.** For a single cash flow, the formula is Future = (Cash Flow) * (1 + Discount Rate/Period)^(Number of Periods). Enter **=B4*(1+B5)^B6** in cell **B15**.

4. **Future Value using the FV Function.** The Excel FV function can be used to calculate the future value of a single cash flow, the future value of an annuity, or the future value of a bond. For a single cash flow, the format is =-FV(Discount Rate / Period, Number of Periods, 0, Single Cash Flow). Enter **=-FV(B5,B6,0,B4)** in cell **B18**.

The Future Value of this Single Cash Flow is $1,000.00. Notice you get the same answer all three ways: using the time line, using the formula, or using the FV function!

Comparing Present Value and Future Value, we see that they are opposite operations. That is, one operation "undoes" the other. The Present Value of $1,000.00 in period 5 is $747.26 in period 0. The Future Value of $747.26 in period 0 is $1,000.00 in period 5.

Problems

Skill-Building Problems.

1. A single cash flow of $1,673.48 will be received in 4 periods. For this cash flow, the appropriate discount rate / period is 7.8%. What is the present value of this single cash flow?

2. A single cash flow of $932.47 is available now (in period 0). For this cash flow, the appropriate discount rate / period is 3.9%. What is the period 4 future value of this single cash flow?

Live In-class Problems.

3. Given the partial Present Value spreadsheet **SinglepZ.xls**, complete step **2 Present Value Using A Timeline**.

4. Given the partial Future Value spreadsheet **SinglefZ.xls**, complete step **2 Future Value Using A Timeline**.

2 Annuity

2.1 Present Value

Problem. An annuity pays $80.00 each period for 5 periods. For these cash flows, the appropriate discount rate / period is 6.0%. What is the present value of this annuity?

Solution Strategy. We will calculate the present value of this annuity in three equivalent ways. First, we will calculate the present value using a time line, where each column corresponds to a period of calendar time. Second, we use a formula for the present value. Third, we use Excel's **PV** function for the present value.

FIGURE 2.1 Spreadsheet for Annuity - Present Value.

	A	B	C	D	E	F	G
1	ANNUITY	Present Value					
2							
3	**Inputs**						
4	Payment	$80.00					
5	Discount Rate / Period	6.0%					
6	Number of Periods	5					
7							
8	**Annuity Present Value using a Time Line**						
9	Period	0	1	2	3	4	5
10	Cash Flows	$0.00	$80.00	$80.00	$80.00	$80.00	$80.00
11	Present Value of Each Cash Flow	$0.00	$75.47	$71.20	$67.17	$63.37	$59.78
12	Present Value	$336.99					
13							
14	**Annuity Present Value using the Formula**						
15	Present Value	$336.99					
16							
17	**Annuity Present Value using the PV Function**						
18	Present Value	$336.99					

How To Build Your Own Spreadsheet Model.

1. **Inputs.** Enter the inputs in the range **B4:B6**.

2. **Annuity Present Value using a Time Line.** Create a time line from period 0 to period 5. Determine the annuity cash flows in periods 1 through 5. Calculate the present value of each cash flow and sum the present values as follows.

    o **Period.** Enter 0, 1, 2, …, 5. in the range **B9:G9**.

    o **Cash Flows.** Enter $0.00 in cell **B10**. Enter =$B$4 in cell **C10** and copy it across.

    o **Present Value of Each Cash Flow** = (Cash Flow) / ((1 + Discount Rate/Period) ^ Period). Enter =B10/((1+$B$5)^B9) in cell **B11** and copy it across. The $ signs in $B$5 lock the column and row when copying.

    o **Present Value** = Sum over all periods of the Present Value of Each Cash Flow. Enter =SUM(B11:G11) in cell **B12**.

4

3. **Annuity Present Value using the Formula.** The formula for Annuity Present Value = (Payment) * (1 - ((1 + Discount Rate/Period) ^ (-Number of Periods))) / (Discount Rate/Period). Enter **=B4*(1-((1+B5)^(-B6)))/B5** in cell **B15**.

4. **Annuity Present Value using the PV Function.** The Excel **PV** function can be used to calculate the present value of an annuity using the following format =-PV(Discount Rate / Period, Number of Periods, Payment, 0). Enter **=-PV(B5,B6,B4,0)** in cell **B18**.

The Present Value of this Annuity is $336.99. Notice you get the same answer all three ways: using the time line, using the formula, or using the PV function.

2.2 Future Value

Problem. An annuity pays $80.00 each period for 5 periods. For these cash flows, the appropriate discount rate / period is 6.0%. What is the period 5 future value of this annuity?

Solution Strategy. We will calculate the future value of this annuity in three equivalent ways. First, we will calculate the future value using a time line, where each column corresponds to a period of calendar time. Second, we use a formula for the future value. Third, we use Excel's **FV** function for the future value.

FIGURE 2.2 Spreadsheet for Annuity - Future Value.

	A	B	C	D	E	F	G
1	ANNUITY	Future Value					
2							
3	Inputs						
4	Payment	$80.00					
5	Discount Rate / Period	6.0%					
6	Number of Periods	5					
7							
8	Annuity Future Value using a Time Line						
9	Period	0	1	2	3	4	5
10	Cash Flows	$0.00	$80.00	$80.00	$80.00	$80.00	$80.00
11	Future Value of Each Cash Flow	$0.00	$101.00	$95.28	$89.89	$84.80	$80.00
12	Future Value						$450.97
13							
14	Annuity Future Value using the Formula						
15	Future Value	$450.97					
16							
17	Annuity Future Value using the FV Function						
18	Future Value	$450.97					

How To Build Your Own Spreadsheet Model.

1. **Inputs.** Enter the inputs in the range **B4:B6**.

2. **Annuity Future Value using a Time Line.** Create a time line from period 0 to period 5. Determine the annuity cash flows in periods 1 through 5. Calculate the present value of each cash flow and sum the present values as follows.

   o **Period.** Enter 0, 1, 2, ..., 5. in the range **B9:G9**.

   o **Cash Flows.** Enter $0.00 in cell **B10**. Enter **=$B$4** in cell **C10** and copy it across.

5

- o **Future Value of Each Cash Flow** = (Cash Flow) * (1 + Discount Rate/Period)^((Number of Periods) - (Current Period)). Enter **=B10*(1+$B$5)^($B$6-B9)** in cell **B11** and copy it across. The exponent **($B$6-B9)** causes the period 0 cash flow to be compounded 5 times into the future, the period 1 cash flow to be compounded 4 times into the future, the period 2 cash flow to be compounded 3 times into the future, etc. The $ signs in **$B$5** and **$B$6** lock the column and the row when copying.

  - o **Future Value** = Sum over all periods of the Future Value of Each Cash Flow. Enter **=SUM(B11:G11)** in cell **B12**.

3. **Annuity Future Value using the Formula.** The formula for Annuity Present Value = (Payment) * (1 - ((1 + Discount Rate/Period) ^ (Number of Periods))) / (Discount Rate/Period). Enter **=B4*(((1+B5)^B6)-1)/B5** in cell **B15**.

4. **Annuity Future Value using the FV Function.** The Excel **FV** function can be used to calculate the future value of an annuity with the using format =-FV(Discount Rate / Period, Number of Periods, Payment, 0). Enter **=-FV(B5,B6,B4,0)** in cell **B18**.

The Future Value of this Annuity is $450.97. Notice you get the same answer all three ways: using the time line, using the formula, or using the FV function.

2.3 System of Four Annuity Variables

Problem. There is a tight connection between all of the inputs and output to annuity valuation. Indeed, they form a system of four annuity variables: (1) Payment, (2) Discount Rate / Period, (3) Number of Periods, and (4) Present Value. Given any three of these variables, find the fourth variable.

Solution Strategy. Given any three of these variable, we will use as many equivalent ways of solving for the fourth variable as possible. In solving for the Payment, use the formula and **PMT** function. In solving for the Discount Rate / Period, use the **RATE** function. In solving for the Number of Periods, use the **NPER** function. In solving for the Present Value, use a Time Line, formula, and the **PV** function.

FIGURE 2.3 Spreadsheet for Annuity - System of Four Annuity Variables.

	A	B	C	D	E	F	G
1	ANNUITY	System of Four Annuity Variables					
2							
3	Inputs						
4	Payment	$80.00					
5	Discount Rate / Period	6.0%					
6	Number of Periods	5					
7	Present Value	$336.99					
8							
9	Payment						
10	Payment using the Formula	$80.00					
11	Payment using the PMT Function	$80.00					
12							
13	Discount Rate / Period						
14	Discount Rate / Per using the RATE Func	6.0%					
15							
16	Number of Periods						
17	Num of Periods using the NPER Function	5					
18							
19	Present Value						
20	Period	0	1	2	3	4	5
21	Cash Flows	$0.00	$80.00	$80.00	$80.00	$80.00	$80.00
22	Present Value of Each Cash Flow	$0.00	$75.47	$71.20	$67.17	$63.37	$59.78
23	Present Value using a Time Line	$336.99					
24							
25	Present Value using the Formula	$336.99					
26	Present Value using the PV Function	$336.99					

How To Build Your Own Spreadsheet Model.

1. **Start with the Present Value Spreadsheet, Then Insert and Delete Rows.** Open the spreadsheet that you created for Annuity - Present Value and immediately save the spreadsheet under a new name using the **File | Save As** command. Select the range **A7:A17** and click on **Insert | Rows.** Select the cell **A25,** click on **Edit | Delete,** select the **Entire Row** radio button on the **Delete** dialog box, and click on **OK.** Select the range **A26:A27,** click on **Edit | Delete,** select the **Entire Row** radio button on the **Delete** dialog box, and click on **OK.**

2. **Inputs.** Enter the inputs in the range **B4:B7.**

3. **Payment.** The formula for the Payment = (Present Value) / ((1 - ((1 + Discount Rate/Period) ^ (-Number of Periods))) / (Discount Rate/Period)). Enter **=B7/((1-((1+B5)^(-B6)))/B5)** in cell **B10.** The Excel **PMT** function can be used to calculate an annuity payment using the following format =PMT(Discount Rate / Period, Number of Periods, -Present Value, 0). Enter **=PMT(B5,B6,-B7,0)** in cell **B11.**

4. **Discount Rate / Period.** The Excel **RATE** function can be used to calculate the discount rate / period for an annuity using the following format =RATE(Number of Periods, Payment, -Present Value, 0). Enter **=RATE(B6,B4,-B7,0)** in cell **B14.**

5. **Number of Periods.** The Excel **NPER** function can be used to calculate an annuity payment using the following format =NPER(Discount Rate / Period, Payment, -Present Value, 0). Enter **=NPER(B5,B4,-B7,0)** in cell **B17.**

We see that the system of four annuity variables is internally consistent. The four outputs in rows **10** through **26** (Payment = $80.00, Discount Rate / Period = 6.0%, Number of Periods = 5, and Present Value = $336.99) are identical to the four inputs in rows **4** through **7**. Thus, any of the four annuity variables can be calculated from the other three in a fully consistent manner.

Problems

Skill-Building Problems.

1. An annuity pays $142.38 each period for 6 periods. For these cash flows, the appropriate discount rate / period is 4.5%. What is the present value of this annuity?

2. An annuity pays $63.92 each period for 4 periods. For these cash flows, the appropriate discount rate / period is 9.1%. What is the period 5 future value of this annuity?

Live In-class Problems.

3. Given the partial Present Value spreadsheet **AnnuitpZ.xls**, complete step **2 Annuity Present Value Using A Timeline**.

4. Given the partial Future Value spreadsheet **AnnuitfZ.xls**, complete step **2 Annuity Future Value Using A Timeline**.

5. Given the partial System of Four Annuity Variables spreadsheet **AnnuitsZ.xls**, do steps **3 Payment**, **4 Discount Rate / Period**, and **5 Number of Periods**.

3 Net Present Value

3.1 Constant Discount Rate

Problem. A project requires a current investment of $100.00 and yields future expected cash flows of $21.00, $34.00, $40.00, $33.00, and $17.00 in periods 1 through 5, respectively. All figures are in thousands of dollars. For these expected cash flows, the appropriate discount rate is 8.0%. What is the net present value of this project?

Solution Strategy. We will calculate the net present value of this project in two equivalent ways. First, we will calculate the net present value using a time line, where each column corresponds to a period of calendar time. Second, we use Excel's **NPV** function for the net present value.

FIGURE 3.1 Spreadsheet for Net Present Value - Constant Discount Rate.

	A	B	C	D	E	F	G
1	NET PRESENT VALUE		Constant Discount Rate				
2	(in thousands of $)						
3							
4	Inputs						
5	Discount Rate	8.0%					
6	Period	0	1	2	3	4	5
7	Current Investment	$100.00					
8	Future Cash Flows		$21.00	$34.00	$40.00	$33.00	$17.00
9							
10	Net Present Value using a Time Line						
11	Period	0	1	2	3	4	5
12	Cash Flows	($100.00)	$21.00	$34.00	$40.00	$33.00	$17.00
13	Present Value of Each Cash Flow	($100.00)	$19.44	$29.15	$31.75	$24.26	$11.57
14	Net Present Value	$16.17					
15							
16	Net Present Value using the NPV Function						
17	Net Present Value	$16.17					

How To Build Your Own Spreadsheet Model.

1. **Inputs.** Enter the Discount Rate in **B5**, the Current Investment in **B7** and the Future Cash Flows in the range **C8:G8**.

2. **Net Present Value using a Time Line.** Create a time line from period 0 to period 5. Determine the project cash flows in periods 0 through 5. Calculate the present value of each cash flow and sum the present values as follows.

   o **Period.** Enter **0, 1, 2, …, 5.** in the range **B11:G11**.

   o **Cash Flows.** The current investment is a negative cash flow. Enter **=-B7** in cell **B12**. Future cash flows are positive cash flows. Enter **=C8** in cell **C12** and copy it across.

   o **Present Value of Each Cash Flow** = (Cash Flow) / ((1 + Discount Rate) ^ Period). Enter **=B12/((1+$B$5)^B11)** in cell **B13** and copy it across. The $ signs in **$B$5** lock the column and row when copying.

9

- **Net Present Value** = Sum over all periods of the Present Value of Each Cash Flow. Enter **=SUM(B13:G13)** in cell **B14**.

3. **Net Present Value using the NPV Function.** The Excel **NPV** function is used to calculate the net present value of a cash flow stream using the following format =-(Current Investment) + NPV(Discount Rate, Future Cash Flows). Enter **=-B7+NPV(B5,C8:G8)** in cell **B17**. An oddity of the Excel **NPV** function is that it only discounts cash flows starting in period 1 and going forward. You must add the present value of the period 0 cash flow separately, which explains the negative cash flow term: -(Current Investment).

The Net Present Value of this project is $16.17. Notice you get the same answer both ways: using the time line or using the NPV function.

3.2 General Discount Rate

Problem. A project requires a current investment of $100.00 and yields future expected cash flows of $21.00, $34.00, $40.00, $33.00, and $17.00 in periods 1 through 5, respectively. All figures are in thousands of dollars. For these expected cash flows, the appropriate discount rate starts at 8.0% in period 1 and declines to 7.0% in period 5. What is the net present value of this project?

Solution Strategy. We will calculate the Net Present Value of this project using a Time Line. This is the *only* possible way to calculate the project NPV in the general case where the discount rate changes over time. Excel's **NPV** function can not be used because it is limited to the special case of a constant discount rate. And there is no simple formula for NPV, short of typing in a term for each cash flow.

FIGURE 3.2 Spreadsheet for Net Present Value - General Discount Rate.

	A	B	C	D	E	F	G
1	**NET PRESENT VALUE**		**General Discount Rate**				
2	(in thousands of $)						
3							
4	**Inputs**						
5	Period	0	1	2	3	4	5
6	Current Investment	$100.00					
7	Future Cash Flows		$21.00	$34.00	$40.00	$33.00	$17.00
8	Discount Rate		8.0%	7.6%	7.3%	7.0%	7.0%
9							
10	**Net Present Value using a Time Line**						
11	Period	0	1	2	3	4	5
12	Cumulative Discount Factor	0.0%	8.0%	16.2%	24.7%	33.4%	42.8%
13	Cash Flows	($100.00)	$21.00	$34.00	$40.00	$33.00	$17.00
14	Present Value of Each Cash Flow	($100.00)	$19.44	$29.26	$32.08	$24.73	$11.91
15	Net Present Value	$17.42					

How To Build Your Own Spreadsheet Model.

1. **Inputs.** Enter the Current Investment in **B6**, the Future Cash Flows in the range **C7:G7**, and the Discount Rates in the range **C8:G8**.

2. **Net Present Value using a Time Line.** Create a time line from period 0 to period 5. Calculate a cumulative discount factor. Determine the project cash flows in periods 0 through 5. Calculate the present value of each cash flow and sum the present values as follows.

   - **Period.** Enter 0, 1, 2, …, 5. in the range **B11:G11**.

10

o **Cumulative Discount Factor.** Enter **0.0%** in the cell **B12**. The (Cumulative Discount Factor on date t) = (1 + Cumulative Discount Factor on date t-1) * (1 + Discount Rate on date t) - 1. Enter **=(1+B12)*(1+C8)-1** in cell **C12** and copy it across.

o **Cash Flows.** The current investment is a negative cash flow. Enter **=-B6** in cell **B13**. Future cash flows are positive cash flows. Enter **=C7** in cell **C13** and copy it across.

o **Present Value of Each Cash Flow** = (Cash Flow on date t) / (1+ Cumulative Discount Factor on date t). Enter **=B13/(1+B12)** in cell **B14** and copy it across.

o **Net Present Value** = Sum over all periods of the Present Value of Each Cash Flow. Enter **=SUM(B14:G14)** in cell **B15**.

The Net Present Value of this project is $17.42. This spreadsheet can handle *any* pattern of discount rates. For example, it can handle the special case of a constant discount rate.

FIGURE 3.3 General Spreadsheet Implementing a Constant Discount Rate.

	A	B	Z	AA	AB	AC	AD	AE	AF
1	LOAN AMORTIZATION								
2									
3	Inputs								
4	Present value	$300,000							
5	Interest rate / year	8.00%							
6	Number of years	30							
7									
8	Outputs								
9	Year	1	25	26	27	28	29	30	31
10	Beg. Principal Balance	$300,000	$123,192	$106,399	$88,262	$68,675	$47,521	$24,674	($0)
11	Payment	$26,648	$26,648	$26,648	$26,648	$26,648	$26,648	$26,648	
12	Interest Component	$24,000	$9,855	$8,512	$7,061	$5,494	$3,802	$1,974	
13	Principal Component	$2,648	$16,793	$18,136	$19,587	$21,154	$22,847	$24,674	

The Net Present Value of this project is $16.17. Notice this is the same answer as the previous spreadsheet for the Net Present Value - Constant Discount Rate. The general discount rate spreadsheet is the most general way to do discounting and is the approach we will use throughout this book.

Problems

Skill-Building Problems.

1. A project requires a current investment of $189.32 and yields future expected cash flows of $45.19, $73.11, $98,54, $72.83, and $58.21 in periods 1 through 5, respectively. All figures are in thousands of dollars. For these expected cash flows, the appropriate discount rate is 6.3%. What is the net present value of this project?

2. A project requires a current investment of $54.39 and yields future expected cash flows of $19.27, $27.33, $34.94, $41.76, and $32.49 in periods 1 through 5, respectively. All figures are in thousands of dollars. For these expected cash flows, the appropriate discount rate starts at 6.4% in period 1 and declines to 5.4% in period 5. What is the net present value of this project?

Live In-class Problems.

3. Given the partial Constant Discount Rate spreadsheet **NpvcondZ.xls**, complete step **2 Net Present Value Using A Timeline**.

11

4. Given the partial General Discount Rate spreadsheet **NpvgendZ.xls**, complete step **2 Net Present Value Using A Timeline**.

4 Real And Inflation

4.1 Constant Discount Rate

Problem. A project requires a current investment of $100.00 and yields future expected cash flows of $21.00, $34.00, $40.00, $33.00, and $17.00 in periods 1 through 5, respectively. All figures are in thousands of dollars. The inflation rate is 3.0%. For these expected cash flows, the appropriate Real Discount Rate is 5.0%. What is the net present value of this project?

Solution Strategy. We begin by calculating the (nominal) discount rate from the inflation rate and the real discount rate. The rest of the net present value calculation is the same as the Net Present Value - Constant Discount Rate spreadsheet.

FIGURE 4.1 Spreadsheet for Real and Inflation - Constant Discount Rate.

	A	B	C	D	E	F	G
1	REAL AND INFLATION	Constant Discount Rate					
2	(in thousands of $)						
3							
4	Inputs						
5	Inflation Rate	3.0%					
6	Real Discount Rate	5.0%					
7	Period	0	1	2	3	4	5
8	Current Investment	$100.00					
9	Future Cash Flows		$21.00	$34.00	$40.00	$33.00	$17.00
10							
11	Outputs						
12	Discount Rate	8.2%					
13							
14	Net Present Value using a Time Line						
15	Period	0	1	2	3	4	5
16	Cash Flows	($100.00)	$21.00	$34.00	$40.00	$33.00	$17.00
17	Present Value of Each Cash Flow	($100.00)	$19.42	$29.07	$31.62	$24.12	$11.49
18	Net Present Value	$15.72					
19							
20	Net Present Value using the NPV Function						
21	Net Present Value	$15.72					

How To Build Your Own Spreadsheet Model.

1. **Start with the Net Present Value - Constant Discount Rate Spreadsheet, Insert Rows, And Move One Item.** Open the spreadsheet that you created for Net Present Value - Constant Discount Rate and immediately save the spreadsheet under a new name using the **File | Save As** command. Select the cell **A5** and click on **Insert | Rows**. Select the range **A11:A13** and click on **Insert | Rows**. Select the range **A6:B6**, click on **Edit | Cut**, select the cell **A12**, and click on **Edit | Paste**.

2. **Inputs.** Enter the inputs in the range **B5:B6**.

3. **Discount Rate.** The formula for the (Nominal) Discount Rate = (1 + Inflation Rate) * (1 + Real Discount Rate) - 1. Enter **=(1+B5)*(1+B6)-1** in cell **B12**.

The Net Present Value of this project is $15.72.

4.2 General Discount Rate

Problem. A project requires a current investment of $100.00 and yields future expected cash flows of $21.00, $34.00, $40.00, $33.00, and $17.00 in periods 1 through 5, respectively. All figures are in thousands of dollars. The forecasted inflation rate starts at 3.0% in period 1 and declines to 2.0% in period 5. For these expected cash flows, the appropriate REAL discount rate starts at 5.0% in period 1 and increases to 6.5% in period 5. What is the net present value of this project?

Solution Strategy. We begin by calculating the (nominal) discount rate for each period from the inflation rate in each period and corresponding real discount rate. The rest of the net present value calculation is the same as the Net Present Value - General Discount Rate spreadsheet.

FIGURE 4.2 Spreadsheet for Real and Inflation - General Discount Rate.

	A	B	C	D	E	F	G
1	REAL AND INFLATION	General Discount Rate					
2	(in thousands of $)						
3							
4	**Inputs**						
5	Period	0	1	2	3	4	5
6	Current Investment	$100.00					
7	Future Cash Flows		$21.00	$34.00	$40.00	$33.00	$17.00
8	Inflation Rate		3.0%	2.8%	2.5%	2.2%	2.0%
9	Real Discount Rate		5.0%	5.5%	6.0%	6.5%	6.5%
10							
11	**Net Present Value using a Time Line**						
12	Period	0	1	2	3	4	5
13	Discount Rate		8.2%	8.5%	8.7%	8.8%	8.6%
14	Cumulative Discount Factor	0.0%	8.2%	17.3%	27.4%	38.7%	50.7%
15	Cash Flows	($100.00)	$21.00	$34.00	$40.00	$33.00	$17.00
16	Present Value of Each Cash Flow	($100.00)	$19.42	$28.99	$31.39	$23.79	$11.28
17	Net Present Value	$14.87					

How To Build Your Own Spreadsheet Model.

1. **Start with the Net Present Value - General Discount Rate Spreadsheet, Insert Rows, And Move One Item.** Open the spreadsheet that you created for Net Present Value - General Discount Rate and immediately save the spreadsheet under a new name using the **File | Save As** command. Select the cell **A8** and click on **Insert | Rows**. Select the cell **A13** and click on **Insert | Rows**. Select the range **A9:G9**, click on **Edit | Cut**, select the cell **A13**, and click on **Edit | Paste**.

2. **Inputs.** Enter the inputs in the range **C8:G9**.

3. **Discount Rate.** The formula for the (Nominal) Discount Rate = (1 + Inflation Rate) * (1 + Real Discount Rate) - 1. Enter **=(1+C8)*(1+C9)-1** in cell **C13** and copy it across.

The Net Present Value of this project is $14.87. This spreadsheet can handle *any* pattern of inflation rates and real discount rates. Of course, it can handle the special case of a constant inflation rates and constant real discount rates.

Problems

Skill-Building Problems.

1. A project requires a current investment of $117.39 and yields future expected cash flows of $38.31, $48.53, $72.80, $96.31, and $52.18 in periods 1 through 5, respectively. All figures are in thousands of dollars. The inflation rate is 2.7%. For these expected cash flows, the appropriate Real Discount Rate is 8.6%. What is the net present value of this project?

2. A project requires a current investment of $328.47 and yields future expected cash flows of $87.39, $134.97, $153.28, $174.99, and $86.41 in periods 1 through 5, respectively. All figures are in thousands of dollars. The forecasted inflation rate starts at 3.4% in period 1 and increases to 4.7% in period 5. For these expected cash flows, the appropriate REAL discount rate starts at 7.8% in period 1 and decreases to 5.4% in period 5. What is the net present value of this project?

Live In-class Problems.

3. Given the partial Constant Discount Rate spreadsheet **ReacondZ.xls**, complete step **3 Discount Rate**.

4. Given the partial General Discount Rate spreadsheet **ReagendZ.xls**, complete step **3 Discount Rate**.

5 Loan Amortization

5.1 Basics

Problem. To purchase a house, you take out a 30 year mortgage. The present value (loan amount) of the mortgage is $300,000. The mortgage charges an interest rate / year of 8.00%. What is the annual payment required by this mortgage? How much of each year's payment goes to paying interest and how much reducing the principal balance?

Solution Strategy. First, we use Excel's **PMT** function to calculate the annual payment of a 30 year annuity (mortgage). Then we will use a time line and simple recursive formulas to split out the payment into the interest component and the principal reduction component.

FIGURE 5.1 Spreadsheet for Loan Amortization - Basics.

	A	B	C	D	E	F	G
1	LOAN AMORTIZATION	Basics					
2							
3	Inputs						
4	Present value	$300,000					
5	Interest rate / year	8.00%					
6	Number of years	30					
7							
8	Outputs						
9	Year	1	2	3	4	5	6
10	Beg. Principal Balance	$300,000	$297,352	$294,492	$291,403	$288,067	$284,464
11	Payment	$26,648	$26,648	$26,648	$26,648	$26,648	$26,648
12	Interest Component	$24,000	$23,788	$23,559	$23,312	$23,045	$22,757
13	Principal Component	$2,648	$2,860	$3,089	$3,336	$3,603	$3,891

How To Build Your Own Spreadsheet Model.

1. **Inputs.** Enter the inputs in the range **B4:AF9**.

2. **Year and Freeze Panes.** Enter **1, 2, 3, ..., 31.** in the range **B9:G11**. A simple way to do this is to enter **1** in cell **B9**, enter **2** in cell **C9**, hover the cursor over the lower right corner of cell **C9**, and when you see the "fill handle" (it looks a "+" sign) drag it all the way across to cell **G11**. Select **C10** and click on **Window | Freeze Panes**. This locks in the column and row titles.

3. **Beg. Principal Balance.** The principal balance at the beginning of Year 1 is the full amount of the loan (i.e., the present value). Enter **=B4** in cell **B10**. We will return to the rest of this line in a moment.

4. **Payment.** The Excel **PMT** function can be used to calculate an annuity payment using the following format =PMT(Interest Rate / Year, Number of Years, -Present Value, 0). Enter **=PMT($B$5,$B$6,-$B$4,0)** in cell **B11**. The $ signs in the formula lock in the row and column when copying.

5. **Interest Component in year t** = (Interest rate/year) * (Beginning Principal Balance in year t). Enter **=$B$5*B10** in cell **B12**.

16

6. **Principal Component in year t** = Payment - (Interest Component). In other words, whatever part of the payment is leftover after paying the interest goes to reducing the principal balance. Enter =B11-B12 in cell **B13**.

7. **Beg. Principal Balance in year t** = (Beg. Principal Balance in year t-1) - (Principal Component in year t-1). Enter =B10-B13 in cell **C10**

8. **Copy The Formulas.** Select the range **B11:B13** and copy it to **C11**. Select the range **C10:C13** and copy it to the range **D10:AE10**. Select the cell **AE10** and copy it to **AF10**.

The Annual Payment is $26,648. Figure 2 shows the final years of the time line for the loan.

FIGURE 5.2 Final Years of the Time Line of Loan Amortization - Basics.

	A	B	Z	AA	AB	AC	AD	AE	AF
1	LOAN AMORTIZATION								
2									
3	**Inputs**								
4	Present value	$300,000							
5	Interest rate / year	8.00%							
6	Number of years	30							
7									
8	**Outputs**								
9	Year	1	25	26	27	28	29	30	31
10	Beg. Principal Balance	$300,000	$123,192	$106,399	$88,262	$68,675	$47,521	$24,674	($0)
11	Payment	$26,648	$26,648	$26,648	$26,648	$26,648	$26,648	$26,648	
12	Interest Component	$24,000	$9,855	$8,512	$7,061	$5,494	$3,802	$1,974	
13	Principal Component	$2,648	$16,793	$18,136	$19,587	$21,154	$22,847	$24,674	

The principal balance drops to zero in year 31 after the final payment is made in year 30. The loan is paid off! It doesn't matter whether the zero amount in cell AF10 displays as positive or negative. The only reason it would display as negative is due to round off error in the eighth decimal or higher, which is irrelevant of our purposes.

The Interest Component depends on the size of the Beg. Principal Balance. In year 1 the interest component starts at its highest level of $24,000 because the Beg. Principal Balance is at its highest level of $300,000. The interest component gradually declines over time as the Principal Balance gradually declines over time. The interest component reaches its lowest level of $1,974 as the Beg. Principal Balance reaches its lowest level of $300,000. The principal repayment component is the residual part of the payment that is left over after the interest component is paid off. In year 1 when the interest component is the highest, the principal component is the lowest. Even though you made a payment of $26,648 in year 1, only $2,648 of it went to paying off the principal! The principal payment gradually increases over time until it reaches its highest level of $24,674 in year 30.

5.2 Sensitivity Analysis

Problem. Examine the same 30 year mortgage for $300,000 as in the previous section. Consider what would happen if the interest rate / year dropped from 8.00% to 7.00%. How much of each year's payment goes to paying interest vs. how much goes to reducing the principal under the two interest rates?

Solution Strategy. Construct a data table for the interest component under the two interest rates. Construct another data table for the principal component under the two interest rates. Create a graph of the two interest components and two principal components.

FIGURE 5.3 Spreadsheet for Loan Amortization - Sensitivity Analysis.

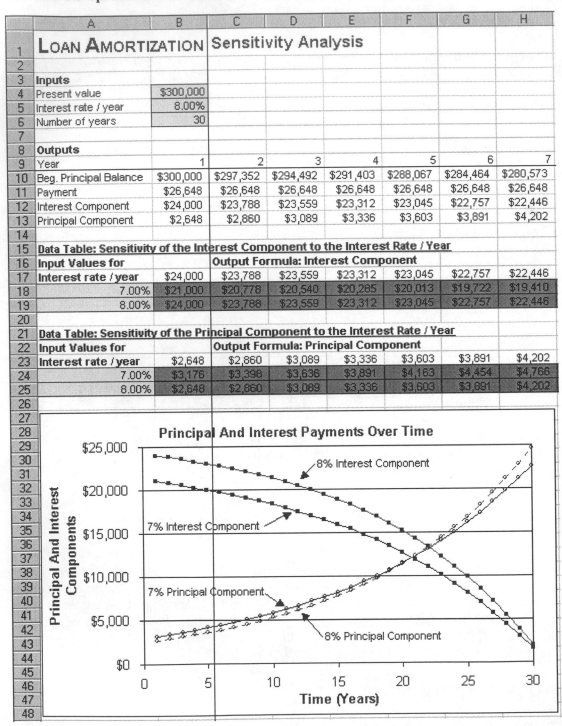

	A	B	C	D	E	F	G	H
1	**LOAN AMORTIZATION**		Sensitivity Analysis					
2								
3	**Inputs**							
4	Present value	$300,000						
5	Interest rate / year	8.00%						
6	Number of years	30						
7								
8	**Outputs**							
9	Year	1	2	3	4	5	6	7
10	Beg. Principal Balance	$300,000	$297,352	$294,492	$291,403	$288,067	$284,464	$280,573
11	Payment	$26,648	$26,648	$26,648	$26,648	$26,648	$26,648	$26,648
12	Interest Component	$24,000	$23,788	$23,559	$23,312	$23,045	$22,757	$22,446
13	Principal Component	$2,648	$2,860	$3,089	$3,336	$3,603	$3,891	$4,202
14								
15	**Data Table: Sensitivity of the Interest Component to the Interest Rate / Year**							
16	**Input Values for**		**Output Formula: Interest Component**					
17	**Interest rate / year**	$24,000	$23,788	$23,559	$23,312	$23,045	$22,757	$22,446
18	7.00%	$21,000	$20,778	$20,540	$20,285	$20,013	$19,722	$19,410
19	8.00%	$24,000	$23,788	$23,559	$23,312	$23,045	$22,757	$22,446
20								
21	**Data Table: Sensitivity of the Principal Component to the Interest Rate / Year**							
22	**Input Values for**		**Output Formula: Principal Component**					
23	**Interest rate / year**	$2,648	$2,860	$3,089	$3,336	$3,603	$3,891	$4,202
24	7.00%	$3,176	$3,398	$3,636	$3,891	$4,163	$4,454	$4,766
25	8.00%	$2,648	$2,860	$3,089	$3,336	$3,603	$3,891	$4,202

How To Build Your Own Spreadsheet Model.

1. **Start with the Basics Spreadsheet.** Open the spreadsheet that you created for Loan Amortization - Basics and immediately save the spreadsheet under a new name using the **File | Save As** command.

2. **Interest Component Data Table.** Create a list of input values for the Interest Rate / Year (7.0% and 8.0%) in the range **A18:A19**. Create an output formula that references the Interest Component row by entering the formula **=B12** in cell **B17** and copy it to the range **C17:AE17**. Select the range **A17:AE19** for the One-Variable Data Table. This range includes both the input values on the left side of the range and the output formula on the top of the range. Then choose **Data | Table** from the main menu and a **Table** dialog box pops up. Enter the cell address **B5** (Interest Rate / Year) in the **Column Input Cell** and click on **OK**.

3. **Principal Component Data Table.** Create a list of input values for the Interest Rate / Year (7.0% and 8.0%) in the range **A24:A25**. Create an output formula that references the Principal Component row by entering the formula **=B13** in cell **B23** and copy it to the range **C23:AE23**. Select the range **A23:AE25** for the One-Variable Data Table. This range includes both the input values on the left side of the range and the output formula on the top of the range. Then choose **Data | Table** from the main menu and a **Table** dialog box pops up. Enter the cell address **B5** (Interest Rate / Year) in the **Column Input Cell** and click on **OK**.

4. **Graph.** Select the range **B9:AE9**, hold down the **Control** button and keep holding it down, select the range **B18:AE19**, continue holding down the **Control** button, and select the range **B24:AE25**. Then choose **Insert | Chart** from the main menu. Select the **XY (Scatter)** chart type and make other selections to complete the Chart Wizard.

From the graph, we see that the Interest Component is much lower at 7% than it is at 8%. Indeed you pay $3,000 less in interest ($21,000 vs. $24,000) in year 1. The difference in interest component gradually declines over time. The principal component nearly the same over time. The principal component is slightly more frontloaded at 7% than at 8%. That is, $528 *more* of your payment goes to principal in year 1 at 7% than at 8%. Then it switches and $2,080 *less* of your payment goes to principal in year 30.

Problems

Skill-Building Problems.

1. To purchase a house, you take out a 30 year mortgage. The present value (loan amount) of the mortgage is $217,832. The mortgage charges an interest rate / year of 9.27%. What is the annual payment required by this mortgage? How much of each year's payment goes to paying interest and how much reducing the principal balance?

2. In purchasing a house, you need to obtain a mortgage with a present value (loan amount) of $175,000. You have a choice of: (A) a 30 year mortgage at an interest rate / year of 9.74% or (B) a 15 year mortgage at an interest rate / year of 9.46%. What is the annual payment required by the two alternative mortgages? How much of each year's payment goes to paying interest and how much reducing the principal balance by the two alternative mortgages? Which mortgage would you prefer?

3. Consider a 30 year mortgage for $442,264 as in the previous section. What would happen if the interest rate / year dropped from 9.21% to 7.95%. How much of each year's payment goes to paying interest vs. how much goes to reducing the principal under the two interest rates?

Live In-class Problems.

4. Given the partial Basics spreadsheet **LoanbasZ.xls**, do steps **4 Payment, 5 Interest Component in year t, 6 Principal Component in year t, 7 Beg. Principal Balance in year t**, and **8 Copy the Formulas**.

5. Given the partial Sensitivity Analysis spreadsheet **LoansenZ.xls**, complete steps **2 Interest Component Data Table** and **3 Principal Component Data Table**.

PART 2 VALUATION

6 Bond Valuation

6.1 Basics

Problem. A bond has a face value of $1,000, an annual coupon rate of 5.0%, a yield to maturity of 9.0%, makes 2 (semiannual) coupon payments per year, and 8 periods to maturity (or 4 years to maturity). What is price of this bond based on the Annual Percentage Rate (APR) convention? What is price of this bond based on the Effective Annual Rate (EAR) convention?

Solution Strategy. We will create a switch that can be used to select either the EAR or APR rate convention. The choice of rate convention will determine the discount rate / period. For a given discount rate / period, we will calculate the bond price in four equivalent ways. First, we will calculate the bond price as the present value of the bond's cash flows. Second, we use a formula for the bond price. Third, we use Excel's **PV** function for a bond price. Fourth, we use Excel's Analysis ToolPak Add-In **PRICE** function, which only works under the APR convention.

FIGURE 6.1 Spreadsheet Model of Bond Valuation - Basics.

	A	B	C	D	E	F	G	H	I	J
1	**BOND VALUATION**	**Basics**		**Annual Percentage Rate**						
2										
3	**Inputs**									
4	Rate Convention: 1 = EAR, 0 = APR	0								
5	Annual Coupon Rate (CR)	5.0%								
6	Yield to Maturity (Annualized) (k$_d$)	9.0%								
7	Number of Payments / Year (NOP)	2								
8	Number of Periods to Maturity (N)	8								
9	Face Value (M)	$1,000								
10										
11	**Outputs**									
12	Discount Rate / Period (DR)	4.5%								
13	Coupon Payment (INT)	$25								
14										
15	**Calculate Bond Price using the Cash Flows**									
16	Period	0	1	2	3	4	5	6	7	8
17	Time (Years)	0.0	0.5	1.0	1.5	2.0	2.5	3.0	3.5	4.0
18	Cash Flows		$25.00	$25.00	$25.00	$25.00	$25.00	$25.00	$25.00	$1,025.00
19	Present Value of Cash Flow		$23.92	$22.89	$21.91	$20.96	$20.06	$19.20	$18.37	$720.76
20	Bond Price	$868.08								
21										
22	**Calculate Bond Price using the Formula**									
23	Bond Price	$868.08								
24										
25	**Calculate Bond Price using the PV Function**									
26	Bond Price	$868.08								
27										
28	**Calculate Bond Price using the PRICE Function (under APR)**									
29	Bond Price	$868.08								

How To Build This Spreadsheet Model.

1. **Enter The Inputs and Name Them.** Enter **0** in cell **B4**. This will serve as a switch between the APR and the EAR rate conventions. To highlight which rate convention is in use, enter

21

=IF($B$4=1,"Effective Annual Rate","Annual Percentage Rate") in cell **D1**. Enter the other inputs into the range **B5:B9** and then name each one. Put the cursor on cell **B5**, click on **Insert | Name | Define**, enter **CR** in the **Names in Workbook** box, and click on **OK**. Put the cursor on cell **B6** and repeat the process to name it **kd**. Repeat the process to give the cells **B7**, **B8**, and **B9** the names **NOP**, **N**, and **M**, respectively.

2. **Calculate the Discount Rate / Period.** The Discount Rate / Period depends on the rate convention being used as follows:

$$\text{Discount Rate / Period} = \begin{cases} (1+\text{Yield To Maturity})^{\wedge}(1/(\text{Number of Payments / Year}))-1 & \text{under EAR} \\ (\text{Yield To Maturity})/(\text{Number of Payments / Year}) & \text{under APR} \end{cases}.$$

Enter **=IF($B$4=1,((1+kd)^(1/NOP))-1,kd/NOP)** in cell **B12** and use the process above to give the cell **B12** the name **DR**.

3. **Calculate the Coupon Payment.** The formula is Coupon Payment = Coupon Rate * Face Value / (Number of Payments / Year). Enter **=CR*M/NOP** in cell **B13** and use the process above to give the cell **B13** the name **INT**.

4. **Calculate Bond Price using the Cash Flows.** Calculate the bond price as the present value of the bond's cash flows. This bond has two cash flows per year for four years or eight periods. Enter the period numbers **0, 1, 2, ..., 8** in the range **B16:J16**. Complete the bond price calculation as follows:

   o Time (years) = (Period) / (Number of Payments / Year) = Period / NOP. Enter **=B16/NOP** in cell **B17** and copy it across.

   o Cash Flows in Periods 1-7 = Coupon Payment. Enter **=INT** in cell **C18** and copy it across.

   o Cash Flow in Period **8** = Coupon Payment + Face Value. Add **+M** to the formula in cell **J18**, so that it reads **=INT+M**.

   o Present Value of Cash Flow = (Cash Flow)/((1+Discount Rate/Period)^ Period). Enter **=C18/((1+DR)^C16)** in cell **C19** and copy it across.

   o Present Value of the Bond = Sum of all the Present Value of Cash Flows (row 19). Enter **=SUM(C19:J19)** in cell **B20**.

5. **Calculate Bond Price using the Formula.** The present value of the bond's cash flows can be simplified down to an equivalent formula. The bond price formula is

$$V_B = \frac{INT \cdot \left(1 - \left((1+DR)^{-N}\right)\right)}{DR} + \frac{M}{(1+DR)^N},$$

where the first term is the present value of an annuity for the string of coupon payments and the second term is the present value of face value payment at the end. Enter **=INT*(1-((1+DR)^(-N)))/DR+M/((1+DR)^N)** in cell **B23**.

6. **Calculate Bond Price using the PV Function.** Excel has a function to calculate the price of a bond. The format is =-PV(Discount Rate / Period, Number of Periods to Maturity, Coupon Payment, Face Value). Enter **=-PV(DR,N,INT,M)** in cell **B26**.

7. **Calculate Bond Price using the PRICE Function (under APR).** Excel's Analysis ToolPak Add-In contains several advanced bond functions, including a Bond Price function assuming the APR convention is being used.

   o Click on **Tools | Add-Ins**, check the **Analysis ToolPak** checkbox on the **Add-Ins** dialog box (see Figure 2 below), and click on **OK**.

   FIGURE 6.2 The Add-Ins dialog box.

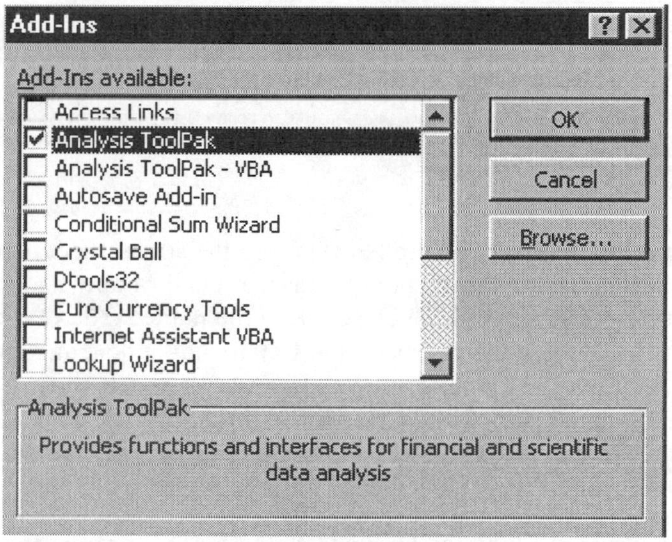

8. The bond price function is =PRICE(Settlement Date, Maturity Date, Annual Coupon Rate, Yield To Maturity, Redemption Value, Number of Payments). The Settlement Date is the date when you exchange money to purchase the bond. Specifying the exact day of settlement and maturity allows a very precise calculation. For our purpose, we simple want the difference between the two dates to equal the (8 Periods To Maturity) / (2 Payments / Year) = 4 Years To Maturity. This is easily accomplished by the use of the DATE function. The DATE Function has the format =DATE(Year, Month, Day). We will enter an arbitrary starting date of 1/1/2000 for the Settlement Date and then specify a formula for 1/1/2000 plus N / NOP for the Maturity Date. We need to add an IF statement to test for the rate convention being used. The bond function is only valid with APR. Enter **=IF($B$4=1,"",PRICE(DATE(2000,1,1),DATE(2000+N/NOP,1,1), CR,kd,100,NOP)*M/100)** in cell **B29**. This uses a conventional Redemption Value of $100.00 and scales the resulting price by the ratio of (M Value) / $100.00.

The resulting bond price is $868.08. Notice you get the same answer all four ways: using the cash flows, using the formula, using the PV function, or using the PRICE function!

6.2 By Yield To Maturity

What is the relationship between bond price and yield to maturity? We can construct a graph to find out.

FIGURE 6.3 Spreadsheet Model of Bond Valuation - By Yield To Maturity.

	A	B	C	D	E	F	G	H	I	J
1	**BOND VALUATION**	**By Yield To Maturity**				**Annual Percentage Rate**				
2										
3	Inputs									
4	Rate Convention: 1 = EAR, 0 = APR	0								
5	Annual Coupon Rate (CR)	5.0%								
6	Yield to Maturity (Annualized) (kd)	9.0%								
7	Number of Payments / Year (NOP)	2								
8	Number of Periods to Maturity (N)	8								
9	Face Value (M)	$1,000								
10										
11	Outputs									
12	Discount Rate / Period (DR)	4.5%								
13	Coupon Payment (INT)	$25								
14										
15	Chart Outputs									
16	Yield to Maturity (Annualized)	1.0%	2.0%	3.0%	4.0%	5.0%	6.0%	7.0%	8.0%	9.0%
17	Discount Rate / Period	0.5%	1.0%	1.5%	2.0%	2.5%	3.0%	3.5%	4.0%	4.5%
18	Bond Price	$1,156	$1,115	$1,075	$1,037	$1,000	$965	$931	$899	$868

Bond Price By Yield To Maturity (chart, placed within C2:J15)

How To Build This Spreadsheet Model.

1. **Start with the Basics Spreadsheet and Delete Rows.** Open the spreadsheet that you created for Bond Pricing – Basics and immediately save the spreadsheet under a new name using the **File | Save As** command. Delete rows **15** through **29** by selecting the range **A15:A29**, clicking on **Edit | Delete**, selecting the **Entire Row** radio button on the **Delete** dialog box, and clicking on **OK**.

2. **Enter Yield To Maturity (Annualized).** Enter Yield To Maturity values **1.0%, 2.0%, 3.0%, 4.0%, …, 20%** in the range **B16:U16**.

3. **Calculate Discount Rate / Period.** Copy the Discount Rate / Period formula from cell **B12** to the cell **B17**. In cell **B17**, change the variable **kd** to **B16**, so that the formula reads **=IF($B$4=1,((1+B16)^(1/NOP))-1,B16/NOP)** and then copy it across.

4. **Calculate Bond Price.** Calculate the bond price using **PV** function and the inputs **N, INT, M**, and the Discount Rate / Period in cell **B17**. Enter **=-PV(B17,N,INT,M)** in cell **B18** and copy it across.

5. **Graph the Bond Price By Yield To Maturity.** Highlight the range **B16:U16** and then while holding down the **Ctrl** button highlight the ranges **B18:U18**. Next choose **Insert | Chart** from the main menu. Select an **XY(Scatter)** chart type and make other selections to complete the Chart Wizard. Place the graph in the range **C2:J15**.

This graph shows the inverse relationship between bond price and yield to maturity. In other word, a higher discount rate (yield to maturity) lowers the present value of the bond's cash flows (price). The graph also that the relationship is curved (nonlinear) rather than being a straight line (linear).

6.3 Dynamic Chart

If you increased the coupon rate of a bond, what would happen to its price? If you increased the yield to maturity of a bond, what would happen to its price? You can answer these questions and more by creating a *Dynamic Chart* using "spinners." Spinners are up-arrow / down-arrow buttons that allow you to easily change the inputs to the model with the click of a mouse. Then the spreadsheet recalculates the model and instantly redraws the model outputs on the graph.

FIGURE 6.4 Spreadsheet Model of Bond Valuation – Dynamic Chart.

	A	B	C	D	E	F	G	H	I	J
1	BOND VALUATION	By Yield To Maturity				Annual Percentage Rate				
2										
3	Inputs									
4	Rate Convention: 1 = EAR, 0 = APR	0								
5	Annual Coupon Rate (CR)	5.0%								
6	Yield to Maturity (Annualized) (kd)	9.0%								
7	Number of Payments / Year (NOP)	2								
8	Number of Periods to Maturity (N)	8								
9	Face Value (M)	$1,000								
10										
11	Outputs									
12	Discount Rate / Period (DR)	4.5%								
13	Coupon Payment (INT)	$25								
14										
15	Chart Outputs									
16	Yield to Maturity (Annualized)	1.0%	2.0%	3.0%	4.0%	5.0%	6.0%	7.0%	8.0%	9.0%
17	Discount Rate / Period	0.5%	1.0%	1.5%	2.0%	2.5%	3.0%	3.5%	4.0%	4.5%
18	Bond Price	$1,156	$1,115	$1,075	$1,037	$1,000	$965	$931	$899	$868

Chart (rows 2–15, columns D–I): "Bond Price By Yield To Maturity" — Bond Price (y-axis, $500 to $1,200) vs Yield To Maturity (x-axis, 0.0% to 20.0%), downward-sloping curve.

How To Build This Spreadsheet Model.

1. **Start with the Basics Spreadsheet and Delete Rows.** Open the spreadsheet that you created for Bond Pricing – Basics and immediately save the spreadsheet under a new name using the **File | Save As** command. Delete rows **15** through **29** by selecting the range **A15:A29**, clicking on **Edit | Delete**, selecting the **Entire Row** radio button on the **Delete** dialog box, and clicking on **OK**. Repeat this procedure to delete row **8**.

2. **Increase Row Height for the Spinners.** Select the range **A4:A8**. Then click on **Format | Row Height** from the main menu. Enter a height of **30** and click on **OK**.

3. **Display the Forms Toolbar.** Click on **View | Toolbars | Forms** from the main menu.

4. **Create the Spinners.** Look for the up-arrow / down-arrow button on the **Forms** toolbar (which will display the word "**Spinner**" if you hover the cursor over it) and click on it. Then draw the box for a spinner from the upper left corner of cell **C4** down to the lower right corner of the cell. Then a spinner appears in the cell **C4**. Right click on the spinner (press the right mouse button while the cursor is above the spinner) and a small menu pops up. Click on **Copy**. Then select the cell **C5** and click on **Paste**. This creates an identical spinner in the cell **C5**. Repeat the process three times more. Select cell **C6** and click on **Paste**. Then select cell **C7** and click on **Paste**. Then select cell **C8** and click on **Paste**. You now have five spinners down column **C**.

5. **Create The Cell Links.** Right click on the first spinner in the cell **C4** and a small menu pops up. Click on **Format Control** and a dialog box pops up. Click on the **Control** tab, then enter the cell link **D4** in the **Cell link** edit box and click on **OK**. Repeat this procedure for the other four spinners. Link the spinner in cell **C5** to cell **D5**. Link the spinner in cell **C6** to cell **D6**. Link the spinner in cell **C7** to cell **D7**. Link the spinner in cell **C8** to cell **D8** and also on the **Control tab**, set the **Minimum value** equal to **1**. Test your spinners by clicking on the up-arrows and down-arrows of the spinners to see how they change the values in the linked cells.

6. **Create Scaled Inputs.** The values in the linked cells are always integers, but they can be scaled appropriately to the problem at hand. Restrict the value in cell **B4** to be either 1 or 0 by entering **=IF(D4>1,1,D4)**. In cell **B5**, enter **=D5/200**. In cell **B6**, enter **=D6/200**. In cell **B7**, enter **=D7**. In cell **B8**, enter **=D8*50**.

7. **Enter Time To Maturity.** Enter Time To Maturity values **1, 2, 3, 4, ..., 30** in the range **B15:AE15**.

8. **Calculate Number of Periods to Maturity.** The Number of Periods to Maturity = (Time to Maturity) * (Number of Periods / Year). Enter **=B15*NOP** In cell **B16** and copy it across.

9. **Calculate Bond Price of a Coupon Bond.** Calculate the duration of a coupon bond using the **PV** bond duration function and the scaled inputs in cells **DR, INT, M** and the Time to Maturity in cell **B16**. Specifically, enter **=-PV(DR,B$16,INT,M)** in cell **B17**. Be sure that **B$16** has a $ in the middle to lock in the row, but not the column.

10. **Calculate Bond Price of a Par Bond.** A par bond is a bond with a coupon rate equal to the yield to maturity. As a benchmark for comparison, calculate the bond price of a par bond using the same inputs for everything else. Copy the formula in cell **B17** to cell **B18**. Then change the coupon payment from **INT** to **DR*M** so that the formula reads **=-PV(DR,B$16,DR*M,M)**. Copy the range **B17:B18** to the range **C17:AE18**.

11. **Graph the Bond Price of a Coupon Bond and Par Bond.** Highlight the range **B15:AE15** and then while holding down the **Ctrl** button highlight the range **B17:AE18**. Next choose **Insert | Chart** from the main menu. Select an **XY(Scatter)** chart type and make other selections to complete the Chart Wizard. Place the graph in the range **E3:J12**.

Your *Dynamic Chart* allows you to change the Bond Price inputs and instantly see the impact on a graph of the price of a coupon bond and par bond by time to maturity. This allows you to perform instant experiments on Bond Price. Below is a list of experiments that you might want to perform:

- What happens when the annual coupon rate is increased?

- What happens when the yield to maturity is increased?

- What happens when the number of payments / year is increased?

- What happens when the face value is increased?

- What is the relationship between the price of a par bond and time to maturity?

- What happens when the annual coupon rate is increased to the point that it equals the yield to maturity? What happens when it is increased further?

6.4 System of Five Bond Variables

There is a system of five bond variables: (1) Number of Periods to Maturity (N), (2) Face Value (M), (3) Discount Rate / Period (DR), (4) Coupon Payments (INT), and (5) Bond Price (VB). Given any four of these variables, the fifth variable can be found by using Excel functions (and in some cases by formulas).

FIGURE 6.5 Spreadsheet Model of Bond Valuation - System of Five Bond Variables.

	A	B	C	D	E	F	G	H	I
1	Bond Valuation	System of Five Bond Variables			Annual Percentage Rate				
2									
3	Inputs								
4	Rate Convention: 1 = EAR, 0 = APR	0							
5	Annual Coupon Rate (CR)	5.0%							
6	Yield to Maturity (Annualized) (k_d)	9.0%							
7	Number of Payments / Year (NOP)	2							
8	(1) Number of Periods to Maturity (N)	8							
9	(2) Face Value (M)	$1,000							
10	(3) Discount Rate / Period (DR)	4.5%							
11	(4) Coupon Payment (INT)	$25							
12	(5) Bond Price (V_b)	$868.08							
13									
14	(1) Number of Periods to Maturity (N)								
15	Number of Periods to Maturity using the NPER Function	8							
16									
17	(2) Face Value (M)								
18	Face Value using the FV Function	$1,000.00							
19	Face Value using the Formula	$1,000.00							
20									
21	(3) Find Discount Rate / Period (DR)								
22	Discount Rate / Period using the RATE Function	4.5%							
23									
24	(4) Coupon Payment (INT)								
25	Coupon Payment using the PMT Function	$25.00							
26	Coupon Payment using the Formula	$25.00							
27									
28	(5) Bond Price (V_b)								
29	Bond Price using the PV Function	$868.08							
30	Bond Price using the Formula	$868.08							

How To Build This Spreadsheet Model.

1. **Start with the Basics Spreadsheet and Delete Rows.** Open the spreadsheet that you created for Bond Pricing – Basics and immediately save the spreadsheet under a new name using the **File | Save As** command. Delete rows **27** through **29** by selecting the range **A27:A29**, clicking on **Edit | Delete**, selecting the **Entire Row** radio button on the **Delete** dialog box, and clicking on **OK**. Then repeat this procedure to delete rows **14** through **25** and repeat this procedure again to delete rows **10** through **11**. This places the five bond variables in rows **8** through **12**, highlighted with **purple labels** above.

2. **Calculate Number of Periods to Maturity (N).** NPER is the Excel function to calculate the number of periods to maturity. The format is =NPER(Discount Rate / Period, Coupon Payment, -Bond Price, Par Value). Enter **=NPER(DR,INT,-VB,M)** in cell **B15**.

3. **Calculate Face Value (M).** There are two ways to calculate the face value of the bond.

   o Use the Excel Function FV. The format is =FV(Discount Rate / Period, Number of Periods to Maturity, Coupon Payment, -Bond Price). Enter **=FV(DR,N,INT,-VB)** in cell **B18**.

   o Use the face value formula

   $$M = V_B \cdot (1+DR)^N - \frac{INT \cdot \left(\left((1+DR)^N \right) - 1 \right)}{DR},$$

   where the first term is the future value of the bond price and the second term is the future values of the string of coupon payments. Enter **=VB*((1+DR)^N)-INT*(((1+DR)^N)-1)/DR** in cell **B19**.

4. **Calculate Discount Rate / Period (DR).** RATE is the Excel function to calculate the discount rate per period. The format is =RATE(Number of Periods to Maturity, Coupon Payment, -Bond Price, Par Value). Enter **=RATE(N,INT,-VB,M)** in cell **B22**.

5. **Calculate Coupon Payment (INT).** There are two ways to calculate the coupon payment of the bond.

   o Use the Excel Function PMT. The format is =PMT(Discount Rate / Period, Number of Periods to Maturity, -Bond Price, Par Value). Enter **=PMT(DR,N,-VB,M)** in cell **B25**.

   o Use the coupon payment formula

   $$INT = \frac{V_B - M/(1+DR)^N}{\left(1 - \left((1+DR)^{-N} \right) \right)/DR},$$

   where the numerator is the bond price minus the present value of the par value and the denominator is the present value of a \$1 coupon payment. Enter **=(VB-M/((1+DR)^N))/((1-((1+DR)^(-N)))/DR)** in cell **B26**.

6. **Calculate Bond Price (VB).** There are two ways to calculate the price of the bond.

   o Use the Excel Function PV. The format is =PV(Discount Rate / Period, Number of Periods to Maturity, Coupon Payment, Par Value). Enter **=-PV(DR,N,INT,M)** in cell **B29**.

   o Use the bond price formula

   $$V_B = \frac{INT \cdot \left(1 - \left((1+DR)^{-N} \right) \right)}{DR} + \frac{M}{(1+DR)^N},$$

   where the first term is the present value of the string of coupon payments and the second term is the present value of the par value. Enter **=INT*(1-((1+DR)^(-N)))/DR+M/((1+DR)^N)** in cell **B30**.

We see that the system of five bond variables is internally consistent. The five outputs in rows **15** through **30** (N=8, M=1000, DR=4.5%, INT=\$25, VB=\$868.08) are identical to the five inputs in rows **8** through **12**. Thus, any of the five bond variables can be calculated from the other four in a fully consistent manner.

28

Problems

Skill-Building Problems

1. A bond has a face value of $1,000, an annual coupon rate of 4.60%, an yield to maturity of 8.1%, makes 2 (semiannual) coupon payments per year, and 10 periods to maturity (or 5 years to maturity). Determine the price of this bond based on the Annual Percentage Rate (APR) convention and the price of this bond based on the Effective Annual Rate (EAR) convention.

2. Determine the relationship between bond price and yield to maturity by constructing a graph of the relationship.

3. Given four of the bond variables, determine the fifth bond variable.
   (a.) Given Number of Periods to Maturity is 10, Face Value is $1,000, Discount Rate / Period is 3.2%, and Coupon Payment is $40, determine the Bond Price.
   (b.) Given Number of Periods to Maturity is 8, Face Value is $1,000, Discount Rate / Period is 4.5%, and the Bond Price is $880.00, determine the Coupon Payment.
   (c.) Given Number of Periods to Maturity is 6, Face Value is $1,000, Coupon Payment is $30, and the Bond Price is $865.00, determine Discount Rate / Period.
   (d.) Given Number of Periods to Maturity is 8, Discount Rate / Period is 3.8%, Coupon Payment is $45, and the Bond Price is $872.00, determine Face Value.
   (e.) Given Face Value is $1,000, Discount Rate / Period is 4.3%, Coupon Payment is $37, and the Bond Price is $887.00, determine the Number of Periods to Maturity.

4. Perform instant experiments on whether changing various inputs causes an increase or decrease in the Bond Price and by how much.
   (a.) What happens when the annual coupon rate is increased?
   (b.) What happens when the yield to maturity is increased?
   (c.) What happens when the number of payments / year is increased?
   (d.) What happens when the face value is increased?
   (e.) What is the relationship between the price of a par bond and time to maturity?
   (f.) What happens when the annual coupon rate is increased to the point that it equals the yield to maturity? What happens when it is increased further?

Live In-class Problems.

5. Given the partial Basics spreadsheet **BondbasZ.xls**, complete step **4 Calculate Bond Price using the Cash Flows**.

6. Given the partial By Yield To Maturity spreadsheet **BondyieZ.xls**, do steps **2 Enter Yield To Maturity (Annualized), 3 Calculate Discount Rate / Period,** and **4 Calculate Bond Price**.

7. Given the partial Dynamic Chart spreadsheet **BonddynZ.xls**, do steps **8 Calculate the Number of Periods to Maturity, 9 Calculate Bond Price of a Coupon Bond,** and **10 Calculate Bond Price of a Par Bond**.

8. Given the partial System of Five Bond Variables spreadsheet **BondsysZ.xls**, complete step **2 Calculate Number of Periods to Maturity** using the NPER function, complete **step 3 Calculate Face Value** using the FV function, complete step **4 Calculate Discount Rate / Period** using the RATE function, complete step **5 Calculate Coupon Payment** using the PMT function, and complete step **6 Calculate Bond Price** using the PV function.

7 Stock Valuation

7.1 Two Stage

Problem. Given the historical data, we can see that over last two years Hot Prospects Inc. has generated a very high real Return On Investment (Real ROI) of 22.3% and 20.7%. Over the last three years, its dividends per share has increased rapidly from $5.10 to $5.84 to $6.64. As the competition catches up over the next five years, the Hot Prospects Real ROI is expected to gradually slow down. The long-run forecast calls for the firm's Real ROI to match the firm's real discount rate (Real k), which is 9.0% per year. Hot Prospects follows a policy of retaining 50.0% of its earnings and paying out the rest as dividends. Going forward, the inflation rate is expected to be 3.0% per year indefinitely. What is the firm's intrinsic value / share?

Solution Strategy. Construct a two-stage discounted dividend model. In stage one, explicitly forecast the firm's dividend over a five-year horizon. In stage two, forecast the firm's dividend from year six to infinity and calculate it's continuation value as the present value of this constant growth annuity. Then, discount the future dividends and the date 5 continuation value back to the present to get the intrinsic value per share.

FIGURE 7.1 Spreadsheet for Stock Valuation - Two Stage.

	A	B	C	D	E	F	G	H	I	J
1	STOCK VALUATION	Two Stage								
2										
3	Inputs									
4	Inflation Rate	3.0%								
5	Real Discount Rate (Real k)	9.0%								
6	Earnings Retention Rate	50.0%								
7										
8	Outputs									Stage 2:
9	Nominal Discount Rate (k)	12.3%								Infinite
10						Stage 1: Explicit Forecast				Horizon
11			Historical Data			Horizon (ROI > k)				(ROI = k)
12	Period	-2	-1	0	1	2	3	4	5	6
13	Inflation Rate		2.8%	3.1%	3.0%	3.0%	3.0%	3.0%	3.0%	3.0%
14	Real Return on Investment (Real ROI)		22.3%	20.7%	19.0%	17.0%	15.0%	13.0%	11.0%	9.0%
15	Nominal Return on Investment (ROI)		25.7%	24.4%	22.6%	20.5%	18.5%	16.4%	14.3%	12.3%
16	Real Growth Rate in Dividend (Real g)		11.2%	10.4%	9.5%	8.5%	7.5%	6.5%	5.5%	4.5%
17	Nominal Growth Rate in Dividend (g)		14.5%	13.7%	12.8%	11.8%	10.7%	9.7%	8.7%	7.6%
18	Nominal Dividend / Share	$5.10	$5.84	$6.64	$7.49	$8.37	$9.27	$10.17	$11.05	$11.89
19	Continuation Value / Share								$256.51	
20	Sum of Future Div. & Cont. Value/Shr				$7.49	$8.37	$9.27	$10.17	$267.56	
21	PV of Future Div. & Cont. Value / Shr				$6.67	$6.64	$6.55	$6.40	$150.00	
22	Intrinsic Value / Share			$176.26						

How To Build This Spreadsheet Model.

1. **Inputs.** Enter the inflation rate, real discount rate, and earnings retention rate into the range **B4:B6**. Enter the historical data in the range **C13:D18** and the cell **B18**. Input the projected inflation rate by entering =$B$4 in cell **E13** and copy it across.

2. **Calculate The Nominal Discount Rate.** The Nominal Discount Rate = (1 + Inflation Rate) * (1 + Real Discount Rate) - 1. Enter =(1+B4)*(1+B5)-1 in cell **B9**.

3. **Forecast Future Real and Nominal ROI.** In the long-run, the firm's Real ROI is forecast to equal the firm's real discount rate. Enter **=B5** in cell **J14**. Given the Real ROI of 20.7% on date 0 and a forecast of 9.0% per year starting in year 6, forecast the intermediate years by entering a smooth declining pattern, such as **19.0%, 17.0%, 15.0%,** etc. from date 1 to date 5 in the range **E14:I14**. For date 6, enter =B5 in cell **J14**. Calculate the Nominal Return On Investment (ROI) = (1 + Inflation Rate) * (1 + Real ROI) - 1. Enter **=(1+E13)*(1+E14)-1** in cell **E15** and copy it across.

4. **Real and Nominal Growth Rate in Dividends.** Calculate the Real Growth Rate in Dividend (Real g) = (Real ROI) * (Earnings Retention Rate). Enter **=E14*$B$6** in cell **E16** and copy it across. Calculate the Nominal Growth Rate in Dividend (g) = (1 + Inflation Rate) (1 + Real g) - 1. Enter **=(1+$B$4)*(1+E16)-1** in cell **E17** and copy it across.

5. **Nominal Dividend / Share.** Calculate the Date t Nominal Dividend = (Date t-1 Nominal Dividend) * (1 + Date t Nominal Growth Rate in Dividend). Enter **=D18*(1+E17)** in cell **E18** and copy it across.

6. **Date 5 Continuation Value.** The Date 5 Continuation Value is the present value of the stream of dividends from date 6 to infinity. Using the present value of an infinitely growing annuity formula, calculate Date 5 Continuation Value = (Date 6 Dividend) / (Nominal Discount Rate – Date 6 Nominal Growth Rate in Dividends). Enter **=J18/(B9-J17)** in cell **I19**.

7. **Sum and PV of Future Dividends and the Continuation Value / Share.** On each date, sum the future dividend and continuation value / share. Enter **=SUM(E18:E19)** in cell **E20** and copy it across. Calculate the Present Value of the Future Dividend and Continuation Value / Share – (Date t Sum) / ((1 + Nominal Discount Rate) ^ t). Enter **=E20/((1+$B$9)^E12)** in cell **E21** and copy it across.

8. **Intrinsic Value Per Share.** Sum the PV of Future Dividends and Continuation Value. Enter **=SUM(E21:I21)** in cell **D22**.

Hot Prospects Inc. is estimated to have an intrinsic value per share of $176.26.

7.2 Dynamic Chart

Problem. How sensitive is the Intrinsic Value to changes in: (1) the Inflation Rate, (2) Earnings Retention Rate, and (3) Real Discount Rate (k)? Said differently, how important is it to be very accurate in forecasting these three inputs?

Solution Strategy. First, we vary the Real Discount Rate input and use Excel's **Data Table** feature to generate the corresponding Intrinsic Value / Share outputs. Second, we construct a **Dynamic Chart** by graphing the Data Table inputs and outputs and by adding spinners to the Inflation Rate and Earnings Retention Rate inputs.

31

FIGURE 7.2 Spreadsheet for Stock Valuation - Dynamic Chart.

	A	B	C	D	E	F	G	H	I	J
1	STOCK VALUATION	Dynamic Chart								
3	Inputs									
4	Inflation Rate	3.0%	[spinner]	6						
5	Earnings Retention Rate	50.0%	[spinner]	5						
14	Outputs									
15	Real Discount Rate (Real k)	9.0%	7.0%	8.0%	9.0%	10.0%	11.0%	12.0%		
16	Intrinsic Value / Share	$176	$235	$202	$176	$156	$139	$125		
18										Stage 2:
19	Nominal Discount Rate (k)	12.3%								Infinite
20						Stage 1: Explicit Forecast				Horizon
21			Historical Data			Horizon (ROI > k)				(ROI = k)
22	Period	-2	-1	0	1	2	3	4	5	6
23	Inflation Rate		2.8%	3.1%	3.0%	3.0%	3.0%	3.0%	3.0%	3.0%
24	Real Return on Investment (Real ROI)		22.3%	20.7%	19.0%	17.0%	15.0%	13.0%	11.0%	9.0%
25	Nominal Return on Investment (ROI)		25.7%	24.4%	22.6%	20.5%	18.5%	16.4%	14.3%	12.3%
26	Real Growth Rate in Dividend (Real g)		11.2%	10.4%	9.5%	8.5%	7.5%	6.5%	5.5%	4.5%
27	Nominal Growth Rate in Dividend (g)		14.5%	13.7%	12.8%	11.8%	10.7%	9.7%	8.7%	7.6%
28	Nominal Dividend / Share	$5.10	$5.84	$6.64	$7.49	$8.37	$9.27	$10.17	$11.05	$11.89
29	Continuation Value / Share								$256.51	
30	Sum of Future Div. & Cont. Value/Shr				$7.49	$8.37	$9.27	$10.17	$267.56	
31	PV of Future Div. & Cont. Value / Shr				$6.67	$6.64	$6.55	$6.40	$150.00	
32	Intrinsic Value / Share			$176.26						

How To Build This Spreadsheet Model.

1. **Open the Two Stage Spreadsheet and Move A Few Things.** Open the spreadsheet that you created for Stock Valuation – Two Stage and immediately save the spreadsheet under a new name using the **File | Save As** command. Insert ten rows above the **Outputs**, by selecting the range **A8:A17** and clicking on **Insert | Rows**. Move The Label "Outputs," by selecting the cell **A18**, clicking on **Edit | Cut**, selecting the cell **A14** and clicking on **Edit | Paste**. Using the same steps, move the range **A5:B5** to the range **A15:B15** and move the range **A6:B6** to the range **A5:B5**.

2. **Increase Row Height for the Spinners.** Select the range **A4:A5**. Then click on **Format | Row Height** from the main menu. Enter a height of **30** and click on **OK**.

3. **Display the Forms Toolbar.** Select **View | Toolbars | Forms** from the main menu.

4. **Create the Spinners.** Look for the up-arrow / down-arrow button on the Forms toolbar (which will display the word "Spinner" if you hover the cursor over it) and click on it. Then draw the box for a spinner from the upper left corner of cell **C4** down to the lower right corner of the cell. Then

a spinner appears in the cell **C4**. Right click on the spinner (press the right mouse button while the cursor is above the spinner) and a small menu pops up. Click on Copy. Then select the cell **C5** and click on Paste. This creates an identical spinner in cell **C5**. You now have two spinners down column **C**.

5. **Create The Cell Links.** Right click on the first spinner in the cell **C4** and a small menu pops up. Click on **Format Control** and a dialog box pops up. Enter the cell link **D4** in the **Cell link** edit box and click on **OK**. Repeat this procedure for the other spinner. Link the spinner in cell **C5** to cell **D5**. Click on the up-arrows and down-arrows of the spinners to see how they change the values in the linked cells.

6. **Create Scaled Inputs.** The values in the linked cells are always integers, but they can be scaled appropriately to the problem at hand. In cell **B4**, enter **=D4/200**. In cell **B5**, enter **=D5/10**.

7. **Enter Real Discount Rate Values.** In the range **C15:H15**, enter the values **7%, 8%, 9%, 10%, 11%,** and **12%**.

8. **Create A Data Table To Calculate Intrinsic Value / Share.** Use Excel's Data Table feature to calculate the Intrinsic Value / Share for each corresponding Real Discount Rate. Specify the output cell by entering **=D32** in cell **B16**. Select the range **B15:H16**, click on **Data | Table**, enter **$B$15** in the **Row Input Cell** box, and click on **OK**.

9. **Graph the Intrinsic Value / Share.** Select the range **C15:H16**, then click on **Insert | Chart** from the main menu. Select an **XY(Scatter)** chart type and make other selections to complete the Chart Wizard. Place the graph in the range **E2:J13**.

The Data Table and the graph indicate that decreasing the Real Discount Rate from 12% to 7% causes the Intrinsic Value / Share to jump from $125 / Share to $235 / Share. Thus, the Intrinsic Value / Share is *very sensitive* to Real Discount Rate. Clicking on the spinner for the Inflation Rate causes no change at all in the Intrinsic Value / Share. This makes sense because the Inflation Rate contributes equally to the Nominal Return on Investment and to the Nominal Discount Rate. The two effects cancel each other out, leaving zero net impact on Intrinsic Value / Share. Clicking on the spinner for the Earnings Retention Rate causes a huge movement in the Intrinsic Value / Share. Hence, it is important to be as accurate as possible about both the Real Discount Rate and the Earnings Retention Rates.

Problems

Skill-Building Problems.

1. Suppose that a firm has generated a real Return On Investment (Real ROI) of 14.6% and 11.9% of the last two year, while the inflation rate as been 3.5% and 2.4%, respectively. Over the last three years, the firm's dividends per share have increased from $15.92 to $16.23 to $17.36. Over the next five years, the firm's Real ROI is expected to gradually slow down. The long-run forecast calls for the firm's Real ROI to match the firm's real discount rate (Real k), which is 6.2% per year. The firm follows a policy of retaining 34.0% of its earnings and paying out the rest as dividends. Going forward, the inflation rate is expected to be 4.1% per year indefinitely. Determine the firm's intrinsic value / share.

2. Perform instant experiments on whether changing various inputs causes an increase or decrease in the firm's intrinsic value / share and by how much.
   (a.) What happens when the inflation rate is increased?
   (b.) What happens when the earnings retention rate is increased?

Live In-class Problems.

3. Given the partial Two Stage spreadsheet **StocktwZ.xls**, do steps **4 Real and Nominal Growth Rate in Dividends, 5 Nominal Dividend / Share, 6 Date 5 Continuation Value, 7 Sum and PV of Future Dividends and Continuation Value / Share,** and **8 Intrinsic Value Per Share**.

4. Given the partial Dynamic Chart spreadsheet **StockdyZ.xls**, complete steps **7 Enter Real Discount Rate Values** and **8 Create A Data Table To Calculate Intrinsic Value / Share**.

8 The Yield Curve

8.1 Obtaining It From Bond Listings

Problem. Given bond prices and yields as published by the financial press or other information sources, obtain the U.S. Treasury Yield Curve.

Solution Strategy. Collect information about Treasury Bills and Treasury Strips for a variety of different maturity dates. Graph the ask yield of these bonds against their time to maturity. See the figure below.

FIGURE 8.1 Spreadsheet Model of The Yield Curve – Obtaining It From Bond Listings.

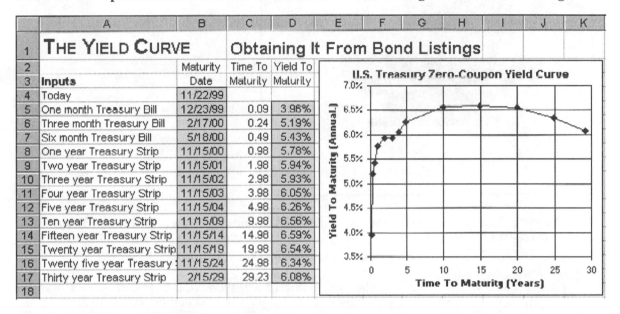

How To Build This Spreadsheet Model.

1. **Inputs.** Enter the today's date in cell **B4**. We wish to graph the *zero-coupon* yield curve, so we will use zero coupon bonds (i.e., bonds that make a single payment on the maturity date and nothing before then). We will use U.S. Treasury Bills for maturities of less than one year and U.S. Treasury Strips for maturities of one year or more. In the financial press, identify 1, 3, and 6 month Treasury Bills and the 1, 2, 3, 4, 5, 10, 15, 20, 25, and 30 year Treasury Strips. We use more frequent maturities at the short end (1, 3, and 6 month), because often there is more curvature in the yield curve for short maturities. For each Treasury Bill or Treasury Strip, enter the maturity date in the range **B5:B17** and yield to maturity (the "ask yield" column in the *Wall Street Journal*) in the range **D5:D17** . When entering the maturity date, be sure to use four-digit years ("2030"), rather than two-digit years ("30"). Excel assumes that two-digit years in the range 00 to 29 are really 2000 to 2029, but that years in the range 30 to 99 are really 1930 to 1999! This distinction doesn't matter for most applications, but it does matter for long-term bonds maturing in 2030 and beyond!

2. **Time To Maturity.** For a given bond, Time To Maturity = Maturity Date - Today's Date. We can calculate the fraction of a year between two calendar dates using Excel's Analysis ToolPak Add-

In **YEARFRAC** function. Excel's Analysis ToolPak Add-In contains several advanced date functions that are useful in finance.

- Click on **Tools**, **Add-Ins**, check the **Analysis ToolPak** checkbox on the **Add-Ins** dialog box (see Figure 2 below), and click on **OK**.

FIGURE 2. The Add-Ins dialog box.

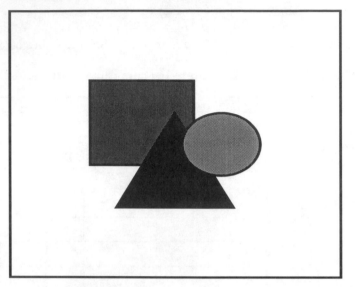

- The date function we will use is **YEARFRAC(Today's Date, Maturity Date)**. Enter **=YEARFRAC($B$4,B5)** in cell **C5**. The two $ in **$B$4** lock in the row and column when the cell formula is copied. Copy cell **C5** to the range **C6:C17**.

3. **Graph the Yield Curve.** Highlight the range **C5:D17** and then choose **Insert Chart** from the main menu. Select an **XY(Scatter)** chart type and make other selections to complete the Chart Wizard.

The November 22nd, 1999 U.S. Treasury Yield Curve demonstrates some frequently-observed properties of the yield curve. Often, there is a sharp rise at the short-end (up to 1 year to maturity), a gentle rise after that, and a small dip at the long-end (past 20 years to maturity).

8.2 Using It To Price A Coupon Bond

Problem. Given the yield curve as published by the financial press, consider a coupon bond has a face value of $1,000, an annual coupon rate of 5.0%, makes 2 (semiannual) coupon payments per year, and 8 periods to maturity (or 4 years to maturity). What is price and yield to maturity of this coupon bond based on the Annual Percentage Rate (APR) convention? What is price and yield to maturity of this coupon bond based on the Effective Annual Rate (EAR) convention?

Solution Strategy. We will use the yield curve you entered in **The Yield Curve - Obtaining It From Bond Listings**. We will calculate the bond price as the present value of the bond's cash flows, where each cash flow is discounted based on the correspond yield on the yield curve (e.g., a cash flow in year three will be discounted based on the yield curve's yield at year three). We will use Excel's **RATE** function to determine the yield to maturity of this coupon bond.

FIGURE 8.2 Spreadsheet Model of The Yield Curve – Using It To Price A Coupon Bond.

	A	B	C	D	E	F	G	H	I	J
1	**THE YIELD CURVE**	Using It To Price A Coupon Bond								
2		Maturity	Time To	Yield To						
3	**Yield Curve Inputs**	Date	Maturity	Maturity						
4	Today	11/22/99								
5	One month Treasury Bill	12/23/99	0.09	3.96%						
6	Three month Treasury Bill	2/17/00	0.24	5.19%						
7	Six month Treasury Bill	5/18/00	0.49	5.43%						
8	One year Treasury Strip	11/15/00	0.98	5.78%						
9	Two year Treasury Strip	11/15/01	1.98	5.94%						
10	Three year Treasury Strip	11/15/02	2.98	5.93%						
11	Four year Treasury Strip	11/15/03	3.98	6.05%						
12	Five year Treasury Strip	11/15/04	4.98	6.26%						
13	Ten year Treasury Strip	11/15/09	9.98	6.56%						
14	Fifteen year Treasury Strip	11/15/14	14.98	6.59%						
15	Twenty year Treasury Strip	11/15/19	19.98	6.54%						
16	Twenty five year Treasury Strip	11/15/24	24.98	6.34%						
17	Thirty year Treasury Strip	2/15/29	29.23	6.08%						
18										
19	**Bond Inputs**									
20	Rate Convention: 1 = EAR, 0 = APR	0	**Annual Percentage Rate**							
21	Annual Coupon Rate (CR)	5.0%								
22	Number of Payments / Year (NOP)	2								
23	Number of Periods to Maturity (N)	8								
24	Face Value (M)	$1,000								
25										
26	**Outputs**									
27	Coupon Payment (INT)	$25								
28										
29	**Calculate the Price and Yield To Maturity of a Coupon Bond using the Cash Flows**									
30	Period	0	1	2	3	4	5	6	7	8
31	Time (Years)	0.0	0.5	1.0	1.5	2.0	2.5	3.0	3.5	4.0
32	Cash Flows		$25.00	$25.00	$25.00	$25.00	$25.00	$25.00	$25.00	$1,025.00
33	Yield to Maturity (Annualized)		5.43%	5.78%	5.86%	5.94%	5.94%	5.93%	5.99%	6.05%
34	Discount Rate / Period		2.72%	2.89%	2.93%	2.97%	2.97%	2.97%	3.00%	3.03%
35	Present Value of Cash Flow		$24.34	$23.62	$22.93	$22.24	$21.60	$20.98	$20.33	$807.58
36	Coupon Bond Price	$963.61								
37	Coupon Bond Discount Rate / Period	3.02%								
38	Coupon Bond Yield to Maturity	6.04%								

The chart in cells E2:J17 is titled "US Treasury Zero-Coupon Yield Curve" with the y-axis "Yield To Maturity (Annual.)" ranging from 3.5% to 7.0% and the x-axis "Time To Maturity (Years)" ranging from 0 to 30.

How To Build This Spreadsheet Model.

1. **Start with the Bond Listings Spreadsheet.** Open the spreadsheet that you created for The Yield Curve – Obtaining It From Bond Listings and immediately save the spreadsheet under a new name using the **File | Save As** command.

2. **Enter The Bond Inputs and Name Them.** Enter **0** in cell **B20**. This will serve as a switch between the APR and the EAR rate conventions. To highlight which rate convention in use, enter **=IF($B$20=1,"Effective Annual Rate","Annual Percentage Rate")** in cell **C20**. Enter the other bond inputs into the range **B21:B25** and then name each one. Put the cursor on cell **B21**, click on **Insert | Name | Define**, enter **CR** in the **Names in Workbook** box, and click on **OK**. Put the cursor on cell **B22** and repeat the process to name it **NOP**. Repeat the process to give the cells **B23**, and **B24** the names **N** and **M**, respectively.

3. **Calculate the Coupon Payment.** The formula is Coupon Payment = Coupon Rate * Face Value / (Number of Payments / Year). Enter **=CR*M/NOP** in cell **B27** and use the process above to give the cell **B27** the name **INT**.

4. **Calculate the Price and Yield To Maturity of a Coupon Bond using the Cash Flows.** Calculate the price as the present value of the coupon bond's cash flows. This bond has two cash flows per year for four years or eight periods. Enter the period numbers **0, 1, 2, ..., 8** in the range **B30:J30**. Complete the bond price calculation as follows:

- Time (years) = (Period) / (Number of Payments / Year) = Period / NOP. Enter **=B30/NOP** in cell **B31** and copy it across.

- Cash Flows in Periods 1-7 = Coupon Payment. Enter **=INT** in cell **C32** and copy it across.

- Cash Flow in Period 8 = Coupon Payment + Face Value. Add **+M** to the formula in cell **J32**, so that it reads **=INT+M**.

- Yield To Maturity = correspond yield on the yield curve. Where there a yield curve Time To Maturity that closely matches the cash flow Time, use the corresponding yield. Enter **=D7** in cell **C33**, **=D8** in cell **D33**, **=D9** in cell **F33**, **=D10** in cell **H33**, and **=D11** in cell **J33**. Otherwise, we will interpolate from the two closest points on the yield curve. For example the yield for the cash flow at year 1.5, take the average of the one year yield and the two year yield. Enter **=(D33+F33)/2** in cell **E33**, **=(F33+H33)/2** in cell **G33**, and **=(H33+J33)/2** in cell **I33**.

- Discount Rate / Period depends on the rate convention being used as follows:
$$\text{Discount Rate / Period} = \begin{cases} (1+\text{Yield To Maturity})^{\wedge}(1/(\text{Number of Payments / Year}))-1 & \text{under EAR} \\ (\text{Yield To Maturity})/(\text{Number of Payments / Year}) & \text{under APR} \end{cases}$$
Enter **=IF($B$20=1,((1+C33)^(1/NOP))-1,C33/NOP)** in cell **C34** and copy it across.

- Present Value of Cash Flow =(Cash Flow)/((1+Discount Rate/Period)^ Period). Enter **=C32/((1+C34)^C30)** in cell **C35** and copy it across.

- Present Value of the Bond = Sum of all the Present Value of Cash Flows (row 19). Enter **=SUM(C35:J35)** in cell **B36**.

- Coupon Bond Discount Rate / Period. RATE is the Excel function to calculate the discount rate per period. The format is =RATE(Number of Periods to Maturity, Coupon Payment, -Bond Price, Par Value). Enter **=RATE(N,INT,-B36,M)** in cell **B37**.

- Coupon Bond Yield To Maturity. Depends on the rate convention being used as follows:
$$\text{Yield To Maturity} = \begin{cases} (1+\text{Discount Rate / Period})^{\wedge}(\text{Number of Payments / Year})-1 & \text{under EAR} \\ (\text{Discount Rate / Period}) \cdot (\text{Number of Payments / Year}) & \text{under APR} \end{cases}$$
Enter **=IF($B$20=1,((1+B37)^(NOP))-1,B37*NOP)** in cell **B38**.

The Coupon Bond's price is $963.61 and its Yield To Maturity is 6.04%. Note that this yield is not the same as four year yield (6.05%) or any other point on the yield curve. The yield of the coupon bond is a weighted average of the yields for each of the eight periods. Since the bond's biggest cash flow is on the maturity date, the biggest weight in the weighted average is on the maturity date. Thus the coupon bond's yield is closest to the yield of the maturity date, but it is not the same.

8.3 Using It To Determine Forward Rates

Problem. Given the yield curve as published by the financial press, calculate the implied forward rates at all maturities.

Solution Strategy. We will use the yield curve that you entered in a spreadsheet for **The Yield Curve - Obtaining It From Bond Listings**. We will calculate the forward rates implied by the yield curve and then graph our results.

FIGURE 8.3 Spreadsheet Model of The Yield Curve – Using It To Determine Forward Rates.

	A	B	C	D	E
1	THE YIELD CURVE		Using It To Determine Forward Rates		
2		Maturity	Time To	Yield To	Forward
3	Inputs	Date	Maturity	Maturity	Rates
4	Today	11/22/99			
5	One month Treasury Bill	12/23/99	0.09	3.96%	3.96%
6	Three month Treasury Bill	2/17/00	0.24	5.19%	5.90%
7	Six month Treasury Bill	5/18/00	0.49	5.43%	5.65%
8	One year Treasury Strip	11/15/00	0.98	5.78%	6.13%
9	Two year Treasury Strip	11/15/01	1.98	5.94%	6.10%
10	Three year Treasury Strip	11/15/02	2.98	5.93%	5.91%
11	Four year Treasury Strip	11/15/03	3.98	6.05%	6.41%
12	Five year Treasury Strip	11/15/04	4.90	6.26%	7.10%
13	Ten year Treasury Strip	11/15/09	9.98	6.56%	6.86%
14	Fifteen year Treasury Stri	11/15/14	14.98	6.59%	6.85%
15	Twenty year Treasury St	11/15/19	19.98	6.54%	6.39%
16	Twenty five year Treasur	11/15/24	24.98	6.34%	5.54%
17	Thirty year Treasury Strip	2/15/29	29.23	6.08%	4.56%
18					
19					

How To Build This Spreadsheet Model.

1. **Start with the Bond Listings Spreadsheet.** Open the spreadsheet that you created for **The Yield Curve - Obtaining It From Bond Listings** and immediately save the spreadsheet under a new name using the **File | Save As** command.

2. **Insert a Column and Format It.** Select the cell **E1** and click on **Insert | Columns**. To get rid of the yellow background, select the range **E5:E17**, click on **Format | Cells**, click on the **Patterns** tab, click on the **No Colors** button, and click on **OK**.

3. **Forward Rates.** The forward rate from date T-1 to date T is given by

$$FR_{T-1,T} = \frac{(1+k_T)^T}{(1+r_{T-1})^{T-1}},$$

where k_T is the date T yield and k_{T-1} is the date T-1 yield. More generally, the forward rate from any date t to date T is given by

$$\left(1 + FR_{t,T}\right)^{T-t} = \frac{\left(1+k_T\right)^T}{\left(1+k_t\right)^t}.$$

Solving for the forward rate, we obtain

$$FR_{T-t} = \left(\frac{\left(1+k_T\right)^T}{\left(1+k_t\right)^t}\right)^{1/(T-t)} - 1.$$

Enter =(((1+D5)^C5)/((1+D4)^C4))^(1/(C5-C4))-1 in cell **E5** and copy it down.

4. **Add The Forward Rates To The Graph.** To add the forward rates, select the range **E5:E17.**, click on **Edit | Copy**, then select the graph by clicking anywhere on the graph, and click on **Edit | Paste**.

Using the forward rates as at least a rough forecast of future interest rates and taking the forward rates at face value, they would suggest that interest rates are going to be in the 6% range in the short run, rising to 7% in five years, and declining below 5% in the long run. One difficulty with taking this interpretation literally has to do with market segmentation in the demand for treasury securities. There is significantly more demand for short-term bonds than bonds of other maturities, for their use in short-term cash management. There is also extra demand by institutional bond funds for the newly-issued, longest maturity treasury bond (the so-called, "on-the-run" bond). High demand means high prices, which means low yields. Thus, the yield curve is typically has lower yields at the short end and the long end due to this segmentation in market demand. It is not clear whether this yield curve would be nearly flat or not in the absence of market segmentation. Ignoring the extreme forward rates generated by the short run and long run segmentation, the forecast seems to be between 6.0% and 6.5%.

Problems

Skill-Building Problems.

1. Given the yield curve as published by the financial press, consider a coupon bond has a face value of $2,000, an annual coupon rate of 4.2%, makes 2 (semiannual) coupon payments per year, and 8 periods to maturity (or 4 years to maturity). Determine the price and yield to maturity of this coupon bond based on the Annual Percentage Rate (APR) convention. Then use it to determine the price and yield to maturity of this coupon bond based on the Effective Annual Rate (EAR) convention.

2. Given the yield curve as published by the financial press, calculate the implied forward rates at all maturities.

Live In-class Problems.

3. Given the partial Obtaining It From Bond Listings spreadsheet **YieldliZ.xls**, do step **2 Time To Maturity**.

4. Given the partial Using It To Price A Coupon Bond spreadsheet **YieldcoZ.xls**, complete step **4 Calculate the Price and Yield To Maturity of a Coupon Bond using the Cash Flows.**

5. Given the partial Using It To Determine Forward Rates spreadsheet **YieldfoZ.xls**, do step **3 Forward Rates**.

9 US Yield Curve Dynamics

9.1 Dynamic Chart

How does the US yield curve change over time? What determines the volatility of changes in the yield curve? Are there differences in the volatility of short rates, medium rates, long rates, etc.? You can answer these questions and more using a *Dynamic Chart* of the yield curve, which is based on 30 years of monthly US zero-coupon, yield curve data.

I have made a major exception for this spreadsheet model and provided the model already built. To load the model, click on Ycdyndyn.xls. I will update this spreadsheet model each month with the latest yield curve data and make it available for free in the "Free Samples" section of http://www.spreadsheetmodeling.com.

The step-by-step instructions below explain how it you can build this model. The dynamic chart uses "spinners," which are up-arrow / down-arrow buttons, that allow you to advance the yield curve graph from month to month. This allows you to see a dynamic "movie" or animation of the yield curve over time. Thus, you can directly observe the volatility of the yield curve and other dynamic properties. For details of what to look for, see the discussion below on "using the spreadsheet model."

FIGURE 9.1 Spreadsheet Model of US Yield Curve Dynamics – Dynamic Chart.

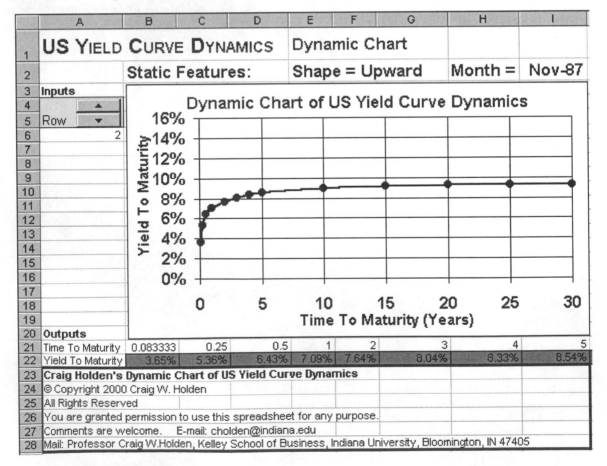

How To Build This Spreadsheet Model.

1. **Start with a Spreadsheet Containing the Yield Curve Database.** Click on Ycdyndat.xls to open a spreadsheet containing the yield curve database (see Figure 2). Select the range **A1:O1** and click on **Insert | Columns**. Columns **P, Q,** and **R** contain three sets of titles for the dataset. Columns **S, T,** and **U** contain yield data for bond maturities of one month, three months, and six months (0.833, 0.25, and 0.50 years, respectively). Columns **V** through **AE** contain yield data for bond maturities of 1, 2, 3, 4, 5, 10, 15, 20, 25, and 30 years. Rows **2** through **9** contain examples of static features yield curve that can be observed from actual data in a particular month. For example, the yield curve is sometimes upward sloping (as it was in Nov 87) or downward sloping (in Nov 80) or flat (in Jan 70) or hump shaped (in Dec 78). Rows **10** through **376** contain monthly US zero-coupon, yield curve data from January 1970 through June 2000. For the period from January 1970 through December 1991, the database is based on the Bliss (1992) monthly estimates of the zero-coupon, yield curve. Bliss fits a parsimonious, nonlinear function that is capable of matching all of the empirically observed shapes of the zero-coupon, yield curve. For more details see Bliss, R., 1992, "Testing Term Structure Estimation Methods," Indiana University Discussion Paper #519. For the period from January 1992 to June 2000, the yield curve is directly observed from Treasury Bills and Strips in the *Wall Street Journal*.

FIGURE 9.2 Spreadsheet Containing the Yield Curve Database.

	P	Q	R	S	T	U	V	W	X
1				Time To Maturity	Time To Maturity	Time To Maturity	Time To Maturity	Time To Maturity	Time To Maturity
2	Title 1	Title 2	Title 3	0.0833	0.25	0.5	1	2	3
3	Static Features:	Shape = Upward	Nov-87	3.65%	5.36%	6.43%	7.09%	7.64%	8.04%
4	Static Features:	Shape = Downward	Nov-80	14.83%	14.60%	14.64%	14.17%	13.22%	12.75%
5	Static Features:	Shape = Flat	Jan-70	7.73%	8.00%	8.03%	7.98%	7.95%	7.94%
6	Static Features:	Shape = Hump	Dec-78	8.82%	9.48%	9.99%	10.18%	9.76%	9.40%
7	Static Features:	Level = Low	Dec-70	4.62%	4.91%	4.95%	5.02%	5.40%	5.69%
8	Static Features:	Level = High	Oct-81	12.65%	13.13%	13.53%	13.85%	14.01%	14.06%
9	Static Features:	Curvature = Little	Dec-72	4.93%	5.24%	5.44%	5.62%	5.86%	6.01%
10	Static Features:	Curvature = Lot	Sep-82	6.67%	7.87%	9.05%	10.29%	11.16%	11.43%
11	Monthly Dynamics:		Jan-70	7.73%	8.00%	8.03%	7.98%	7.95%	7.94%
12	Monthly Dynamics:		Feb-70	6.23%	6.99%	6.97%	6.96%	7.02%	7.04%
13	Monthly Dynamics:		Mar-70	6.33%	6.44%	6.53%	6.67%	6.85%	6.95%
14	Monthly Dynamics:		Apr-70	6.48%	7.03%	7.35%	7.50%	7.60%	7.67%
15	Monthly Dynamics:		May-70	6.22%	7.03%	7.28%	7.45%	7.58%	7.63%
16	Monthly Dynamics:		Jun-70	6.14%	6.47%	6.81%	7.17%	7.43%	7.53%
17	Monthly Dynamics:		Jul-70	6.32%	6.38%	6.55%	6.87%	7.19%	7.31%
18	Monthly Dynamics:		Aug-70	6.22%	6.38%	6.57%	6.83%	7.07%	7.18%
19	Monthly Dynamics:		Sep-70	5.32%	6.04%	6.49%	6.63%	6.64%	6.77%
20	Monthly Dynamics:		Oct-70	5.23%	5.91%	6.23%	6.33%	6.50%	6.69%
21	Monthly Dynamics:		Nov-70	4.86%	5.05%	5.11%	5.10%	5.29%	5.59%

2. **Create a Spinner.** Click on **View | Toolbars | Forms** from the main menu. Look for the up-arrow / down-arrow button on the **Forms** toolbar (which will display the word "**Spinner**" if you hover the cursor over it) and click on it. Then draw the box for a spinner in the range **A4:A5**.

3. **Create The Cell Link.** Right click on the spinner and a small menu pops up. Click on **Format Control** and a dialog box pops up. Click on the **Control** tab, then enter the cell link **A6** in the **Cell link** edit box, set the **Minimum value** equal to **2**, and click on **OK**. Test your spinner by clicking on the up-arrows and down-arrows of the spinner to see how it changes the value in the linked cell.

4. **Time To Maturity.** Reference the Database's Time To Maturity values in the range **S2:AE2**, by entering =S2 in cell **B21** and copy it to the range **C21:N21**.

5. **Yield To Maturity.** Reference the Database's Yield To Maturity values using the Excel **HLOOKUP** function. The format is =HLOOKUP(Lookup value, Database, Row). The Lookup value is the corresponding Time To Maturity, the database is the range **P2:AE600**, which has already been given the range name "**Database**," and the Row is the linked cell **A6**. Enter **=HLOOKUP(B21,Database,$A$6)** in cell **B22** and copy it across.

6. **Graph the Yield To Maturity by Time To Maturity.** Highlight the range **B21:N22**. Next choose **Insert | Chart** from the main menu. Select an **XY(Scatter)** chart type and make other selections to complete the Chart Wizard. Place the graph in the range **B3:I20**.

7. **Three Titles.** Reference the Database's three columns of Title values using the Excel **HLOOKUP** function. The format is same as above, except that the Lookup value will be the column headings ("Title 1", etc.) that we wish to reference. Enter **=HLOOKUP("Title 1",Database,$A$6)** in cell **B2**, **=HLOOKUP("Title 2",Database,$A$6)** in cell **E2**, and **=HLOOKUP("Title 3",Database,$A$6)** in cell **I2**. To format the date title, select cell **I2**, click on **Format | Cells,** click on **Date** in the Category list box, click on **Mar-98** format in the Type list box, and click on **OK**.

Using The Spreadsheet Model.

To run the Dynamic Chart, click on the up arrow of the spinner. The movie / animation begins with some background on the yield curve's static features. In the 30 year database we observe:

- four different **shapes**: upward-sloping, downward-sloping, flat, and hump-shaped,

- the overall **level** of the yield curve ranges from low to high, and

- the amount of **curvature** at the short end ranges from a little to a lot.

Keep clicking on the spinner and you will get to the section of the Dynamic Chart covering 30 years of the US yield curve history. This section shows the yield curve on a month by month basis. For example, Figure 3 shows the US yield curve in November 1970.

FIGURE 9.3 Spreadsheet Containing the Month By Month History – Dynamic Chart.

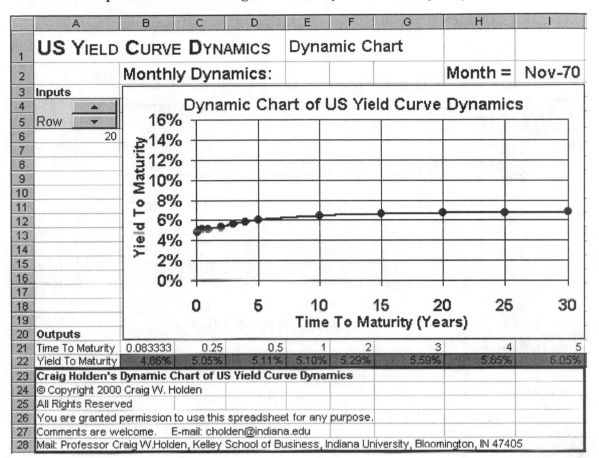

	A	B	C	D	E	F	G	H	I
1	US Yield Curve Dynamics				Dynamic Chart				
2		Monthly Dynamics:						Month =	Nov-70
3	Inputs								
4	▲								
5	Row ▼								
6	20								
7									
8									
9									
10									
11									
12									
13									
14									
15									
16									
17									
18									
19									
20	Outputs								
21	Time To Maturity	0.083333	0.25	0.5	1	2	3	4	5
22	Yield To Maturity	4.86%	5.05%	5.11%	5.10%	5.29%	5.59%	5.85%	6.05%
23	Craig Holden's Dynamic Chart of US Yield Curve Dynamics								
24	© Copyright 2000 Craig W. Holden								
25	All Rights Reserved								
26	You are granted permission to use this spreadsheet for any purpose.								
27	Comments are welcome. E-mail: cholden@indiana.edu								
28	Mail: Professor Craig W.Holden, Kelley School of Business, Indiana University, Bloomington, IN 47405								

Keep clicking on the spinner and you will see the yield curve move around over time. By observing this movie / animation, you should be able to recognize the following key **dynamic** properties of the yield curve:

- short rates (the 0 to 5 year piece of the yield curve) are more volatile than long rates (the 15 to 30 year piece),

- the overall volatility of the yield curve is higher when the level is higher (especially in the early 80's), and

- sometimes there are sharp reactions to government intervention.

As an example of the later, consider what happened in 1980. Figure 4 shows the yield curve in January 1980.

FIGURE 9.4 Spreadsheet Showing The Yield Curve in January 1980.

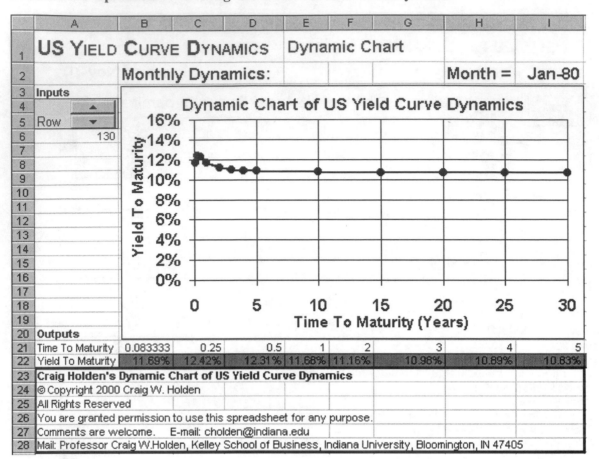

Short rates were around 12% and long rates were at 10.7%. President Jimmy Carter was running for re-election. He wished to manipulate the election year economy to make it better for his re-election bid. His strategy for doing this was to impose credit controls on the banking system. Click on the spinner to see what the reaction of the financial market was.

FIGURE 9.5 Spreadsheet Showing The Yield Curve in March 1980.

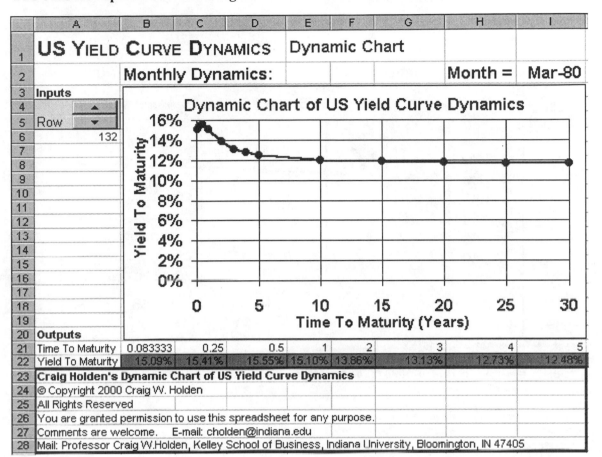

	A	B	C	D	E	F	G	H	I
1	US YIELD CURVE DYNAMICS				Dynamic Chart				
2		Monthly Dynamics:						Month =	Mar-80
3	Inputs								
4	▲								
5	Row ▼								
6	132								
7									
20	Outputs								
21	Time To Maturity	0.083333	0.25	0.5	1	2	3	4	5
22	Yield To Maturity	15.09%	15.41%	15.55%	15.10%	13.86%	13.13%	12.73%	12.48%
23	Craig Holden's Dynamic Chart of US Yield Curve Dynamics								
24	© Copyright 2000 Craig W. Holden								
25	All Rights Reserved								
26	You are granted permission to use this spreadsheet for any purpose.								
27	Comments are welcome. E-mail: cholden@indiana.edu								
28	Mail: Professor Craig W.Holden, Kelley School of Business, Indiana University, Bloomington, IN 47405								

In two months time, the short rate when up to 15.5%, an increase of 3.5%! What a disaster! This was the opposite of the reaction the Carter had intended. Notice that long rates when up to 11.7%, an increase of only 1%. Apparently, the market expected that this intervention would only be a short-lived phenomena. Carter quickly realized what a big political mistake he had made and announced that the credit controls were being dropped. Click on the spinner to see what the reaction of the financial market was.

47

FIGURE 9.6 Spreadsheet Showing The Yield Curve in April 1980.

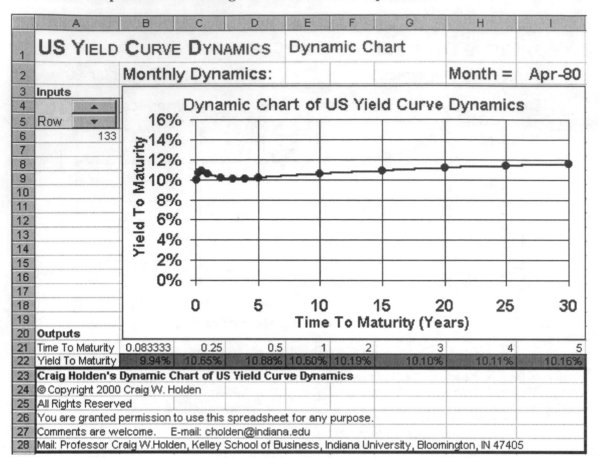

	A	B	C	D	E	F	G	H	I
1	US YIELD CURVE DYNAMICS			Dynamic Chart					
2		Monthly Dynamics:						Month =	Apr-80
3	Inputs								
4	▲								
5	Row ▼								
6	133								
21	Time To Maturity	0.083333	0.25	0.5	1	2	3	4	5
22	Yield To Maturity	9.94%	10.65%	10.86%	10.60%	10.19%	10.10%	10.11%	10.16%
23	Craig Holden's Dynamic Chart of US Yield Curve Dynamics								
24	© Copyright 2000 Craig W. Holden								
25	All Rights Reserved								
26	You are granted permission to use this spreadsheet for any purpose.								
27	Comments are welcome. E-mail: cholden@indiana.edu								
28	Mail: Professor Craig W.Holden, Kelley School of Business, Indiana University, Bloomington, IN 47405								

Short rates dropped to 10.9%! A drop of 4.6% in one month! The high interest rates went away, but the political damage was done. This is the single biggest change in the yield curve in 30 years.

Problems

Skill-Building Problems.

1. How volatile are short rates versus medium rates versus long rates?

   (a.) Get a visual sense of the answer to this question by clicking on the spinner (up/down arrow) to run through all of the years of US Yield Curve history in the database.

   (b.) Calculate the variance of the time series of: (i) one-month yields, (ii) five-year yields, (iii) fifteen-year yields, and (iv) thirty year yields. Use Excel's VAR function to calculate the variance of the yields in columns **S**, **Z**, **AB**, and **AE** in the US Yield Curve Dynamics - Dynamic Chart spreadsheet.

2. Determine the relationship between the volatility of the yield curve and the level of the yield curve. Specifically, for each five year time period (70-74, 75-79, 80-84, etc.) calculate the variance and the average level of the time series of: (i) one-month yields, (ii) five-year yields, (iii) fifteen-year yields, and (iv) thirty year yields. Use Excel's VAR and AVERAGE functions to

calculate the variance and the average of five-year ranges of the yields in columns **S**, **Z**, **AB**, and **AE** in the US Yield Curve Dynamics - Dynamic Chart spreadsheet. For example:

- The 70-74 time series of one-month yields is in the range **S11-S70**.

- The 75-79 time series of one-month yields is in the range **S71-S130**.

- The 80-84 time series of one-month yields is in the range **S131-S190**.

- And so on.

Summarize what you have learned from this analysis.

Live In-class Problems.

3. Given the partial Dynamic Chart spreadsheet **YcdyndyZ.xls**, complete steps **4 Time To Maturity** and **5 Yield To Maturity**.

PART 3 CAPITAL BUDGETING

10 Project NPV

10.1 Basics

Problem. Suppose a firm is considering the following project, where all of the dollar figures are in thousands of dollars. In year 0, the project requires $11,350 investment in plant and equipment, is depreciated using the straight-line method over seven years, and there is a salvage value of $1,400 in year 7. The project is forecast to generate sales of 2,000 units in year 1, rising to 7,400 units in year 5, declining to 1,800 units in year 7, and dropping to zero in year 8. The inflation rate is forecast to be 2.0% in year 1, rising to 4.0% in year 5, and then leveling off. The real cost of capital is forecast to be 11.0% in year 1, rising to 12.2% in year 7. The tax rate is forecast to be a constant 35.0%. Sales revenue per unit is forecast to be $9.70 in year 1 and then grow with inflation. Variable cost per unit is forecast to be $7.40 in year 1 and then grow with inflation. Cash fixed costs are forecast to be $5,280 in year 1 and then grow with inflation. What is the project NPV?

Solution Strategy. Forecast key assumptions, discounting, sales revenue per unit, variable costs per unit, and fixed costs over the seven year horizon. Then, forecast the project income and expense items. Calculate the net cash flows. Discount each cash flow back to the present and sum to get the NPV.

Modeling Issue. The inflation rate is forecast separately and explicitly enters into the calculation of: (1) the discount rate (= cost of capital) and (2) price or cost / unit items. This guarantees that we are *consistent* in the way we are treating the inflation component of cash flows in the numerator of the NPV calculation and the inflation component of the discount rate in the denominator of the NPV calculation. This avoids a common error in practice that people often treat the cash flows and discount rates *as if* they were unrelated to each other and thus they are *inconsistent* in way that they implicitly treat the inflation component of each.

FIGURE 10.1 Spreadsheet for Project NPV - Basics.

	A	B	C	D	E	F	G	H	I
1	**PROJECT NPV**	**Basics**							
2	(in thousands of $)	2001	2002	2003	2004	2005	2006	2007	2008
3		Year 0	Year 1	Year 2	Year 3	Year 4	Year 5	Year 6	Year 7
4	**Key Assumptions**								
5	Unit Sales		2000	4000	5600	6800	7400	3700	1800
6	Inflation Rate		2.0%	2.5%	3.0%	3.5%	4.0%	4.0%	4.0%
7	Real Cost of Capital		11.0%	11.2%	11.4%	11.6%	11.8%	12.0%	12.2%
8	Tax Rate		35.0%	35.0%	35.0%	35.0%	35.0%	35.0%	35.0%
9									
10	**Discounting**								
11	Discount Rate = Cost of Capital		13.2%	14.0%	14.7%	15.5%	16.3%	16.5%	16.7%
12	Cumulative Discount Factor	0.0%	13.2%	29.0%	48.1%	71.0%	98.9%	131.6%	170.3%
13									
14	**Price or Cost / Unit**								
15	Sales Revenue / Unit		$9.70	$9.94	$10.24	$10.60	$11.02	$11.46	$11.92
16	Variable Cost / Unit		$7.40	$7.59	$7.81	$8.09	$8.41	$8.75	$9.10
17	Cash Fixed Costs		$5,280	$5,412	$5,574	$5,789	$6,000	$6,240	$6,490
18									
19	**Cash Flow Forecasts**								
20	Sales Revenue		$19,400	$39,770	$57,348	$72,075	$81,571	$42,417	$21,461
21	Variable Costs		$14,800	$30,340	$43,750	$54,985	$62,230	$32,359	$16,372
22	Gross Margin		$4,600	$9,430	$13,598	$17,090	$19,342	$10,058	$5,089
23									
24	Cash Fixed Costs		$5,280	$5,412	$5,574	$5,769	$6,000	$6,240	$6,490
25	Depreciation		$1,621	$1,621	$1,621	$1,621	$1,621	$1,621	$1,621
26	Total Fixed Costs		$6,901	$7,033	$7,196	$7,391	$7,622	$7,862	$8,111
27									
28	Operating Profit		($2,301)	$2,397	$6,402	$9,699	$11,720	$2,196	($3,023)
29	Taxes		($806)	$839	$2,241	$3,395	$4,102	$769	($1,058)
30	Net Profit		($1,496)	$1,558	$4,161	$6,304	$7,618	$1,427	($1,965)
31									
32	Add Back Depreciation		$1,621	$1,621	$1,621	$1,621	$1,621	$1,621	$1,621
33	Operating Cash Flow		$126	$3,179	$5,783	$7,926	$9,239	$3,049	($343)
34									
35	Investment in Plant & Equip	($11,350)							$1,400
36	Cash Flows	($11,350)	$126	$3,179	$5,783	$7,926	$9,239	$3,049	$1,057
37	Present Value of Each Cash Flow	($11,350)	$111	$2,464	$3,905	$4,634	$4,646	$1,316	$391
38	Net Present Value	$6,117							

How To Build Your Own Spreadsheet Model.

1. **Set-up Titles and Freeze Panes.** Enter column titles, such as **2001, 2002**, etc. in row **2** and **Year 0, Year 1**, etc. in row **3**. Then, place the cursor in cell **B4** and click on **Window | Freeze Panes**. This freezes the top three rows to provide column titles and freezes the first column to provide row titles.

2. **Inputs.** Enter the key assumptions in the range **C5:I8**, the year 1 price and cost inputs in the range **C15:C17**, the year 0 investment in plant and equipment (as a negative number) in cell **B35**, and the year 7 salvage value in cell **I35**.

3. **Discounting.** Calculate the (nominal) discount rate, which is the (nominal) cost of capital. Then calculate the cumulative discount rate.

51

- o **Discount Rate = Cost of Capital.** The formula for the (Nominal) Discount Rate = (1 + Inflation Rate) * (1 + Real Discount Rate) - 1. Enter **=(1+C6)*(1+C7)-1** in cell **C11** and copy it across.

- o **Cumulative Discount Factor.** This is the product of the year-by-year discount factors cumulated to a given date. Enter **0.0%** in cell **B12**. The rest are calculated as (This Year's Cumulative Discount Factor) = (1 + Last Year's Cumulative Discount Factor) * (1 + This Year's Discount Rate) - 1. Enter **=(1+B12)*(1+C11)-1** in cell **C12** and copy across.

4. **Forecast Price and Cost Items.** The price and cost items are projected by growing the item at the inflation rate. This Year's Price/Cost = (Last Year's Price/Cost) * (1 + This Year's Inflation Rate). Enter **=C15*(1+D$6)** in cell **D15** and copy the it to the range **D15:I17**. The $ signs in **D$6** locks in row **6**, which the inflation rate row.

5. **Cash Flow Forecasts.** Forecast each of the cash flow items as appropriate.

- o **Sales Revenue** = (Sales Revenue / Unit) * (Units sold). Enter **=C5*C15** in cell **C20** and copy across.

- o **Variable Costs** = (Variable Costs / Unit) * (Units sold). Enter **=C5*C16** in cell **C21** and copy across.

- o **Gross Margin** = Sales Revenue - Variable Costs. Enter **=C20-C21** in cell **C22** and copy across.

- o **Cash Fixed Costs** = Cash Fixed Costs. Enter **=C17** in cell **C24** and copy across.

- o **Depreciation** = -(Investment in Plant and Equipment) / (Number of years to fully depreciate). Depreciation is held constant each year, because the straight-line method is being used. Enter **=-$B$35/7** in cell **C25** and copy across.

- o **Total Fixed Costs** = Cash Fixed Costs + Depreciation. Enter **=C24+C25** in cell **C26** and copy across.

- o **Operating Profit** = Gross Margin - Total Fixed Costs. Enter **=C22-C26** in cell **C28** and copy across.

- o **Taxes** = Operating Profit * Tax Rate. Enter **=C28*C8** in cell **C29** and copy across.

- o **Net Profit** = Operating Profit - Taxes. Enter **=C28-C29** in cell **C30** and copy across.

- o **Add Back Depreciation** = Depreciation. Enter **=C25** in cell **C32** and copy across.

- o **Operating Cash Flow** = Net Profit + Add Back Depreciation. Enter **=C30+C32** in cell **C33** and copy across.

- o **Cash Flows** = Operating Cash Flow + Investment in Plant and Equipment. Enter **=B33+B35** in cell **B36** and copy across.

6. **Present Value and NPV.** Discount the forecasted cash flows back to the present as follows:

- o **Present Value of Each Cash Flow** = (Cash Flow) / (1 + Cumulative Discount Factor). Enter **=B36/(1+B12)** in cell **B37** and copy across.

- o **Net Present Value** = Sum of Present Value of the Cash Flows. Enter **=SUM(B37:I37)** in cell **B38**.

The Net Present Value of the project is $6,117. The project should be accepted.

10.2 Forecasting Cash Flows

Problem. Consider the same project as Project NPV - Basics. Let's examine the details of how you forecast the project cash flows. Suppose that Direct Labor, Materials, Selling Expenses, and Other Variable Costs are forecast to be $3.50, $2.00, $1.20, and $0.70, respectively, in year 1 and then grow with inflation. Lease Payment, Property Taxes, Administration, Advertising, and Other cash fixed costs are forecast to be $2,800, $580, $450, $930, and $520, respectively, in year 1 and then grow with inflation. What is the Total Variable Cost / Unit, the Total Cash Fixed Costs, and the project NPV?

Solution Strategy. Forecast the variable cost / unit and cash fixed costs in more detail. Then sum up all of the items in each category to get the total. Feed these sums into the previous analysis of the project NPV.

FIGURE 10.2 Spreadsheet for Forecasting Project Assumptions, Discounting, & Price or Cost / Unit.

	A	B	C	D	E	F	G	H	I
1	**PROJECT NPV**		**Forecasting Cash Flows**						
2	(in thousands of $)	2001	2002	2003	2004	2005	2006	2007	2008
3		Year 0	Year 1	Year 2	Year 3	Year 4	Year 5	Year 6	Year 7
4	**Key Assumptions**								
5	Unit Sales		2000	4000	5600	6800	7400	3700	1800
6	Inflation Rate		2.0%	2.5%	3.0%	3.5%	4.0%	4.0%	4.0%
7	Real Cost of Capital		11.0%	11.2%	11.4%	11.6%	11.8%	12.0%	12.2%
8	Tax Rate		35.0%	35.0%	35.0%	35.0%	35.0%	35.0%	35.0%
9									
10	**Discounting**								
11	Discount Rate = Cost of Capital		13.2%	14.0%	14.7%	15.5%	16.3%	16.5%	16.7%
12	Cumulative Discount Factor	0.0%	13.2%	29.0%	48.1%	71.0%	98.9%	131.6%	170.3%
13									
14	**Price or Cost / Unit**								
15	Sales Revenue / Unit		$9.70	$9.94	$10.24	$10.60	$11.02	$11.46	$11.92
16									
17	Variable Costs / Unit:								
18	Direct Labor		$3.50	$3.59	$3.70	$3.82	$3.98	$4.14	$4.30
19	Materials		$2.00	$2.05	$2.11	$2.19	$2.27	$2.36	$2.46
20	Selling Expenses		$1.20	$1.23	$1.27	$1.31	$1.36	$1.42	$1.47
21	Other		$0.70	$0.72	$0.74	$0.76	$0.80	$0.83	$0.86
22	Total Variable Cost / Unit		$7.40	$7.59	$7.81	$8.09	$8.41	$8.75	$9.10
23									
24	Cash Fixed Costs:								
25	Lease Payment		$2,800	$2,870	$2,956	$3,060	$3,182	$3,309	$3,442
26	Property Taxes		$580	$595	$612	$634	$659	$685	$713
27	Administration		$450	$461	$475	$492	$511	$532	$553
28	Advertising		$930	$953	$982	$1,016	$1,057	$1,099	$1,143
29	Other		$520	$533	$549	$568	$591	$615	$639
30	Total Cash Fixed Costs		$5,280	$5,412	$5,574	$5,769	$6,000	$6,240	$6,490

How To Build Your Own Spreadsheet Model.

1. **Open the Basics Spreadsheet and Add Rows.** Open the spreadsheet that you created for Project NPV - Basics and immediately save the spreadsheet under a new name using the **File | Save As** command. Select **A16:A21** and click on **Insert | Row**. Select **A23:A29** and click on **Insert | Row**.

2. **Inputs.** Enter the Variable Cost / Unit inputs in the range **C18:C21** and the Cash Fixed Cost inputs in the range **C25:C29**.

3. **Forecast The Detailed Items.** The detailed Variable Cost / Unit items and Cash Fixed Cost items are projected by growing the item at the inflation rate. Copy the cell **D15** to the range **D18:I21**. Copy the cell **D21** to the range **D25:I29**.

4. **Totals.** Sum up the Variable Cost / Unit and Cash Fixed Cost categories.

   o **Total Variable Cost / Unit.** Enter =SUM(C18:C21) in cell **C22** and copy across.

   o **Total Cash Fixed Costs.** Enter =SUM(C25:C29) in cell **C30** and copy across.

FIGURE 10.3 Spreadsheet for Cash Flow Forecasts.

	A	B	C	D	E	F	G	H	I
1	PROJECT NPV	Forecasting Cash Flows							
2	(in thousands of $)	2001	2002	2003	2004	2005	2006	2007	2008
3		Year 0	Year 1	Year 2	Year 3	Year 4	Year 5	Year 6	Year 7
32	Cash Flow Forecasts								
33	Sales Revenue		$19,400	$39,770	$57,348	$72,075	$81,571	$42,417	$21,461
34	Variable Costs		$14,800	$30,340	$43,750	$54,985	$62,230	$32,359	$16,372
35	Gross Margin		$4,600	$9,430	$13,598	$17,090	$19,342	$10,058	$5,089
36									
37	Cash Fixed Costs		$5,280	$5,412	$5,574	$5,769	$6,000	$6,240	$6,490
38	Depreciation		$1,621	$1,621	$1,621	$1,621	$1,621	$1,621	$1,621
39	Total Fixed Costs		$6,901	$7,033	$7,196	$7,391	$7,622	$7,862	$8,111
40									
41	Operating Profit		($2,301)	$2,397	$6,402	$9,699	$11,720	$2,196	($3,023)
42	Taxes		($806)	$839	$2,241	$3,395	$4,102	$769	($1,058)
43	Net Profit		($1,496)	$1,558	$4,161	$6,304	$7,618	$1,427	($1,965)
44									
45	Add Back Depreciation		$1,621	$1,621	$1,621	$1,621	$1,621	$1,621	$1,621
46	Operating Cash Flow		$126	$3,179	$5,783	$7,926	$9,239	$3,049	($343)
47									
48	Investment in Plant & Equip	($11,350)							$1,400
49	Cash Flows	($11,350)	$126	$3,179	$5,783	$7,926	$9,239	$3,049	$1,057
50	Present Value of Each Cash Flow	($11,350)	$111	$2,464	$3,905	$4,634	$4,646	$1,316	$391
51	Net Present Value	$6,117							

The Net Present Value of the project remains $6,117 as before.

10.3 Working Capital

Problem. Consider the same project as Project NPV - Forecasting Cash Flows. Suppose we add that the project will require working capital in the amount of $0.87 in year 0 for every unit of next year's forecasted sales and this amount will grow with inflation going forward. What is the project NPV?

Solution Strategy. Forecast the working capital amount per next year's unit sales. Then multiply by the forecasted unit sales to determined the required working capital each year. Include the investment in working capital to the total investment cash flows and calculate the project NPV.

FIGURE 10.4 Spreadsheet for Forecasting Project Assumptions, Discounting, & Price or Cost / Unit.

	A	B	C	D	E	F	G	H	I
1	PROJECT NPV	Working Capital							
2	(in thousands of $)	2001	2002	2003	2004	2005	2006	2007	2008
3		Year 0	Year 1	Year 2	Year 3	Year 4	Year 5	Year 6	Year 7
4	**Key Assumptions**								
5	Unit Sales		2000	4000	5600	6800	7400	3700	1800
6	Inflation Rate		2.0%	2.5%	3.0%	3.5%	4.0%	4.0%	4.0%
7	Real Cost of Capital		11.0%	11.2%	11.4%	11.6%	11.8%	12.0%	12.2%
8	Tax Rate		35.0%	35.0%	35.0%	35.0%	35.0%	35.0%	35.0%
9									
10	**Discounting**								
11	Discount Rate = Cost of Capital		13.2%	14.0%	14.7%	15.5%	16.3%	16.5%	16.7%
12	Cumulative Discount Factor	0.0%	13.2%	29.0%	48.1%	71.0%	98.9%	131.6%	170.3%
13									
14	**Price or Cost / Unit**								
15	Sales Revenue / Unit		$9.70	$9.94	$10.24	$10.60	$11.02	$11.46	$11.92
16									
17	Variable Costs / Unit:								
18	Direct Labor		$3.50	$3.59	$3.70	$3.82	$3.98	$4.14	$4.30
19	Materials		$2.00	$2.05	$2.11	$2.19	$2.27	$2.36	$2.46
20	Selling Expenses		$1.20	$1.23	$1.27	$1.31	$1.36	$1.42	$1.47
21	Other		$0.70	$0.72	$0.74	$0.76	$0.80	$0.83	$0.86
22	Total Variable Cost / Unit		$7.40	$7.59	$7.81	$8.09	$8.41	$8.75	$9.10
23									
24	Cash Fixed Costs:								
25	Lease Payment		$2,800	$2,870	$2,956	$3,060	$3,182	$3,309	$3,442
26	Property Taxes		$580	$595	$612	$634	$659	$685	$713
27	Administration		$450	$461	$475	$492	$511	$532	$553
28	Advertising		$930	$863	$902	$1,018	$1,057	$1,099	$1,143
29	Other		$520	$533	$549	$568	$591	$615	$639
30	Total Cash Fixed Costs		$5,280	$5,412	$5,574	$5,769	$6,000	$6,240	$6,490
31									
32	Work Cap / Next Yr Unit Sales	$0.87	$0.89	$0.91	$0.94	$0.97	$1.01	$1.05	$1.09
33	Working Capital	$1,740	$3,550	$5,094	$6,371	$7,176	$3,731	$1,888	$0

How To Build Your Own Spreadsheet Model.

1. **Open the Forecasting Cash Flows Spreadsheet and Add Rows.** Open the spreadsheet that you created for Project NPV - Forecasting Cash Flows and immediately save the spreadsheet under a new name using the **File | Save As** command. Select **A32:A34** and click on **Insert | Row**. Select **A51** and click on **Insert | Row**. Select **A53:A54** and click on **Insert | Row**.

2. **Forecast Working Capital / Next Year's Unit Sales.** Enter the input in cell **B32.** This item is projected by growing it at the inflation rate. This Year's Work Cap/Next Yr Unit Sales = (Last Year's Work Cap/Next Yr Unit Sales) * (1 + This Year's Inflation Rate). Enter **=B32*(1+C$6)** in cell **C32** and copy it across.

3. **Forecast Working Capital.** Working Capital = (This Year's Work Cap/Next Yr Unit Sales) * (Next Yr Unit Sales). Enter **=B32*C5** in cell **B33** and copy it across.

55

FIGURE 10.5 Spreadsheet for Cash Flow Forecasts.

	A	B	C	D	E	F	G	H	I
1	**PROJECT NPV**	**Working Capital**							
2	(in thousands of $)	2001	2002	2003	2004	2005	2006	2007	2008
3		Year 0	Year 1	Year 2	Year 3	Year 4	Year 5	Year 6	Year 7
35	**Cash Flow Forecasts**								
36	Sales Revenue		$19,400	$39,770	$57,348	$72,075	$81,571	$42,417	$21,461
37	Variable Costs		$14,800	$30,340	$43,750	$54,985	$62,230	$32,359	$16,372
38	Gross Margin		$4,600	$9,430	$13,598	$17,090	$19,342	$10,058	$5,089
39									
40	Cash Fixed Costs		$5,280	$5,412	$5,574	$5,769	$6,000	$6,240	$6,490
41	Depreciation		$1,621	$1,621	$1,621	$1,621	$1,621	$1,621	$1,621
42	Total Fixed Costs		$6,901	$7,033	$7,196	$7,391	$7,622	$7,862	$8,111
43									
44	Operating Profit		($2,301)	$2,397	$6,402	$9,699	$11,720	$2,196	($3,023)
45	Taxes		($806)	$839	$2,241	$3,395	$4,102	$769	($1,058)
46	Net Profit		($1,496)	$1,558	$4,161	$6,304	$7,618	$1,427	($1,965)
47									
48	Add Back Depreciation		$1,621	$1,621	$1,621	$1,621	$1,621	$1,621	$1,621
49	Operating Cash Flow		$126	$3,179	$5,783	$7,926	$9,239	$3,049	($343)
50									
51	Investment in Working Capital	($1,740)	($1,810)	($1,544)	($1,277)	($805)	$3,444	$1,843	$1,888
52	Investment in Plant & Equip	($11,350)							$1,400
53	Investment Cash Flow	($13,090)	($1,810)	($1,544)	($1,277)	($805)	$3,444	$1,843	$3,288
54									
55	Cash Flows	($13,090)	($1,684)	$1,635	$4,506	$7,121	$12,684	$4,892	$2,945
56	Present Value of Each Cash Flow	($13,090)	($1,487)	$1,267	$3,043	$4,164	$6,378	$2,112	$1,089
57	Net Present Value	$3,476							

4. **Cash Flows.** Track the working capital through the rest of the project analysis.
   - **Investment in Working Capital** = (Last Year's Working Capital) - (This Year's Working Capital). It is negative cash flow as new working capital is added and a positive cash flow as working capital is recaptured. The first year requires a special formula to get started. Enter =-B33 in cell B51. Then, enter =B33-C33 in C51 and copy it across.

   - **Investment Cash Flow** = (Investment in Working Capital) + (Investment in Plant & Equip). Enter =SUM(B51:B52) in cell B53 and copy it across.

   - **Cash Flows** = (Operating Cash Flow) + (Investment Cash Flow). Enter =B49+B53 in B55 and copy it across.

The Net Present Value of the project drops to $3,476, because of the additional investment in working capital.

10.4 Sensitivity Analysis

Problem. Consider the same project as Project NPV - Working Capital. Assume that the product life-cycle of seven years is viewed as a safe bet, but that the scale of demand for the product is highly uncertain. Analyze the sensitivity of the project NPV to the units sales scale factor and to the cost of capital.

Solution Strategy. Copy the pattern of unit sales in the base case to a new location and multiply this pattern by a scale factor to get the new unit sales scenario. Assume that the real cost of capital is constant. Thus, forecast the future cost of capital by taking the year 1 cost of capital and adding the change in the inflation rate. Create a two-way data table using a range of input values for units sales scale factor and a range of input values for the year 1 cost of capital. Using the data table results, create a 3-D surface chart.

FIGURE 10.6 Spreadsheet for Two-Way Data Table and 3-D Surface Chart.

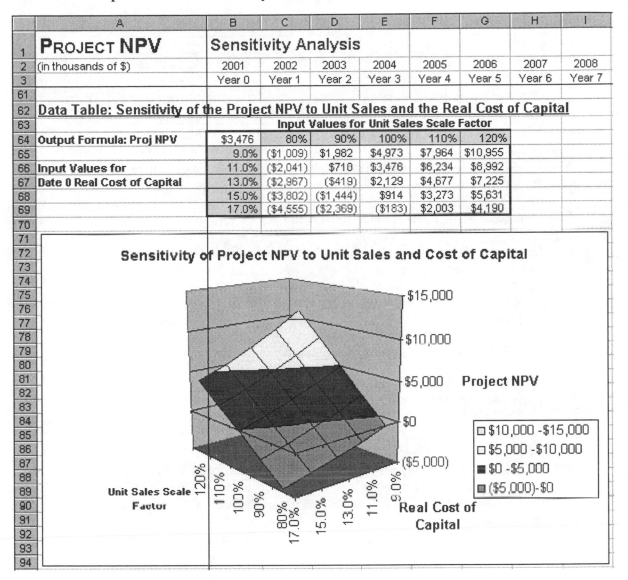

	A	B	C	D	E	F	G	H	I
1	**PROJECT NPV**	**Sensitivity Analysis**							
2	(in thousands of $)	2001	2002	2003	2004	2005	2006	2007	2008
3		Year 0	Year 1	Year 2	Year 3	Year 4	Year 5	Year 6	Year 7
61									
62	**Data Table: Sensitivity of the Project NPV to Unit Sales and the Real Cost of Capital**								
63			Input Values for Unit Sales Scale Factor						
64	Output Formula: Proj NPV	$3,476	80%	90%	100%	110%	120%		
65		9.0%	($1,009)	$1,982	$4,973	$7,964	$10,955		
66	Input Values for	11.0%	($2,041)	$710	$3,476	$6,234	$8,992		
67	Date 0 Real Cost of Capital	13.0%	($2,967)	($419)	$2,129	$4,677	$7,225		
68		15.0%	($3,802)	($1,444)	$914	$3,273	$5,631		
69		17.0%	($4,555)	($2,369)	($183)	$2,003	$4,190		

How To Build Your Own Spreadsheet Model.

1. **Open the Working Capital Spreadsheet and Insert Rows.** Open the spreadsheet that you created for Project NPV - Working Capital and immediately save the spreadsheet under a new name using the **File | Save As** command. Select the range **A5:A6** and click on **Insert | Row**. Select the cell **A9** and click on **Insert | Row**.

FIGURE 10.7 Spreadsheet showing modified Key Assumptions.

	A	B	C	D	E	F	G	H	I
1	PROJECT NPV	Sensitivity Analysis							
2	(in thousands of $)	2001	2002	2003	2004	2005	2006	2007	2008
3		Year 0	Year 1	Year 2	Year 3	Year 4	Year 5	Year 6	Year 7
4	Key Assumptions								
5	Base Case Unit Sales		2000	4000	5600	6800	7400	3700	1800
6	Unit Sales Scale Factor		100.0%						
7	Unit Sales		2000	4000	5600	6800	7400	3700	1800
8	Inflation Rate		2.0%	2.5%	3.0%	3.5%	4.0%	4.0%	4.0%
9	Real Cost of Capital Increment			0.2%	0.4%	0.6%	0.8%	1.0%	1.2%
10	Real Cost of Capital		11.0%	11.2%	11.4%	11.6%	11.8%	12.0%	12.2%
11	Tax Rate		35.0%	35.0%	35.0%	35.0%	35.0%	35.0%	35.0%

2. **Unit Sales.** Save the base case pattern and multiply it by a scale factor to determine unit sales.

   o **Base Case Unit Sales** = the original sales pattern. Copy the range **C7:I7** to **C5**.

   o **Unit Sales Scale Factor.** Enter **100.0%** in **C6**.

   o **Unit Sales** = (Base Case Unit Sales) * (Unit Sales Scale Factor). Enter **=C5*$C$6** in **C7** and copy it across.

3. **Real Cost of Capital.** Save the base case changes as a set of increments and add the increments to the date 0 real cost of capital to determine the current real cost of capital.

   o **Real Cost of Capital Increment.** Enter input increments in the range **D9:I9**.

   o **Real Cost of Capital on date t** = (Date 0 Real Cost of Capital) + (Increment on date t). Enter **=$C$10+D9** in **D10** and copy it across.

4. **Two-Way Data Table.** Create a list of input values for Unit Sales Scale Factor (**80%, 90%, 100%,** etc.) in the range **C64:G64**. Create a list of input values for Cost of Capital (**9.0%, 11.0%, 13.0%,** etc.) in the range **B65:B69**. Create an output formula that references the product NPV by entering the formula **=B60** in cell **B64**. Select the range **B64:G69** for the **Data Table**. This range includes both the input values at the top of the data table and on the left of the data table. Then choose **Data | Table** from the main menu and a **Table** dialog box pops up. Enter the cell address **C6** (for **Unit Sales Scale Factor**) in the **Row Input Cell**, the cell address **C10** (for the **Date 0 Real Cost of Capital**) in the **Column Input Cell**, and click on **OK**.

5. **3D Graph of the Sensitivity Analysis.** Highlight the range **C65:G69** and then choose **Insert | Chart** from the main menu. Select a **Surface** chart type and make other selections to complete the Chart Wizard. To label the x-axis and y-axis, right-click on the chart, select **Source Data ...** from the pop-up menu, enter **C64:G64** in the **Category (X) axis labels** text box, select **Series1** in the **Series** pick list, enter **B65** in the **Name** text box, select **Series2** in the **Series** pick list, enter **B66** in the **Name** text box, and so on until every series has a label.

The sensitivity analysis shows that the Project NPV is highly sensitive to the Unit Sales Scale Factor and the Cost of Capital. If the sales forecast is overly optimistic and/or cost of capital estimate is too low, then the project might actually have a negative NPV. Hence, it is worth spending extra resources to verify the accuracy of the sales forecast and the cost of capital estimate.

Problems

Skill-Building Problems.

1. Suppose a firm is considering the following project, where all of the dollar figures are in thousands of dollars. In year 0, the project requires $37,500 investment in plant and equipment, is depreciated using the straight-line method over seven years, and there is a salvage value of $5,600 in year 7. The project is forecast to generate sales of 5,700 units in year 1, rising to 24,100 units in year 5, declining to 8,200 units in year 7, and dropping to zero in year 8. The inflation rate is forecast to be 1.5% in year 1, rising to 2.8% in year 5, and then leveling off. The real cost of capital is forecast to be 9.3% in year 1, rising to 10.6% in year 7. The tax rate is forecast to be a constant 42.0%. Sales revenue per unit is forecast to be $15.30 in year 1 and then grow with inflation. Variable cost per unit is forecast to be $9.20 in year 1 and then grow with inflation. Cash fixed costs are forecast to be $7,940 in year 1 and then grow with inflation. What is the project NPV?

2. Consider the same project as problem 1, but modify it as follows. Suppose that Direct Labor, Materials, Selling Expenses, and Other Variable Costs are forecast to be $5.20, $3.70, $2.30, and $0.80, respectively, in year 1 and then grow with inflation. Lease Payment, Property Taxes, Administration, Advertising, and Other cash fixed costs are forecast to be $4,100, $730, $680, $1,120, and $730, respectively, in year 1 and then grow with inflation. What is the Total Variable Cost / Unit, the Total Cash Fixed Costs, and the project NPV?

3. Consider the same project as problem 2, but modify it as follows. Suppose we add that the project will require working capital in the amount of $1.23 in year 0 for every unit of next year's forecasted sales and this amount will grow with inflation going forward. What is the project NPV?

4. Consider the same project as problem 3. Assume that the product life-cycle of seven years is viewed as a safe bet, but that the scale of demand for the product is highly uncertain. Analyze the sensitivity of the project NPV to the units sales scale factor and to the cost of capital.

Live In-class Problems.

5. Given the partial Basics spreadsheet **ProjbasZ.xls**, do steps **5 Cash Flow Forecasts** and **6 Present Value and NPV**.

6. Given the partial Forecasting Cash Flows spreadsheet **ProjforZ.xls**, complete steps **2 Inputs, 3 Forecast The Detail Items,** and **4 Totals**.

7. Given the partial Working Capital spreadsheet **ProjworZ.xls**, complete steps **2 Forecast Work Capital / Next Year's Unit Sales, 3 Forecast Working Capital,** and **4 Cash Flows**.

8. Given the partial Sensitivity Analysis spreadsheet **ProjsenZ.xls**, complete step **4 Two-Way Data Table**.

11 Cost-Reducing Project

11.1 Basics

Problem. Suppose a firm is considering a labor-saving investment. In year 0, the project requires a $6,300 investment in equipment (all figures are in thousands of dollars). This investment is depreciated using the straight-line method over five years and there is salvage value in year 5 of $1,200. With or without the cost-reducing investment, all cash flows start in year 1 and end in year 5. The inflation rate is 3.0% in year 2 and declines to 2.0% in year 5. The real growth rate is 16.0% in year 2 and declines to 7.0% in year 5. The tax rate is 38.0% in all years. The real cost of capital is 9.5% in year 1 and declines to 8.9% in year 5. Without the cost-reducing investment, the firm's existing investments will generate year 1 revenue, labor costs, other cash expenses, and depreciation of $11,500, $3,200, $4,500, and $1,800, respectively. With the cost-reducing investment, the firm's year 1 labor costs will be $1,300 and revenues and other cash expenses will remain the same. What is the cost-reducing project NPV?

Solution Strategy. Forecast revenues and expenses both without the cost-reducing investment and with it. Calculate the Net Cash Flow both without and with the cost-reducing investment. Subtract one from the other to obtain the incremental Difference Due to Investment. Discount the project net cash flows back to the present and determine the NPV.

FIGURE 11.1 Spreadsheet for Cost-Reducing Project - Basics.

	A	B	C	D	E	F	G
1	COST-REDUCING PROJECT			Basics			
2	(in thousands of $)	2001	2002	2003	2004	2005	2006
3		Year 0	Year 1	Year 2	Year 3	Year 4	Year 5
4	**Key Assumptions**						
5	Inflation Rate		3.0%	2.8%	2.5%	2.2%	2.0%
6	Real Cost of Capital		9.5%	9.3%	9.1%	9.0%	8.9%
7	Real Growth Rate			16.0%	13.0%	9.0%	7.0%
8	Tax Rate		38.0%	38.0%	38.0%	38.0%	38.0%
9							
10	**Discounting**						
11	Discount Rate = Cost of Capital		12.8%	12.4%	11.8%	11.4%	11.1%
12	Cumulative Discount Factor	0.0%	12.8%	26.7%	41.7%	57.9%	75.4%
13							
14	**Without Investment**						
15	Revenue		$11,500	$13,714	$15,884	$17,694	$19,311
16	Labor Costs		$3,200	$3,816	$4,420	$4,924	$5,374
17	Other Cash Expenses		$4,500	$5,366	$6,215	$6,924	$7,557
18	Gross Margin		$3,800	$4,531	$5,249	$5,847	$6,381
19							
20	Depreciation		$1,800	$1,800	$1,800	$1,800	$1,800
21	Pretax Profit		$2,000	$2,731	$3,449	$4,047	$4,581
22							
23	Income Taxes		$760	$1,038	$1,310	$1,538	$1,741
24	After-tax Profit		$1,240	$1,693	$2,138	$2,509	$2,840
25							
26	Add Back Depreciation		$1,800	$1,800	$1,800	$1,800	$1,800
27	Cash Flows		$3,040	$3,493	$3,938	$4,309	$4,640
28							
29	**With Investment**						
30	Revenue		$11,500	$13,714	$15,884	$17,694	$19,311
31	Labor Costs		$1,300	$1,550	$1,796	$2,000	$2,183
32	Other Cash Expenses		$4,500	$5,366	$6,215	$6,924	$7,557
33	Gross Margin		$5,700	$6,797	$7,873	$8,770	$9,572
34							
35	Depreciation		$3,060	$3,060	$3,060	$3,060	$3,060
36	Pretax Profit		$2,640	$3,737	$4,813	$5,710	$6,512
37							
38	Income Taxes		$1,003	$1,420	$1,829	$2,170	$2,474
39	After-tax Profit		$1,637	$2,317	$2,984	$3,540	$4,037
40							
41	Add Back Depreciation		$3,060	$3,060	$3,060	$3,060	$3,060
42	Cash Flows		$4,697	$5,377	$6,044	$6,600	$7,097
43							
44	**Project Difference**						
45	Difference Due to Investment		$1,657	$1,884	$2,106	$2,291	$2,457
46	Investment and Salvage Value	($6,300)					$1,200
47	Project Cash Flows	($6,300)	$1,657	$1,884	$2,106	$2,291	$3,657
48	Present Value of Each Cash Flow	($6,300)	$1,469	$1,486	$1,486	$1,451	$2,085
49	Project Net Present Value	$1,678					

How To Build Your Own Spreadsheet Model.

1. **Set-up Row and Column Titles.** Enter column titles, such as **2001, 2002**, etc. in row **2** and **Year 0, Year 1**, etc. in row **3**. Then, place the cursor in cell **B4** and click on **Window | Freeze Panes**. This freezes the top two rows as column titles and freezes the first column as row titles.

2. **Inputs.** Enter the key assumptions in the range **C5:G8**. Enter the year 1 revenues and expenses *without* the investment into the range **C15:C17**. Enter the existing depreciation in cell **C20**. Enter the year 1 revenues and expenses *with* the investment into the range **C30:C32**. Enter the year 0 investment as a negative cash flow in cell **B46** and the year 5 salvage value as a positive cash flow in cell **G46**.

3. **Discounting.** Calculate the (nominal) discount rate, which is the (nominal) cost of capital. Then calculate the cumulative discount rate.

   o **Discount Rate = Cost of Capital.** The formula for the (Nominal) Discount Rate = (1 + Inflation Rate) * (1 + Real Discount Rate) - 1. Enter **=(1+C5)*(1+C6)-1** in cell **C11** and copy it across.

   o **Cumulative Discount Factor.** This is the product of the year-by-year discount factors cumulated to a given date. Enter **0.0%** in cell **B12**. The rest are calculated as (This Year's Cumulative Discount Factor) = (1 + Last Year's Cumulative Discount Factor) * (1 + This Year's Discount Rate) - 1. Enter **=(1+B12)*(1+C11)-1** in cell **C12** and copy across.

4. **Forecast Without Investment Cash Flows.** Forecast each item of the Cash Flows spreadsheet as appropriate.

   o **Revenue This Year** = (Revenue Last Year) * (1 + Inflation Rate) * (1 + Real Growth Rate). Enter **=C15*(1+D$5)*(1+D$7)** in cell **D15**. **Labor Costs** and **Other Cash Expenses** are forecast similarly, so copy cell **D15** to the range **D15:G17**.

   o **Gross Margin** = Revenue - (Labor Costs) - (Other Cash Expenses). Enter **=C15-C16-C17** in cell **C18** and copy it across.

   o **Depreciation** is constant over time due to the use of the straight line method. Enter **=C20** in cell **D20** and copy it across.

   o **Pretax Profit** = (Gross Margin) - Depreciation. Enter **=C18-C20** in cell **C21** and copy it across.

   o **Income Taxes** = Operating Income * Tax Rate. Enter **=C21*C$8** in cell **C23** and copy it across.

   o **After Tax Profit** = Pretax Profit - Income Taxes. Enter **=C21-C23** in cell **C24** and copy it across.

   o **Add Back Depreciation** = Depreciation. Enter **=C20** in cell **C26** and copy it across.

   o **Cash Flows** = After-tax Profit + Add Back Depreciation. Enter **=C24+C26** in cell **C27**.

5. **Forecast With Investment Cash Flows.** The With Investment formulas are identical to the Without Investment formulas with two exception. Start by copying the range **A15:G27** to the cell **A30**. The first exception is that the **With Investment Labor Cost** input needs to be reset to **$1,300** in cell **C31**. The second exception is the **With Investment Depreciation** needs to pick up the addition depreciation from the new investment. With Investment Depreciation = Without Investment Depreciation -(New Investment) / (Number of years to fully depreciate). The new

investment is subtracted in order offset the negative sign on the New Investment. Enter =C20-$B$46/5 in cell **C35** and copy it across.

6. **Difference Due to Investment and NPV.** The Difference Due to Investment = With Investment Net Cash Flows - Without Investment Net Cash Flows. Enter =C42-C27 in cell **C45** and copy it across. Project Net Cash Flows = Difference Due To Investment + Investment and Salvage Value. Enter =B45+B46 in cell **B47** and copy it across.

7. **Present Value and NPV.** Discount each cash flow back to the present and calculate the NPV as follows:

   o **Present Value of Each Cash Flow** = (Project Cash Flows) / (1 + Cumulative Discount Factor). Enter =B47/(1+B12) in cell **B48** and copy across.

   o **Project Net Present Value** = Sum of Present Value of the Cash Flows. Enter =SUM(B48:I48) in cell **B49**.

The Net Present Value of this Cost-reducing Project is $1,678. The project should be accepted.

11.2 Sensitivity Analysis

Problem. For the same cost-reducing project as the previous section, analyze the sensitivity of the Project NPV to the assumed With Investment Labor Costs.

Solution Strategy. Create a Data Table using With Investment Labor Costs as the input variable and Project NPV as the output variable. Then graph the relationship.

FIGURE 11.2 Spreadsheet for Cost-Reducing Project - Sensitivity Analysis.

	A	B	C	D	E	F	G	H
1	COST-REDUCING PROJECT			Sensitivity Analysis				
2	(in thousands of $)	2001	2002	2003	2004	2005	2006	
3		Year 0	Year 1	Year 2	Year 3	Year 4	Year 5	
50								
51	Data Table: Sensitivity of Project Net Present Value to With Investment Labor Costs							
52			Input Values for With Investment Labor Costs					
53	Output Formula:		$900	$1,100	$1,300	$1,500	$1,700	
54	Project Net Present Value	$1,678	$2,852	$2,265	$1,678	$1,091	$504	
55								

How To Build Your Own Spreadsheet Model.

1. **Open the Basics Spreadsheet.** Open the spreadsheet that you created for Cost-Reducing Project NPV - Basics and immediately save the spreadsheet under a new name using the **File | Save As** command.

2. **Data Table.** Create a list of input values for With Investment Labor Costs ($900, $1,100, $1,300, etc.) in the range **C53:G53**. Create an output formula that references the Project Net Present Value by entering the formula =**B49** in cell **B54**. Select the range **B53:G54** for the One-Variable Data Table. This range includes both the input values on the top of the range and the output formula on the left side of the range. Then choose **Data | Table** from the main menu and a **Table** dialog box pops up. Enter the cell address **C31** (With Investment Labor Costs) in the **Row Input Cell** and click on **OK**.

3. **Graph.** Highlight the interior of the data table (excluding the top or side) in the range **C54:G54** and then choose **Insert | Chart** from the main menu. Select the **XY (Scatter)** chart type and make other selections to complete the Chart Wizard.

The sensitivity analysis indicates that the Project NPV is not very sensitive to a wide range of values of With Investment Labor Costs. It all cases the project has a positive NPV. This provides confidence that the project's positive NPV is robust to any reasonable error in estimating the labor cost savings.

Problems

Skill-Building Problems.

1. Suppose a firm is considering a labor-saving investment. In year 0, the project requires a $11,700 investment in equipment (all figures are in thousands of dollars). This investment is depreciated using the straight-line method over five years and there is salvage value in year 5 of $4,500. With or without the cost-reducing investment, all cash flows start in year 1 and end in year 5. The inflation rate is 2.6% in year 2 and declines to 1.4% in year 5. The real growth rate is 21.3% in year 2 and declines to 9.5% in year 5. The tax rate is 41.0% in all years. The real cost of capital is 8.7% in year 1 and declines to 7.5% in year 5. Without the cost-reducing investment, the firm's existing investments will generate year 1 revenue, labor costs, other cash expenses, and depreciation of $15,200, $4,100, $5,300, and $3,300, respectively. With the cost-reducing investment, the firm's year 1 labor costs will be $1,600 and revenues and other cash expenses will remain the same. What is the cost-reducing project NPV?

2. For the same cost-reducing project as problem 1, analyze the sensitivity of the Project NPV to the assumed With Investment Labor Costs.

Live In-class Problems.

3. Given the partial Basics spreadsheet **CostbasZ.xls**, do steps **5 Forecast With Investment Cash Flows** and **6 Difference Due to Investment and NPV**.

4. Given the partial Sensitivity Analysis spreadsheet **CostsenZ.xls**, do step **2 Data Table**.

12 Break-Even Analysis

12.1 Based On Accounting Profit

Problem. A project has a fixed cost of $30,000, variable costs of $4.00 per unit, and generates sales revenue of $6.00 per unit. What is the break-even point in unit sales, where accounting profit exactly equals zero, and what is the intuition for it?

Solution Strategy. First, we solve for the break-even point in unit sales using the formula. Second, we use Excel's Solver to back solve for the break-even point using the income statement. Lastly, we will determine the sensitivity of costs, revenues, and accounting profits to unit sales. This will allow us to graphically illustrate the intuition of the break-even point.

FIGURE 12.1 Spreadsheet for Break-Even Analysis - Based On Accounting Profit.

	A	B	C	D	E	F	G
1	BREAK-EVEN ANALYSIS	Based On Accounting Profit					
2							
3	Inputs						
4	Fixed Costs	$30,000					
5	Sales Revenue / Unit	$6.00					
6	Variable Costs / Unit	$4.00					
7							
8	Calculate the Break-even Point using the Formula						
9	Break-even Point (Unit Sales)	15,000					
10							
11	Back solve for the Break-even Point using the Income Statement						
12	Unit Sales	15,000					
13	Sales Revenue	$90,000					
14	Variable Costs	$60,000					
15	Gross Margin	$30,000					
16	Fixed Costs	$30,000					
17	Accounting Profit	$0					

How To Build This Spreadsheet Model.

1. **Inputs. Enter the inputs into the range B4:B6.**

2. **Break-Even Point using the Formula.** The formula is: Break-Even Point = Fixed Costs / (Sales Revenue/Unit - Variable Costs/Unit). In cell **B9**, enter **=B4/(B5-B6)**   We see that the Break-Even Point is 15,000 units.

3. **Back solve for the Break-even Point using the Income Statement.** Create the Income Statement using these simple steps.
    - o   Unit Sales. Enter a trial value for the break-even point. In cell **B12**, enter **12000**
    - o   Sales Revenue = (Sales Revenue/Unit) * (Unit Sales). In cell **B13**, enter **=B12*B5**
    - o   Variable Costs = (Variable Costs/Unit) * (Unit Sales). In cell **B14**, enter **=B12*B6**
    - o   Gross Margin = Sales Revenue - Variable Costs. In cell **B15**, enter **=B13-B14**
    - o   Fixed Costs = input value for Fixed Costs. In cell **B16**, enter **=B4**
    - o   Accounting Profit = Gross Margin - Fixed Costs. In cell **B17**, enter **=B15-B16**

    Then call up Excel's Solver from Excel's main menu by clicking on **Tools** and then **Solver**. (If you don't see **Solver** on the **Tools** Menu, then click on **Tools | Add-Ins**, check the **Solver Add-In** box, and click on **OK**.) Set-up the Solver dialog box by entering Accounting Profit in cell **B17** as the Set Target Cell. In the Equal to row, click on the option button for Value of and enter **0** in the adjacent box. Enter Unit Sales in cell **B12** as the By Changing Cell. See the figure below.

FIGURE 12.2 Solver dialog box.

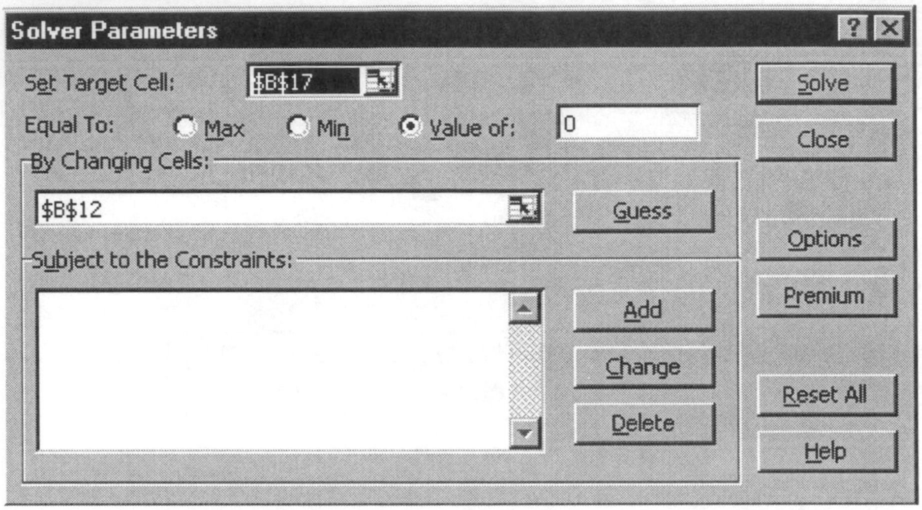

Then run Solver by clicking on the Solve button. By trial and error, the Solver adjusts the value of Unit Sales in cell **B12** until the Accounting Profit in cell **B17** equals zero (within a very small error tolerance). This results in an Break-even Point of 15,000, where Accounting Profit equals zero. Your results may differ by a slight amount depending on Solver's error tolerance. This verifies that the Break-Even Point is 15,000 units.

4. **Create A List of Input Values and An Output Formula.** Create a list of input values for Unit Sales (0, 5,000, 10,000, etc.) in the range **C21:G21**. Create output formulas that reference the pieces of the accounting profit calculation. Specifically:
    o   for Fixed Cost, enter =**B16** in cell **B22**
    o   for Variable Costs, enter   =**B14** in cell **B23**
    o   for Total Costs, enter =**B16+B14** in cell **B24**
    o   for Sales Revenue, enter =**B13** in cell **B25**
    o   for Accounting Profit, enter =**B17** in cell **B26**

FIGURE 12.3 Spreadsheet for Sensitivity of Costs, Revenues, and Accounting Profits to Unit Sales.

	A	B	C	D	E	F	G
19	**Data Table: Sensitivity of Costs, Revenues, and Acct. Profit to Unit Sales**						
20			**Input Values for Unit Sales**				
21	**Output Formulas:**		0	5,000	10,000	15,000	20,000
22	**Fixed Costs**	$30,000	$30,000	$30,000	$30,000	$30,000	$30,000
23	**Variable Costs**	$60,000	0	20000	40000	60000	80000
24	**Total Costs**	$90,000	30000	50000	70000	90000	110000
25	**Sales Revenue**	$90,000	0	30000	60000	90000	120000
26	**Accounting Profit**	$0	-30000	-20000	-10000	0	10000

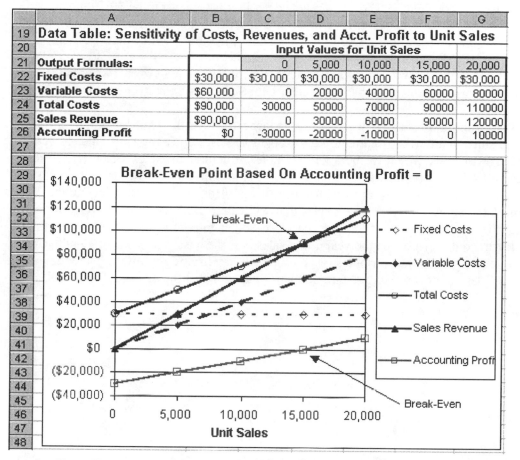

5. **Data Table.** Select the range **B21:G26** for the **Data Table**. This range includes both the list of input values at the top of the data table and the output formulas on the side of the data table. Then choose **Data Table** from the main menu and a **Table** dialog box pops up. Enter the cell address **B12** (Unit Sales) in the **Row Input Cell** and click on **OK**.

6. **Graph the Data Table Results.** Highlight the data table **C21:G26** and then choose **Insert Chart** from the main menu. Select an **XY(Scatter)** chart type and make other selections to complete the Chart Wizard.

The graph shows visually that the Break-Even Point is 15,000 units. The graph illustrates two equivalent intuitions for this result. First, the Break-Even Point is where the Sales Revenue line (in blue) crosses Total Costs line (in red). Second, the Break-Even Point is where Accounting Profit (in orange) hits zero and thus decisively switches from negative to positive.

12.2 Based On NPV

Problem. Suppose a firm is considering the following project, where all of the dollar figures are in thousands of dollars. In year 0, the project requires $11,350 investment in plant and equipment, is depreciated using the straight-line method over seven years, and there is a salvage value of $1,400 in year 7. The project is forecast to generate sales of 2,100 units in year 1 and grow at a sales growth rate of 55.0% in year 2. The sales growth rate is forecast to decline by 15.0% in years 3 and 4, to decline by 20.0% in year 5, to decline by 25.0% in year 6, to decline by 30.0% in year 7. Unit sales will drop to zero in year 8. The inflation rate is forecast to be 2.0% in year 1, rising to 4.0% in year 5, and then leveling off.

67

The real cost of capital is forecast to be 11.0% in year 1, rising to 12.2% in year 5, and then leveling off. The tax rate is forecast to be a constant 35.0%. Sales revenue per unit is forecast to be $9.70 in year 1 and then grow with inflation. Variable cost per unit is forecast to be $7.40 in year 1 and then grow with inflation. Cash fixed costs are forecast to be $5,280 in year 1 and then grow with inflation. What is the project NPV? What is the NPV Break-Even Point in Year 1 Unit Sales, where NPV equals zero? What is the NPV Break-Even Point in the Year 2 Sales Growth Rate, where NPV equals zero? What is the NPV Break-Even Contour in the two-dimensional space of Year 1 Unit Sales and Year 2 Sales Growth Rate?

Solution Strategy. Start with the Project NPV - Basics spreadsheet. Move the Unit Sales line out of the Key Assumptions area, since that is what we are going to solve for. Restructure the Unit Sales forecast to depend on the Sales Growth Rate, which we be a key variable. Structure the Sales Grow Rate forecast over the entire to period to depend on how fast the growth rate is initially. This will make it easy to use Solver and to create a Data Table later on. Project the cash flows of the project and calculate the NPV. Use Solver to determine the amount of year 1 unit sales that will cause the NPV to equal zero, when the sales growth rate is at the base case level of 5% per year. Use Solver to determine the sales growth rate that will cause the NPV to equal zero, when the year 1 unit sales is at the base case level of 39,000. Create a two-variable data table using two input variables (year 1 unit sales and sales growth rate) and the output variable: NPV. Use the data table to create a three-dimensional graph showing the NPV Break-Even Contour.

FIGURE 12.4 Spreadsheet for Break-Even Analysis Based On Net Present Value.

	A	B	C	D	E	F	G	H	I
1	**BREAK-EVEN ANALYSIS**		Based On NPV						
2	(in thousands of $)	2001	2002	2003	2004	2005	2006	2007	2008
3		Year 0	Year 1	Year 2	Year 3	Year 4	Year 5	Year 6	Year 7
4	**Key Assumptions**								
5	Sales Growth Rate			55.0%	40.0%	25.0%	5.0%	-20.0%	-50.0%
6	Change in Sales Growth Rate				-15.0%	-15.0%	-20.0%	-25.0%	-30.0%
7	Inflation Rate		2.0%	2.5%	3.0%	3.5%	4.0%	4.0%	4.0%
8	Real Cost of Capital		11.0%	11.2%	11.4%	11.6%	11.8%	12.0%	12.2%
9	Tax Rate		35.0%	35.0%	35.0%	35.0%	35.0%	35.0%	35.0%
10									
11	**Discounting**								
12	Discount Rate = Cost of Capital		13.2%	14.0%	14.7%	15.5%	16.3%	16.5%	16.7%
13	Cumulative Discount Factor	0.0%	13.2%	29.0%	48.1%	71.0%	98.9%	131.6%	170.3%
14									
15	**Price or Cost / Unit**								
16	Unit Sales		1,853	2872	4020	5026	5277	4222	2111
17	Sales Revenue / Unit		$9.70	$9.94	$10.24	$10.60	$11.02	$11.46	$11.92
18	Variable Cost / Unit		$7.40	$7.59	$7.81	$8.09	$8.41	$8.75	$9.10
19	Cash Fixed Costs		$5,280	$5,412	$5,574	$5,769	$6,000	$6,240	$6,490
20									
21	**Cash Flow Forecasts**								
22	Sales Revenue		$17,972	$28,553	$41,173	$53,268	$58,168	$48,396	$25,166
23	Variable Costs		$13,710	$21,782	$31,410	$40,637	$44,376	$36,921	$19,199
24	Gross Margin		$4,261	$6,770	$9,763	$12,630	$13,792	$11,475	$5,967
25									
26	Cash Fixed Costs		$5,280	$5,412	$5,574	$5,769	$6,000	$6,240	$6,490
27	Depreciation		$1,621	$1,621	$1,621	$1,621	$1,621	$1,621	$1,621
28	Total Fixed Costs		$6,901	$7,033	$7,196	$7,391	$7,622	$7,862	$8,111
29									
30	Operating Profit		($2,640)	($263)	$2,567	$5,240	$6,171	$3,614	($2,144)
31	Taxes		($924)	($92)	$898	$1,834	$2,160	$1,265	($750)
32	Net Profit		($1,716)	($171)	$1,668	$3,406	$4,011	$2,349	($1,394)
33									
34	Add Back Depreciation		$1,621	$1,621	$1,621	$1,621	$1,621	$1,621	$1,621
35	Operating Cash Flow		($95)	$1,450	$3,290	$5,027	$5,632	$3,970	$228
36									
37	Investment in Plant & Equip	($11,350)							$1,400
38	Cash Flows	($11,350)	($95)	$1,450	$3,290	$5,027	$5,632	$3,970	$1,628
39	Present Value of Each Cash Flow	($11,350)	($84)	$1,124	$2,222	$2,939	$2,832	$1,714	$602
40	Net Present Value	($0)							

How To Build This Spreadsheet Model.

1. **Open the Basics Spreadsheet and Add Rows.** Open the spreadsheet that you created for Project NPV - Basics and immediately save the spreadsheet under a new name using the **File | Save As** command. Select the cell **A15** and click on **Insert | Row**. Select the range **A5:I5**, click on **Edit | Cut**, select the cell **A15**, and click on **Edit | Paste**.

2. **Inputs.** Enter the year 2 sales growth rate into the cell **D5**, the change in the sales growth rate into the range **E6:I6**, and the year 1 unit sales of **2,100** in cell **C16**.

3. **Sales Growth Rate on date t** = (Sales Growth Rate on date t-1) + (Change in Sales Growth Rate on date t). Enter **=D5+E6** in cell **E5** and copy it across.

4. **Unit Sales on date t** = (Unit Sales on date t-1) * (1 + Unit Sales Growth Rate). Enter **=C16*(1+D5)** in cell **D16** and copy it across.

The project NPV is $3,217 and should be accepted. But how sure are you of this result? How sensitive is this result to small changes in the assumptions? The Break-Even Point gives you an idea of the robustness of this result.

5. **NPV Break-Even Point in Year 1 Unit Sales.** Use the built-in Solver tool to numerically solve for the NPV Break-Even Point in Year 1 Unit Sales. From Excel's main menu, click on **Tools** and then **Solver**. (If **Solver** does not appear on the **Tools** menu, then click on **Add-Ins**, check **Solver Add-In**, and click on **OK**.) In the Solver dialog box, enter the Net Present Value cell **B40** as the Set Target Cell. In the Equal To row, click on the option button for Value of and enter **0** in the adjacent box. Enter the Year 1 Unit Sales cell **C16** as the By Changing Cell. See figure below. Click on the Solve button.

FIGURE 12.5 Solver dialog box.

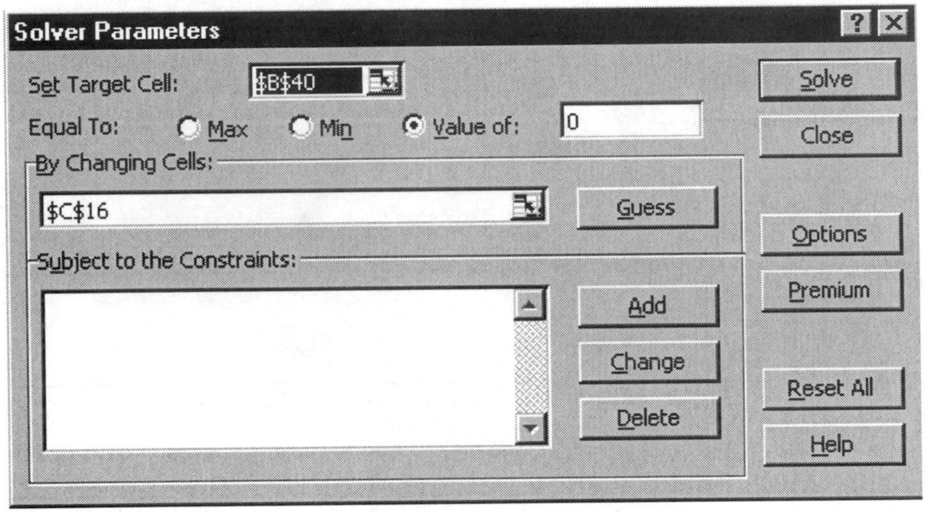

By trial and error, the Solver adjusts the value of the Year 1 Unit Sales in cell **C16** until the Net Present Value in cell **B40** equals zero (within a very small error tolerance). This results in a NPV Break-Even Point in Year 1 Unit Sales (shown in cell **C16**) of 1,853.

6. **NPV Break-Even Point in Sales Growth Rate.** Repeat the NPV Break-Even Analysis only using Year 2 Sales Growth Rate as the changing cell. Enter **2100** in cell **C16** in order to restore the default assumption for Year 1 Unit Sales. From Excel's main menu, click on **Tools** and then **Solver**. In the Solver dialog box, enter Year 2 Sales Growth Rate cell **D5** as the By Changing Cell. Click on the Solve button. By trial and error, the Solver adjusts the value of the Sales Growth Rate in cell **D5** until the Net Present Value in cell **B40** equals zero. This results in a NPV Break-Even Point in Sales Growth Rate (shown in cell **D5**) of 49.5%.

FIGURE 12.6 Two Way Data Table and 3D Graph.

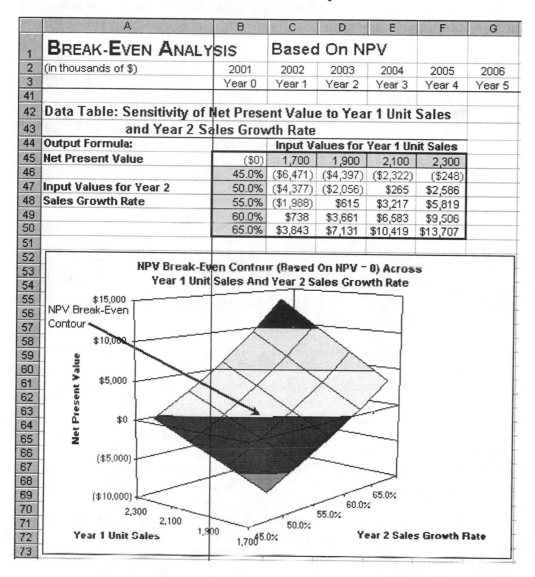

	A	B	C	D	E	F	G
1	**BREAK-EVEN ANALYSIS**		**Based On NPV**				
2	(in thousands of $)	2001	2002	2003	2004	2005	2006
3		Year 0	Year 1	Year 2	Year 3	Year 4	Year 5
41							
42	**Data Table: Sensitivity of Net Present Value to Year 1 Unit Sales**						
43	**and Year 2 Sales Growth Rate**						
44	Output Formula:		**Input Values for Year 1 Unit Sales**				
45	Net Present Value	($0)	1,700	1,900	2,100	2,300	
46		45.0%	($6,471)	($4,397)	($2,322)	($248)	
47	Input Values for Year 2	50.0%	($4,377)	($2,056)	$265	$2,586	
48	Sales Growth Rate	55.0%	($1,988)	$615	$3,217	$5,819	
49		60.0%	$738	$3,661	$6,583	$9,506	
50		65.0%	$3,843	$7,131	$10,419	$13,707	

7. **Create A List of Input Values and An Output Formula.** Create a list of input values for the Year 1 Unit Sales (1,700, 1,900, 2,100, etc.) in the range **C45:F45**. Similarly, create a list of input values for the Year 2 Sales Growth Rate (45.0%, 50.0%, 55.0%, etc.) in the range **B46:B50**. Create an output formula that references the Net Present Value by entering the formula **=B40** in cell **B45**.

8. **Two-Variable Data Table.** Select the range **B45:F50** for the Two-Variable Data Table. This range includes both the list of input values at the top and side of the data table and the output formula in the upper left corner. Then choose **Data | Table** from the main menu and a **Table** dialog box pops up. Enter the cell address **C16** (Year 1 Unit Sales) in the **Row Input Cell**, enter the cell address **D5** (Year 2 Sales Growth Rate) in the **Column Input Cell**, and click on **OK**. The data table shows what combinations of Year 1 Unit Sales and Year 2 Sales Growth yield a positive NPV. Thus, you can assess how optimistic vs. pessimistic your assumptions have to be in order to a get a positive NPV. Thus, you see how *robust* your conclusions are to variations in the inputs.

9. **3-D Graph.** Highlight the interior of the data table (excluding the top or side) in the range C46:F50 and then choose **Insert | Chart** from the main menu. Select a **Surface** chart type and make other selections to complete the Chart Wizard.

The 3-D Graph shows the Net Present Value of the project for combinations of Year 1 Unit Sales and Year 2 Sales Growth Rate. The multi-color surface illustrates various ranges of NPV. In the top corner, the dark blue color is for NPV > $15,000. Below it, a light red section is for a NPV of $10,000 to $15,000. And so on. At the intersection of the Light Green section ($0 to $5,000) and the Light Yellow section (-$5,000 to $0) is a contour highlighted by the arrow. This is the NPV Break-Even Contour, where NPV = 0. Every point on this contour represents a combination of Year 1 Unit Sales and Year 2 Sales Growth Rate for which the NPV = 0. The 3-D Graph shows that project's positive NPV is *very sensitive*. If the Year 1 Unit Sales are a little bit lower than assumed or if the year 2 Sale Growth Rate is a little bit lower than assumed, then the whole project could have a negative NPV.

Problems

Skill-Building Problems.

1. A project has a fixed cost of $73,000, variable costs of $9.20 per unit, and generates sales revenue of $15.40 per unit. What is the break-even point in unit sales, where accounting profit exactly equals zero, and what is the intuition for it?

2. Suppose a firm is considering the following project, where all of the dollar figures are in thousands of dollars. In year 0, the project requires $24,490 investment in plant and equipment, is depreciated using the straight-line method over seven years, and there is a salvage value of $5,800 in year 7. The project is forecast to generate sales of 4,800 units in year 1 and grow at a sales growth rate of 72.0% in year 2. The sales growth rate is forecast to decline by 12.0% in years 3, to decline by 15.0% in year 4, to decline by 18.0% in year 5, to decline by 23.0% in year 6, to decline by 29.0% in year 7. Unit sales will drop to zero in year 8. The inflation rate is forecast to be 2.7% in year 1 and rising to 3.5% in year 7. The real cost of capital is forecast to be 10.2% in year 1, rising to 11.9% in year 7. The tax rate is forecast to be a constant 38.0%. Sales revenue per unit is forecast to be $12.20 in year 1 and then grow with inflation. Variable cost per unit is forecast to be $7.30 in year 1 and then grow with inflation. Cash fixed costs are forecast to be $6,740 in year 1 and then grow with inflation. What is the project NPV? What is the NPV Break-Even Point in Year 1 Unit Sales, where NPV equals zero? What is the NPV Break-Even Point in the Year 2 Sales Growth Rate, where NPV equals zero? What is the NPV Break-Even Contour in the two-dimensional space of Year 1 Unit Sales and Year 2 Sales Growth Rate?

Live In-class Problems.

3. Given the partial Based On Accounting Profit spreadsheet **BevenacZ.xls**, do step **3 Back Solve for the Break-Even Point using the Income Statement**.

4. Given the partial Based On NPV spreadsheet **BevennpZ.xls**, do steps **7 Create a List of Input Variables and an Output Formula** and **8 Two-Variable Data Table**.

13 Three Valuation Methods

13.1 Adjusted Present Value

Problem. A firm has the opportunity to do a one-shot project. It requires a date 0 initial outlay for new investment of $250,000. During the initial five-years, it will generate the following before-tax cash flows: date 1 = $120,000, date 2 = $140,000, date 3 = $180,000, date 4 = $130,000, date 5 = $80,000, and $40,000 each year thereafter. The project's tax rate is 40.0%, it's unlevered cost of capital is 10.0%, and the riskfree rate (= cost of debt) is 3.0%. The company has precommitted to a particular quantity of debt on the following dates to support this project: date 0 = $150,000, date 1 = $130,000, date 2 = $110,000, date 3 = $90,000, date 4 = $70,000, and $40,000 each year thereafter. What is the project's NPV as calculated using the APV method? What is the present value of future cash flows to both debt and equity? Other modules in this chapter will analyze the same problem using the FTE and WACC methods and verify that all three methods yield the same results.

Solution Strategy. Value this two-stage project under the APV method by calculating the NPV of the unlevered investments plus the present value of the debt tax shield. Then use the project NPV result to calculate the PV of Future Cash Flows for each date in the future. This will be used by the other modules in this chapter to calculate the amount of Equity and Cost of Equity Capital for each date.

FIGURE 13.1 Spreadsheet for Three Valuation Methods Using The APV Method.

	A	B	C	D	E	F	G	H
1	THREE VALUATION METHODS			Adjusted Present Value				
2								
3	**Inputs**							
4	Initial Outlay for New Investment	$250.00						
5	Tax Rate	40.0%						
6	Unlevered Cost of Capital	10.0%						
7	Riskfree Rate	3.0%						
8								
9	**Adjusted Present Value (APV)**							Infinite
10	(A.) NPV of Unlevered Investment			Explicit Forecast Horizon				Horizon
11	Date	0	1	2	3	4	5	6
12	Before-tax Cash Flow		$120.00	$140.00	$180.00	$130.00	$80.00	$40.00
13	Taxes		$48.00	$56.00	$72.00	$52.00	$32.00	$16.00
14	After-tax Cash Flow		$72.00	$84.00	$108.00	$78.00	$48.00	$24.00
15								
16	PV of Future Cash Flows	$448.12	$420.93	$379.02	$308.93	$261.82	$240.00	
17	Initial Outlay for New Investment	($250.00)						
18	(A.) NPV of Unlevered Investment	$198.12						
19								Infinite
20	(B.) PV of Debt Tax Shield			Explicit Forecast Horizon				Horizon
21	Date	0	1	2	3	4	5	6
22	Debt (D)	$150.00	$130.00	$110.00	$90.00	$70.00	$50.00	$50.00
23	Tax Shield		$1.80	$1.56	$1.32	$1.08	$0.84	$0.60
24								
25	(B.) PV of Future Tax Shield	$23.36	$22.26	$21.37	$20.69	$20.23	$20.00	
26	NPV of Project (APV) = (A.) + (B.)	$221.48						
27	PV of Future Cash Flows (APV)	$471.48	$443.19	$400.39	$329.62	$282.05	$260.00	

How To Build This Spreadsheet Model.

1. **Inputs.** Enter the overall project inputs in the range **B4:B7**, the Before-Tax Cash flows in the range **C12:H12**, and the Debt amounts in the range **B22:G22**. Lock in the first seven rows as titles by selecting cell **A8** and clicking on **Window | Freeze Panes**.

2. **Taxes and After-Tax Cash Flow.** Taxes paid is the (Before-tax Cash Flow) * (Tax Rate). Enter **=C12*$B$5** in the cell **C13** and copy it across. The $ sign on **$B$5** lock in the absolute cell reference for the Tax Rate. After-tax Cash Flow is Before-tax Cash Flow less Taxes. Enter **=C12-C13** in cell **C14** and copy it across.

3. **Present Value of Future Cash Flows.** Using the unlevered cost of capital, discount an infinite series of constant cash flows using the infinite annuity formula: (After-tax Cash Flow) / (Unlevered Cost of Capital). Enter **=H14/$B$6** in cell **G16**. Discount the explicitly forecast horizon cash flows using a recursive, one-period-at-a-time approach: PV of Future Cash Flow (t) = [After-tax Cash Flow (t+1) + PV of Future Cash Flow (t+1)] / (1 + Unlevered Cost of Capital). Enter **=(G14+G16)/(1+$B$6)** in cell **F16** and copy it leftwards to the range **B16:E16**.

4. **New Investment and NPV of Unlevered Investment.** To get the NPV of the Unlevered Investment, subtract the Initial Outlay for New Investment. Enter **=-$B$4** in cell **B17** and **=B16+B17** in cell **B18**.

5. **Tax Shield.** We adopt the convention that interest to be paid on date t+1 based on debt which issued on date t. A tax shield is defined as the quantity of taxes avoided by deducing interest expense. It is calculated as Tax Shield (t+1) = Debt (t) * (Riskfree Rate) * (Tax Rate). Enter **=B22*$B$7*$B$5** in cell **C23** and copy it across.

6. **PV of Future Tax Shield.** Using the riskfree rate, discount an infinite series of constant tax shields using the infinite annuity formula: (Tax Shield) / (Riskfree Rate). Enter **=H23/$B$7** in cell **G25**. Discount the explicitly forecast horizon tax shields using a recursive, one-period-at-a-time approach: PV of Future Tax Shield (t) = [Current Date Tax Shield (t+1) + PV of Future Tax Shield (t+1)] / (1 + Riskfree Rate). Enter **=(G23+G25)/(1+$B$7)** in cell **F25** and copy it leftwards to the range **B25:E25**.

7. **NPV of the Project and PV of Future Cash Flows.** The NPV of the Project under APV is the sum of: (A.) NPV of the Unlevered Investment and (B.) PV of Debt Tax Shield. Enter **=B18+B25** in cell **B26**. The PV of Future Cash Flows under APV is the sum of the PV of Future Cash Flows and PV of Debt Tax Shield. Enter **=B16+B25** in cell **B27** and copy it across.

We see that the NPV of the Project under APV is $221.48 and the PV of Future Cash Flows under APV starts at $471.48 and declines to $260.00. As a special case, the same spreadsheet model can be used for a single-stage, infinite horizon project. This is implemented by holding the Cash Flows and Debt amounts constant over the Explicit Forecast Horizon (the first stage) and identical to the Cash Flows and Debt amounts over the Infinite Horizon (the second stage).

13.2 Flows To Equity

Problem. Given the same firm and same project as the APV case, calculate the project's NPV using the Flows To Equity method. Compare this result to the APV result. On each date, calculate the present value of future cash flows to both debt and equity. Verify that this result is the same as the APV case.

Solution Strategy. Use the PV of Future Cash Flows from the APV case to determine the about of Equity used on each date and the resulting Cost of Equity Capital on each date. Calculate the amount of cash flows available to equityholders after debtholders are paid off. Discount these flows to equity and subtract the initial outlay by shareholders to get the project NPV under FTE. Then calculate the present value of future cash flows to both debt and equity.

FIGURE 13.2 Spreadsheet for Three Valuation Methods Using The FTE Method.

	A	B	C	D	E	F	G	H
1	THREE VALUATION METHODS			Flows To Equity				
2								
3	Inputs							
4	Initial Outlay for New Investment	$250.00						
5	Tax Rate	40.0%						
6	Unlevered Cost of Capital	10.0%						
7	Riskfree Rate	3.0%						
28								
29	Flows To Equity (FTE)							
30	Debt (D)	$150.00	$130.00	$110.00	$90.00	$70.00	$50.00	$50.00
31	Equity (E)	$321.48	$313.19	$290.39	$239.62	$212.05	$210.00	
32	Debt + Equity (D+E)	$471.48	$443.19	$400.39	$329.62	$282.05	$260.00	
33	Cost of Equity Capital	12.8%	12.4%	12.1%	12.0%	11.6%	11.0%	
34								Infinite
35				Explicit Forecast Horizon				Horizon
36	Date	0	1	2	3	4	5	6
37	EBIT		$120.00	$140.00	$180.00	$130.00	$80.00	$40.00
38	Interest Expense		$4.50	$3.90	$3.30	$2.70	$2.10	$1.50
39	Before-tax Cash Flow		$115.50	$136.10	$176.70	$127.30	$77.90	$38.50
40	Taxes		$46.20	$54.44	$70.68	$50.92	$31.16	$15.40
41	After-tax Cash Flow		$69.30	$81.66	$106.02	$76.38	$46.74	$23.10
42	New Borrowing (Repayment)		($20.00)	($20.00)	($20.00)	($20.00)	($20.00)	$0.00
43	Flows To Equity (FTE)		$49.30	$61.66	$86.02	$56.38	$26.74	$23.10
44								
45	PV of Future FTE = Equity (E)	$321.48	$313.19	$290.39	$239.62	$212.05	$210.00	
46	Initial Outlay from Shareholders	($100.00)						
47	NPV of Project (FTE)	$221.48						
48	PV of Future Cash Flows (FTE)	$471.48	$443.19	$400.39	$329.62	$282.05	$260.00	

How To Build This Spreadsheet Model.

1. **Open the APV Spreadsheet.** Open the spreadsheet that you created for Corporate Financial Planning - Adjusted Present Value and immediately save the spreadsheet under a new name using the **File | Save As** command.

2. **Debt, Equity, and the Total.** The Debt row is a repeat of the Debt input. Enter **=B22** in cell **B30** and copy it across. Equity is the Present Value of Future Cash Flows (APV) less Debt. Enter **=B27-B30** in cell **B31** and copy it across. Sum these two rows to get Debt + Equity. Enter **=B30+B31** in cell **B32** and copy it across.

3. **Cost of Equity.** The infinite horizon formula is Cost of Equity = (Unlevered Cost of Capital) + (1 - Tax Rate) * (Unlevered Cost of Capital - Riskfree Rate) * (Debt / Equity). Enter **=$B$6+(1-$B$5)*($B$6-$B$7)*(G30/G31)** in cell **G33**. The finite horizon formula for is Date t Cost of Equity

75

= (Unlevered Cost of Capital) + (Unlevered Cost of Capital - Riskfree Rate)
* {(Date t Debt) * [1 + (Riskfree Rate)*(1 - Tax Rate)] - PV of Future Tax Shield (t+1) }
/ [(Date t Equity) * (1 + Riskfree Rate)]

Enter =$B$6+(($B$6-$B$7)*(B30*(1+$B$7*(1-$B$5))-C25))/(B31*(1+$B$7)) in cell **B33** and copy it to the range **C33:F33**. The term PV of Future Tax Shield (t+1) is the present value of future tax shields as of date t+1. We simply reference the identical calculation done under the APV method in cell **C25**.

4. **Flows to Equity.** Calculate the cash flows to the equityholders (net of the debtholders) as follows:

   o EBIT repeats Before-Tax Cash Flows. Enter =C12 in cell **C37**.

   o Interest Expense (t+1) is Debt (t) * (Riskfree Rate). Enter =B22*$B$7 in cell **C38**.

   o Before-Tax Cash Flow is the difference. Enter =C37-C38 in cell **C39**.

   o Taxes is Before Tax Cash Flow * (Tax Rate). Enter =C39*$B$5 in cell **C40**.

   o After-Tax Cash Flow is the difference. Enter =C39-C40 in cell **C41**.

   o New Borrowing (Repayment) is Debt (t+1) – Debt (t). Enter =C30-B30 in cell **C42**.

   o Flows to Equity is the sum. Enter =C41+C42 in cell **C43**.

   o Copy the range **C37:C43** to the range **D37:H43**.

5. **Present Value of Future FTE.** Using the cost of equity capital, discount an infinite series of constant cash flows using the infinite annuity formula: (Flows To Equity) / (Cost of Equity Capital). Enter =IF(H43=0,0,H43/G33) in cell **G45**. The IF statement avoids an error message that occurs when a cell in the formula is undefined. This occurs when the Infinite Horizon Flow to Equity (**H43**) is zero causing the prior period sum of Debt and Equity to be zero and thus causing the Cost of Equity Capital calculation in cell **G33** to be undefined. Discount the explicitly forecast horizon cash flows using a recursive, one-period-at-a-time approach: PV of Future Flows To Equity (t) = [Flows To Equity (t+1) + PV of Future Flows To Equity (t+1)] / (1 + Cost of Equity Capital). Enter =IF(G43+G45=0,0,(G43+G45)/(1+F33)) in cell **F45** and copy it leftwards to the range **B45:E45**. Again the IF statement avoids an error message that occurs when a cell in the formula is undefined. You can verify by comparing row **45** to row **31** that Present Value of the Future FTE is equal to the Equity (E).

6. **Initial Outlay from Shareholders, NPV of the Project, and PV of Future Cash Flows.** The Initial Outlay from Shareholders = -(Initial Outlay for the New Investment) + (Initial Outlay from the Debtholders). Enter =-$B$4+B30 in cell **B46**. The NPV of the Project using the FTE method = (Present Value of Future FTE) + (Initial Outlay from Shareholders). Enter =B45+B46 in cell **B47**. The PV of Future Cash Flows (FTE) = Debt + Present Value of Future FTE = Debt + Equity. Enter =B30+B45 in cell **B48** and copy it across.

We see that the NPV of the Project under FTE is $221.48, which is the same as the APV calculation. We see that the PV of Future Cash Flows under FTE starts at $471.48 and declines to $260.00, which is the same as under APV.

13.3 Weighted Average Cost of Capital

Problem. Given the same firm and same project as the APV and FTE cases, calculate the project's NPV using the Weighted Average Cost of Capital method. Compare this result to the APV and FTE results. On each date, calculate the present value of future cash flows to both debt and equity. Verify that this result is the same as the APV and FTE cases.

Solution Strategy. Use the Debt and Equity amounts calculated for the FTE case to determine the Debt Weight, Equity Weight, and the Weighted Average Cost of Capital on each date. Calculate the after-tax cash flows available to firm, discount these cash flows, and then subtract the initial outlay for the new investment to get the project NPV under WACC. Then calculate the present value of future cash flows to the firm.

FIGURE 13.3 Spreadsheet for Three Valuation Methods Using The WACCapital Method.

	A	B	C	D	E	F	G	H
1	THREE VALUATION METHODS			Weighted Average Cost of Capital				
2								
3	Inputs							
4	Initial Outlay for New Investment	$250.00						
5	Tax Rate	40.0%						
6	Unlevered Cost of Capital	10.0%						
7	Riskfree Rate	3.0%						
49								
50	Weighted Ave Cost of Capital (WACC)							
51	Equity Weight (E / (D+E))	68.2%	70.7%	72.5%	72.7%	75.2%	80.8%	
52	Debt Weight (D / (D+E))	31.8%	29.3%	27.5%	27.3%	24.8%	19.2%	
53	WACC	9.27%	9.30%	9.30%	9.23%	9.20%	9.23%	
54								Infinite
55				Explicit Forecast Horizon				Horizon
56	Date	0	1	2	3	4	5	6
57	Before-tax Cash Flow		$120.00	$140.00	$180.00	$130.00	$80.00	$40.00
58	Taxes		$48.00	$56.00	$72.00	$52.00	$32.00	$16.00
59	After-tax Cash Flow		$72.00	$84.00	$108.00	$78.00	$48.00	$24.00
60								
61	PV of Net Cash Flows (at WACC)	$471.48	$443.19	$400.39	$329.62	$282.05	$260.00	
62	Initial Outlay for New Investment	($250.00)						
63	NPV of Project (WACC)	$221.48						
64	PV of Future Cash Flows (WACC)	$471.48	$443.19	$400.39	$329.62	$282.05	$260.00	

How To Build This Spreadsheet Model.

1. **Open the FTE Spreadsheet.** Open the spreadsheet that you created for Corporate Financial Planning - Flows To Equity and immediately save the spreadsheet under a new name using the **File | Save As** command.

2. **Equity and Debt Weights.** Using the Debt (D) calculated in row **30** and the Equity (E) calculated in row **31**, determine Equity Weight = E / (D+E). Enter **=B31/(B30+B31)** in cell **B51** and copy it across. Similarly, calculate the Debt Weight = D / (D+E). Enter **=B30/(B30+B31)** in cell **B52** and copy it across.

3. **WACC.** The formula for WACC = (Cost of Equity Capital) (Equity Weight) + (1 − Tax Rate) (Riskfree Rate) (Debt Weight). Enter **=B33*B51+(1-$B$5)*$B$7*B52** in cell **B53** and copy it across.

4. **WACC Method.** Calculate the firm's net cash flows and then discount them at WACC as follows:

    o Before-Tax Cash Flows repeats row **12**. Enter **=C12** in cell **C57** and copy it across.

    o Taxes is Before Tax Cash Flow * (Tax Rate). Enter **=C57*$B$5** in cell **C58** and copy it across.

    o After-Tax Cash Flow is the difference. Enter **=C57-C58** in cell **C59** and copy it across.

5. **Present Value of Net Cash Flows (at WACC).** Using the weighted average cost of capital (WACC), discount the infinite series of constant cash flows using the infinite annuity formula: (After-tax Cash Flow) / WACC. Enter **=IF(H59=0,0,H59/G53)** in cell **G61**. The IF statement avoids an error message that occurs when a cell in the formula is undefined. This occurs when the Infinite Horizon After-tax Cash Flow (**H59**) is zero causing the Equity Weight and Debt Weight to be undefined and thus causing WACC in cell **G53** to be undefined. Discount the explicitly forecast horizon cash flows using a recursive, one-period-at-a-time approach: PV of Future Net Cash Flows (t) = [Net Cash Flow (t+1) + PV of Future Net Cash Flows (t+1)] / (1+WACC). Enter **=IF(G59+G61=0,0,(G59+G61)/(1+F53))** in cell **F61** and copy it leftwards to the range **B61:E61**. Again the IF statement avoids an error message.

6. **Initial Outlay from New Investment, NPV of the Project, and PV of Future Cash Flows.** To get the NPV of the Project using the WACC method, subtract the Initial Outlay for New Investment. Enter **=-$B$4** in cell **B62** and **=B61+B62** in cell **B63**. The PV of Future Cash Flows (WACC) is a repeat of row **61**. Enter **=B61** in cell **B64** and copy it across.

We see that the NPV of the Project under WACC is $221.48, which is the same as the APV and FTE calculation. We see that the PV of Future Cash Flows under WACC starts at $471.48 and declines to $260.00, which is the same as under APV and FTE.

Finally, all of the discussion so far has focused on valuing projects. However, the same Two-Stage spreadsheet model can be used value companies simply by zeroing out the Investment amount and entering the *firm's total* Before-tax Cash Flows and the *firm's total* Debt amount. Again, all three valuation methods will generate the same valuation of the firm.

Problems

Skill-Building Problems.

1. A firm has the opportunity to do a one-shot project. It requires a date 0 initial outlay for new investment of $250,000. During the initial five-years, it will generate the following before-tax cash flows: date 1 = $380,000, date 2 = $430,000, date 3 = $520,000, date 4 = $460,000, date 5 = $280,000, and $120,000 each year thereafter. The project's tax rate is 36.0%, it's unlevered cost of capital is 11.6%, and the riskfree rate (= cost of debt) is 3.7%. The company has precommitted to a particular quantity of debt on the following dates to support this project: date 0 = $130,000, date 1 = $220,000, date 2 = $270,000, date 3 = $240,000, date 4 = $150,000, and $70,000 each year thereafter. What is the project's NPV as calculated using the APV method? What is the present value of future cash flows to both debt and equity?

2. Given the same firm and same project as problem 1, calculate the project's NPV using the Flows To Equity method. Compare this result to the APV result. On each date, calculate the present

value of future cash flows to both debt and equity. Verify that this result is the same as the APV case.

3. Given the same firm and same project as problem 1 and 2, calculate the project's NPV using the Weighted Average Cost of Capital method. Compare this result to the APV and FTE results. On each date, calculate the present value of future cash flows to both debt and equity. Verify that this result is the same as the APV and FTE cases.

Live In-class Problems.

4. Given the partial Adjusted Present Value spreadsheet **ThreeapZ.xls**, do steps **5 Tax Shield** and **6 Present Value of Future Tax Shield** and the first part of step **7 NPV of the Project and PV of Future Cash Flows**.

5. Given the partial Flows To Equity spreadsheet **ThreeftZ.xls**, do steps **5 Present Value of Future FTE** and the first two parts of step **6 Initial Outlay from Shareholders, NPV of the Project, and PV of Future Cash Flows**.

6. Given the partial Weighted Average Cost of Capital spreadsheet **ThreewaZ.xls**, do steps **2 Equity and Debt Weights** and **3 WACC**.

PART 4 FINANCIAL PLANNING

14 Corporate Financial Planning

14.1 Actual

Problem. Construct actual (historical) financial statements for **Cutting Edge B2B Inc.** in preparation for forecasting their financial statements.

Solution Strategy. Enter actual values in the yellow input sections. Enter appropriate additions and substractions to complete the Income Statement and Balance sheet. Then calculate the Key Assumptions over the actual years.

FIGURE 14.1 Actual Assumptions & Income Statement for Cutting Edge B2B Inc.

	A	B	C	D	E	F	G	H	I
1	CORPORATE FINANCIAL PLANNING				Actual				
2	Cutting Edge B2B Inc.	1997	1998	1999	2000	2001	2002	2003	Ave Hist.
3	Financial Plan	Actual	Actual	Actual	Actual	Forecast	Forecast	Forecast	% of Sales
4	Key Assumptions								
5	Sales Growth Rate			24.3%	19.8%				
6	Tax Rate		43.5%	42.1%	37.9%				
7	Int Rate on Short-Term Debt		6.7%	6.9%	7.1%				
8	Int Rate on Long-Term Debt		7.9%	8.1%	8.3%				
9	Dividend Payout Rate		35.0%	35.0%	35.0%				
10	Price / Earnings		29.3	29.0	29.0				
11									
12	Income Statement (Mil.$)								
13	Sales		$93.28	$115.93	$138.84				
14	Cost of Goods Sold		$58.39	$75.49	$89.83				
15	Gross Margin		$34.89	$40.44	$49.01				
16									
17	Selling, Gen & Adm Expenses		$7.28	$8.56	$10.21				
18	Depreciation		$6.37	$7.31	$9.86				
19	EBIT		$21.24	$24.57	$28.94				
20									
21	Interest Expense		$5.23	$6.69	$8.88				
22	Taxes		$6.96	$7.52	$7.60				
23	Net Income		$9.05	$10.36	$12.46				
24	Shares Outstanding (Millions)		40.36	44.93	53.91				
25	Earnings Per Share		$0.22	$0.23	$0.23				
26									
27	Allocation of Net Income:								
28	Dividends		$3.17	$3.63	$4.36				
29	Change in Equity		$5.88	$6.73	$8.10				

How To Build Your Own Spreadsheet Model.

1. **Set-up Row and Column Titles.** Enter column titles, such as 1997, 1998, etc. in row **2** and "Actual" vs. "Forecast" in row **3**. Then, place the cursor in cell **B4** and click on **Window | Freeze Panes**. This freezes the top three rows as column titles at the top and freezes Column A as a row title at the left. This step is essential to navigation in a large spreadsheet model.

2. **Enter Actual Values.** Enter three years of actual interest rates into the range **C7:E8**. Enter three years of actual Income Statement values for Cutting Edge B2B Inc into the yellow input sections of the range **C13:E22** (see Figure 14.1). Enter the shares outstanding into the range **C24:E24**. Enter dividends into the range **C28:E28**. Enter four years of actual Balance Sheet values into the yellow input sections of the range **B34:E55** (see Figure 14.2). Enter the observed market price / share into the range **B62:E62**.

FIGURE 14.2 Actual Balance Sheet for Cutting Edge B2B Inc.

	A	B	C	D	E	F	G	H	I
1	CORPORATE FINANCIAL PLANNING				Actual				
2	Cutting Edge B2B Inc.	1997	1998	1999	2000	2001	2002	2003	Ave Hist.
3	Financial Plan	Actual	Actual	Actual	Actual	Forecast	Forecast	Forecast	% of Sales
31	Balance Sheet (Mil.$)								
32	Assets								
33	Current Assets								
34	Cash & Equivalents	$4.27	$6.38	$7.62	$8.83				
35	Receivables	$20.58	$24.39	$28.77	$34.11				
36	Inventories	$26.73	$30.45	$36.75	$43.27				
37	Total Current Assets	$51.58	$61.22	$73.14	$86.21				
38									
39	Property, Plant & Equip. (PPE)	$331.64	$423.92	$503.87	$613.28				
40	Accumulated Depreciation	$98.72	$105.09	$112.40	$122.26				
41	Net PPE	$232.92	$318.83	$391.47	$491.02				
42									
43	Total Assets	$284.50	$380.05	$464.61	$577.23				
44									
45	Liabilities and Shareholders' Equity								
46	Current Liabilities								
47	Accounts Payable	$31.83	$63.43	$83.84	$94.41				
48	Short-term Debt	$30.86	$43.03	$64.85	$79.49				
49	Total Current Liabilities	$62.69	$106.46	$148.69	$173.90				
50									
51	Long-term Debt	$40.00	$45.90	$51.50	$70.81				
52	Total Liabilities	$102.69	$152.36	$200.19	$244.71				
53									
54	Shareholders' Equity								
55	Paid-in Capital	$90.00	$130.00	$160.00	$220.00				
56	Retained Earnings	$91.81	$97.69	$104.42	$112.52				
57	Total Shareholders' Equity	$181.81	$227.69	$264.42	$332.52				
58									
59	Total Liab. & Share. Equity	$284.50	$380.05	$464.61	$577.23				
60									
61	Debt / (Debt + Equity)	28.0%	28.1%	30.6%	31.1%				
62	Market Price / Share	$6.21	$6.57	$6.68	$6.71				
63	External Funds Needed		$58.07	$57.42	$93.95				

3. **The Income Statement and Earnings Per Share.** Some Income Statement items are based on the Key Assumptions section, others are forecasted as a percentage of sales, and others are simple additions or subtractions.

   o Gross Margin = Sales - Cost of Good Sold. Enter =C13-C14 in cell **C15** and copy it across.

- Earnings Before Interest and Taxes (EBIT) = Gross Margin - SG&A Expense. - Depreciation. Enter =C15-C17-C18 in cell C19 and copy it across.

- Net Income = EBIT- Interest Expense - Taxes. Enter =C19-C21-C22 in cell C23 and copy it across.

- Earnings Per Share = Net Income / Shares Outstanding. Enter =C23/C24 in cell C25 and copy it across.

- Change in Equity = Net Income - Dividends. Enter =C23-C28 in cell C29 and copy it across.

4. **The Balance Sheet and the Plug Item.** A Balance Sheet, by definition, must balance. Therefore, one line on the forecasted balance sheet must be a slack or plug item. There is some discretion in what you choose to be the plug item. In this case, the plug item is Long-term Debt. It is the residual item after everything else is forecast. Specifically, the Balance Sheet works as follows:

- Total Current Assets = Sum of the Current Asset Items. Enter =SUM(B34:B36) in cell B37 and copy it across.

- Net PPE = Property, Plant and Equipment – Accumulated Depreciation. Enter =B39-B40 in cell B41 and copy it across.

- Total Assets = Total Current Assets + Net PPE. Enter =B37+B41 in cell B43 and copy it across.

- Total Liabilities and Shareholders Equity is set equal to Total Assets. Enter =B43 in cell B59 and copy it across.

- Retained Earnings on the First Date is set directly. Enter $91.81 in cell B56. Retained Earnings on date t = (Retained Earnings on date t-1) + (Change in Equity from the Income Statement). Enter =B56+C29 in cell C56 and copy it across.

- Total Shareholders' Equity = Paid-in Capital + Retained Earnings. Enter =B55+B56 in cell B57 and copy it across.

- Total Liabilities = Total Liabilities and Shareholders Equity - Total Shareholders' Equity. Enter =B59-B57 in cell B52 and copy it across.

- Total Current Liabilities = Accounts Payable + Short-term Debt. Enter =B47+B48 in cell B49 and copy it across.

- Long-term Debt = Total Liabilities – Total Current Liabilities. Enter =B52-B49 in cell B51 and copy it across.

5. **Other Comparisons.** Debt / (Debt + Equity) = (Short-term Debt + Long-term Debt) / (Short-term Debt + Long-term Debt + Total Shareholders' Equity). Enter =(B48+B51)/ (B48+B51+B57) in cell B61 and copy it across. The formula for the firm's External Funds Needed = (Increase in Total Assets) – (Increase in Retained Earnings) – (Increase in Accounts Payable). Enter =(C43-B43)-(C56-B56)-(C47-B47) in cell C63 and copy it across.

6. **Key Assumptions.** It is helpful to analyze key growth rates and ratios for past few years in order to forecast those same items into the future.

- o Sales Growth Rate(date t) = (Sales(date t) – Sales(date t-1)) / Sales(date t-1). Enter =**(D13-C13)/C13** in cell **D5** and copy it across.

- o Tax Rate = Taxes / (Before-Tax Income) = Taxes / (EBIT – Interest Expense). Enter =**C22/(C19-C21)** in cell **C6** and copy it across.

- o Dividend Payout Rate = Dividends / Net Income. Enter =**C28/C23** in cell **C9** and copy it across.

- o Price / Earnings = (Market Price Per Share) / (Earnings Per Share). Enter =**C62/C25** in cell **C10** and copy it across.

Now you are ready to Forecast the Financial Statements.

14.2 Forecast

Problem. Given actual financial statements for **Cutting Edge B2B Inc.**, forecast their financial statements for the next three years. Explore the impact of the financing *choice variables*: debt or equity.

Solution Strategy. Analyze the historical financial statements to determine which income statement and balance sheet items are close to being a constant percentage of sales and which items are not. Then, forecast sales as accurately as possible. Then, apply the average historical percentage of sales to generate most of the income statement and balance sheet items. Forecast other key assumptions to generate most of the rest and work out the implications for additional financing. Make the Balance Sheet balance by calculating long-term debt as the plug item. Raise (or lower) the portion of equity relative to the portion of debt by raising (or lowering) paid-in capital.

FIGURE 14.3 Forecast Percent of Sales for Cutting Edge B2B Inc.

	A	B	C	D	E	F	G	H	I
1	CORPORATE FINANCIAL PLANNING				Forecast				
2	Cutting Edge B2B Inc.	1997	1998	1999	2000	2001	2002	2003	Ave Hist.
3	Financial Plan	Actual	Actual	Actual	Actual	Forecast	Forecast	Forecast	% of Sales
65	Income Statement (% of Sales)								
66	Sales		100.0%	100.0%	100.0%	100.0%	100.0%	100.0%	100.0%
67	Cost of Goods Sold		62.6%	65.1%	64.7%	64.1%	64.1%	64.1%	64.1%
68	Gross Margin		37.4%	34.9%	35.3%	35.9%	35.9%	35.9%	35.9%
69									
70	Selling, Gen & Adm Expenses		7.8%	7.4%	7.4%	7.5%	7.5%	7.5%	7.5%
71	Depreciation		6.8%	6.3%	7.1%	6.7%	6.7%	6.7%	6.7%
72	EBIT		22.8%	21.2%	20.8%	21.6%	21.6%	21.6%	21.6%
73									
74	Interest Expense		5.6%	5.8%	6.4%	7.1%	6.7%	6.7%	5.9%
75	Taxes		7.5%	6.5%	5.5%	5.8%	6.0%	6.0%	6.5%
76	Net Income		9.7%	8.9%	9.0%	8.7%	8.9%	8.9%	9.2%
77	Shares Outstanding (Millions)		43.3%	38.8%	38.8%	37.2%	36.1%	34.5%	40.3%
78	Earnings Per Share		0.2%	0.2%	0.2%	0.1%	0.1%	0.1%	0.2%
80	Allocation of Net Income:								
81	Dividends		3.4%	3.1%	3.1%	3.1%	3.1%	3.1%	3.2%
82	Change in Equity		6.3%	5.8%	5.8%	5.7%	5.8%	5.8%	6.0%
84	Balance Sheet (% of Sales)								
85	Assets								
86	Current Assets								
87	Cash & Equivalents		6.8%	6.6%	6.4%	6.6%	6.6%	6.6%	6.6%
88	Receivables		26.1%	24.8%	24.6%	25.2%	25.2%	25.2%	25.2%
89	Inventories		32.6%	31.7%	31.2%	31.8%	31.8%	31.8%	31.8%
90	Total Current Assets		65.6%	63.1%	62.1%	63.6%	63.6%	63.6%	63.6%
92	Property, Plant & Equip. (PPE)		454.5%	434.6%	441.7%	427.0%	424.3%	423.1%	443.6%
93	Accum Depreciation		112.7%	97.0%	88.1%	82.7%	79.9%	78.7%	99.2%
94	Net PPE		341.8%	337.7%	353.7%	344.4%	344.4%	344.4%	344.4%
96	Total Assets		407.4%	400.8%	415.8%	408.0%	408.0%	408.0%	408.0%
98	Liabilities and Shareholders' Equity								
99	Current Liabilities								
100	Accounts Payable		68.0%	72.3%	68.0%	69.4%	69.4%	69.4%	69.4%
101	Short-term Debt		46.1%	55.9%	57.3%	53.1%	53.1%	53.1%	53.1%
102	Total Current Liabilities		114.1%	128.3%	125.3%	122.5%	122.5%	122.5%	122.5%
103									
104	Long-term Debt		49.2%	44.4%	51.0%	48.5%	47.9%	50.8%	48.2%
105	Total Liabilities		163.3%	172.7%	176.3%	171.0%	170.5%	173.4%	170.8%
107	Shareholders' Equity								
108	Paid-in Capital		139.4%	138.0%	158.5%	161.4%	164.8%	163.4%	145.3%
109	Retained Earnings		104.7%	90.1%	81.0%	75.5%	72.7%	71.3%	91.9%
110	Total Shareholders' Equity		244.1%	228.1%	239.5%	237.0%	237.5%	234.6%	237.2%
112	Total Liabilities and Equity		407.4%	400.8%	415.8%	408.0%	408.0%	408.0%	408.0%

How To Build Your Own Spreadsheet Model.

1. **Calculate the Percent of Sales.** For the historical financials, calculate each Income Statement and Balance sheet item as a percentage of sales (see Figure 14.3). In cell **C66**, enter **=C13/C$13** The $ sign in **C$13** locks in Sales in row **13**. Copy the formula in cell **C66** across the entire range

C66:H112. This calculates the historical percent of sales and it sets up the forecasted percent of sales. Delete ranges that correspond to blank sections of the Income Statement and Balance Sheet. That is, delete ranges **C69:H69**, **C73:H73**, **C79:H79**, **C83:H86**, **C91:H91**, **C95:H95**, **C97:H99**, **C103:H103**, **C106:H107**, and **C111:H111**. Looking at the historical financial statements, we see that most Income Statement and Balance Sheet items are nearly a constant percentage of sales. The main exceptions are: **Interest Expense, Taxes, Accumulated Depreciation, Short-term Debt, Long-term Debt**, and **Shareholders' Equity**.

2. **Average Historical Percent of Sales.** In Figure 14.3, column **I** is the average historical percent of sales. This is simply the average of the percent of sales for the three historical years (1997 – 1999). In cell **I66**, enter **=AVERAGE(C66:E66)**. Copy the formula in cell **I66** across the entire range **I67:I112**. Average historical percent of sales are used to forecast all financial items that are nearly constant as a percentage of sales. Delete cells and ranges that correspond to blank parts of the Income Statement and Balance Sheet. That is, delete cells **I69, I73, I91, I95, I103,** and **I111** and delete ranges **I79:I80, I83:I86, I97:I99,** and **I106:I107**.

FIGURE 14.4 Forecast Assumptions & Income Statement for Cutting Edge B2B Inc.

	A	B	C	D	E	F	G	H	I
1	CORPORATE FINANCIAL PLANNING				Forecast				
2	Cutting Edge B2B Inc.	1997	1998	1999	2000	2001	2002	2003	Ave Hist.
3	Financial Plan	Actual	Actual	Actual	Actual	Forecast	Forecast	Forecast	% of Sales
4	Key Assumptions								
5	Sales Growth Rate			24.3%	19.8%	16.0%	13.0%	11.0%	
6	Tax Rate		40.0%	40.0%	40.0%	40.0%	40.0%	40.0%	
7	Int Rate on Short-Term Debt		6.7%	6.9%	7.1%	7.0%	6.9%	6.8%	
8	Int Rate on Long-Term Debt		7.9%	8.1%	8.3%	8.2%	8.1%	8.0%	
9	Dividend Payout Rate		35.0%	35.0%	35.0%	35.0%	35.0%	35.0%	
10	Price / Earnings		29.3	29.0	29.0	29.4	29.4	29.4	
11									
12	Income Statement (Mil.$)								
13	Sales		$93.28	$115.93	$138.84	$161.05	$181.99	$202.01	
14	Cost of Goods Sold		$58.39	$75.49	$89.83	$103.30	$116.73	$129.57	64.1%
15	Gross Margin		$34.89	$40.44	$49.01	$57.76	$65.27	$72.45	
16									
17	Selling, Gen & Adm Expenses		$7.28	$8.56	$10.21	$12.10	$13.67	$15.18	7.5%
18	Depreciation		$6.37	$7.31	$9.86	$10.86	$12.28	$13.63	6.7%
19	EBIT		$21.24	$24.57	$28.94	$34.79	$39.32	$43.64	
20									
21	Interest Expense		$5.23	$6.69	$8.88	$11.37	$12.22	$13.55	
22	Taxes		$6.96	$7.52	$7.60	$9.37	$10.84	$12.04	
23	Net Income		$9.05	$10.36	$12.46	$14.05	$16.25	$18.05	
24	Shares Outstanding (Millions)		40.36	44.93	53.91	59.87	65.67	69.79	
25	Earnings Per Share		$0.22	$0.23	$0.23	$0.23	$0.25	$0.26	
26									
27	Allocation of Net Income:								
28	Dividends		$3.17	$3.63	$4.36	$4.92	$5.69	$6.32	
29	Change in Equity		$5.88	$6.73	$8.10	$9.13	$10.57	$11.73	

3. **Forecasting Sales and Other Key Assumptions.** Looking at the historical sales growth rate in Figure 14.1, it is clear that the rate of growth is slowing down. This may reflect such factors as increasing competition or relative saturation of the market. It seems prudent to forecast a continued slowdown in the rate of growth. Hence, sales are forecast to grow at 16%, 13% and 11% over the next three years. Enter these sales forecasts in the range **F5:H5**. Interest rates on

short-term and long-term debt are forecasted based on their current levels with a slight declining trend. The rest of the key assumptions are forecasted at or near their average historical levels. Enter the forecast values shown in Figure 14.4 in the range **F6:H10**.

4. **The Income Statement.** Some Income Statement items are based on the Key Assumptions section, others are forecasted as a percentage of sales, and others are simple additions or subtractions.

   o Sales on date t = (Sales on date t-1) * (1 + Sales Growth Rate). Enter =**E13*(1+F5)** in cell **F13** and copy it across.

   o Cost of Goods Sold = (Ave. Hist. Goods Sold / Sales) * Sales. For convenience, reference the Ave. Hist. Goods Sold / Sales by entering =**I67** in cell **I14**. Then enter =**$I14*F$13** in cell **F14** and copy it across. The $ sign in **$I14** locks in column **I**, which is the Ave. Hist. Goods Sold / Sales and the $ sign in **F$13** locks in row **13**, which is Sales.

   o Gross Margin = Sales - Cost of Good Sold. This is the same as the Actual Gross Margin. Copy cell **E15** across.

   o Selling, Gen and Adm Expense = (Ave. Hist. SG&A / Sales) * Sales. Depreciation is forecast in the same way. This is the same format as the Cost of Good Sold. Copy the range **F14:I14** to the range **F17:F18**.

   o Earnings Before Interest and Taxes (EBIT) = Gross Margin - SG&A Expense. - Depreciation. This is the same as the Actual EBIT. Copy cell **E19** across.

   o Interest Expense = (Interest Rate on Short-term Debt) * (Amount of Short-term Debt at the End of the Previous Year) + (Interest Rate on Long-term Debt) * (Amount of Short-term Debt at the End of the Previous Year). Enter =**F7*E48+F8*E51** in cell **F21** and copy it across.

   o Taxes = (EBIT- Interest Expense) * (Tax Rate). Enter =**(F19-F21)*F6** in cell **F22** and copy it across.

   o Net Income = EBIT- Interest Expense - Taxes. This is the same as the Actual Net Income. Copy cell **E23** across.

   o Dividends = (Net Income) * (Dividend Payout Rate). Enter =**F23*F9** in cell **F28** and copy it across.

   o Change in Equity = Net Income - Dividends. This is the same as the Actual Change in Equity. Copy cell **E29** across.

FIGURE 14.5 Forecast Balance Sheet for Cutting Edge B2B Inc.

	A	B	C	D	E	F	G	H	I
1	CORPORATE FINANCIAL PLANNING				Forecast				
2	Cutting Edge B2B Inc.	1997	1998	1999	2000	2001	2002	2003	Ave Hist.
3	Financial Plan	Actual	Actual	Actual	Actual	Forecast	Forecast	Forecast	% of Sales
31	Balance Sheet (Mil.$)								
32	Assets								
33	Current Assets								
34	Cash & Equivalents	$4.27	$6.38	$7.62	$8.83	$10.61	$11.99	$13.31	6.6%
35	Receivables	$20.58	$24.39	$28.77	$34.11	$40.55	$45.82	$50.86	25.2%
36	Inventories	$26.73	$30.45	$36.75	$43.27	$51.27	$57.94	$64.31	31.8%
37	Total Current Assets	$51.58	$61.22	$73.14	$86.21	$102.44	$115.75	$128.49	
38									
39	Property, Plant & Equip. (PPE)	$331.64	$423.92	$503.87	$613.28	$687.76	$772.14	$854.71	
40	Accumulated Depreciation	$98.72	$105.09	$112.40	$122.26	$133.12	$145.40	$159.03	
41	Net PPE	$232.92	$318.83	$391.47	$491.02	$554.64	$626.74	$695.68	344.4%
42									
43	Total Assets	$284.50	$380.05	$464.61	$577.23	$657.07	$742.49	$824.17	
44									
45	**Liabilities and Shareholders' Equity**								
46	Current Liabilities								
47	Accounts Payable	$31.83	$63.43	$83.84	$94.41	$111.84	$126.37	$140.27	69.4%
48	Short-term Debt	$30.86	$43.03	$64.85	$79.49	$85.53	$96.65	$107.28	53.1%
49	Total Current Liabilities	$62.69	$106.46	$148.69	$173.90	$197.37	$223.02	$247.56	
50									
51	Long-term Debt	$40.00	$45.90	$51.50	$70.81	$78.05	$87.25	$102.66	
52	Total Liabilities	$102.69	$152.36	$200.19	$244.71	$275.42	$310.27	$350.21	
53									
54	Shareholders' Equity								
55	Paid-in Capital	$90.00	$130.00	$160.00	$220.00	$260.00	$300.00	$330.00	
56	Retained Earnings	$91.81	$97.69	$104.42	$112.52	$121.65	$132.22	$143.95	
57	Total Shareholders' Equity	$181.81	$227.69	$264.42	$332.52	$381.65	$432.22	$473.95	
58									
59	Total Liab. & Share. Equity	$284.50	$380.05	$464.61	$577.23	$657.07	$742.49	$824.17	
60									
61	Debt / (Debt + Equity)	28.0%	28.1%	30.6%	31.1%	30.0%	29.8%	30.7%	
62	Market Price / Share	$6.21	$6.57	$6.68	$6.71	$6.90	$7.28	$7.60	
63	External Funds Needed		$58.07	$57.42	$93.95	$53.28	$60.32	$56.04	

5. **The Balance Sheet.** The Balance Sheet works as follows:

- Current Asset Item = (Ave. Hist. Current Asset Item / Sales) * Sales. This is the same format as Depreciation. Copy the range **F18:I18** to the range **F34:F36**.

- Total Current Assets = Sum of the Current Asset Items. This is the same as the Actual Total Current Assets. Copy cell **E37** across.

- Net PPE = (Ave. Hist. PPE / Sales) * Sales. This is the same format as Inventories. Copy the range **F36:I36** to the cell **F41**.

- Accumulated Depreciation on date t = (Accumulated Depreciation on date t-1) + Depreciation. Enter **=E40+F18** in cell **F40** and copy it across.

- Property Plant and Equipment = Net PPE + Accumulated Depreciation. Enter **=F40+F41** in cell **F39** and copy it across.

87

o Total Assets = Total Current Assets + Net PPE. This is the same as the Actual Total Assets. Copy cell **E43** across.

o Total Liabilities and Shareholders Equity is set equal to Total Assets. This is the same as the Actual Total Liabilities and Shareholders Equity. Copy cell **E59** across.

o Paid-in Capital is a key choice variable. Enter any values for right now. Perhaps you want to continue the trend of recent years. At the end, we will come back and adjust this category to achieve the desired mix of debt and equity.

o Retained Earnings on date t = (Retained Earnings on date t-1) + (Change in Equity from the Income Statement). This is the same as the Actual Retained Earnings. Copy cell **E56** across.

o Total Shareholders' Equity = Paid-in Capital + Retained Earnings. This is the same as the Actual Total Shareholders' Equity. Copy cell **E57** across.

o Total Liabilities = Total Liabilities and Shareholders Equity - Total Shareholders' Equity. This is the same as the Actual Total Liabilities. Copy cell **E52** across.

o Accounts Payable is forecasted based on the Percentage of Sales. This is the same format as Net PPE. Copy the range **F41:I41** to the cell **F47**.

o Short-term Debt = (Ave. Hist. Short-term Debt / Sales) * Sales. This is the same format as Inventories. Copy the range **F36:I36** to the cell **F48**.

o Total Current Liabilities = Accounts Payable + Short-term Debt. This is the same as the Actual Total Current Liabilities. Copy cell **E52** across.

o Long-term Debt = Total Liabilities − Total Current Liabilities. This is the same as the Actual Long-term Debt. Copy cell **E51** across.

6. **Adjust Paid in Capital and Check Long-Term Debt.** Most companies try to maintain a target proportion of debt vs. equity. Adjustment Paid in Capital, which is a component of equity, will accomplish this. Debt / (Debt + Equity) is the same as the Actual ratio. Copy cell **E61** across. Historically, the company has maintained a Debt / (Debt + Equity) proportion between 28.0% and 30.2%. In this forecast, the company chooses to maintain a Debt / (Debt + Equity) proportion of slightly more than 29%. Raise (or lower) Paid in Capital in the range **F55:H55** to the percentages shown in Figure 14.5, in order to lower (or raise) the Debt / (Debt + Equity) proportion. After all of the forecasting is done, it is important to check Long-term Debt to make sure that it isn't growing explosively or dropping rapidly (perhaps going negative!). If it is going wild, then backtrack to identify the source of sharp up or down movements and check for errors.

7. **Shares Outstanding and Earnings Per Share.** The formula for Shares Outstanding on date t = (Shares Outstanding on date t-1) + (Paid in Capital on date t - Paid in Capital on date t-1) * (Market Price / Share on date t-1). This assumes that you issue shares at the beginning of the year. Enter =**E24+(F55-E55)/E62** in cell **F24** and copy it across. Earnings Per Share = Net Income / Shares Outstanding. This is the same as the Actual Earnings Per Share. Copy cell **E25** across. Some of these cells will temporarily display an error message until the Market Price / Share is calculated in the step below.

8. **Other Comparisons.** The formula for Market Price / Share = (Price / Earnings) * (Earnings / Share). Enter **=F10*F25** in cell **F62** and copy it across. The formula for the firm's External Funds Needed = (Increase in Total Assets) – (Increase in Retained Earnings) – (Increase in Accounts Payable). This is the same as the Actual External Funds Needed. Copy cell **E63** across. We see that there continues to be a significant amount of External Funds Needed.

The forecast for the next three years is a steady increase in Earnings Per Share from $0.23 to $0.25 to $0.26.

14.3 Cash Flow

Problem. Given historical and forecasted Income Statements and Balance Sheets for **Cutting Edge B2B Inc.**, create the historical and forecasted Cash Flow Statement.

Solution Strategy. Construct the cash flow statement by starting with Net Income from the Income Statement and then picking up the year to year changes from the Balance Sheets.

FIGURE 14.6 Historical and Forecasted Cash Flow Statement for Cutting Edge B2B Inc.

	A	B	C	D	E	F	G	H	I
1	CORPORATE FINANCIAL PLANNING				Cash Flow				
2	Cutting Edge B2B Inc.	1997	1998	1999	2000	2001	2002	2003	Ave Hist.
3	Financial Plan	Actual	Actual	Actual	Actual	Forecast	Forecast	Forecast	% of Sales
114	Cash Flow Statement (Mil.$)								
115	Cash Flow From Operating Activities								
116	Net Income		$9.05	$10.36	$12.46	$14.05	$16.25	$18.05	
117	+ Depreciation		$6.37	$7.31	$9.86	$10.86	$12.28	$13.63	
118	- Increase in Accounts Receivable		($3.81)	($4.38)	($5.34)	($6.44)	($5.27)	($5.04)	
119	- Increase in Inventories		($3.72)	($6.30)	($6.52)	($8.00)	($6.67)	($6.37)	
120	+ Increase in Accounts Payable		$31.60	$20.41	$10.57	$17.43	$14.54	$13.90	
121	Cash Flow From Operating Activity		$39.49	$27.40	$21.03	$27.90	$31.13	$34.17	
122									
123	Cash Flow From Investing Activities								
124	- Investment in Plant and Equipment		($92.28)	($79.95)	($109.41)	($74.48)	($84.38)	($82.57)	
125	Cash Flow From Investing Activities		($92.28)	($79.95)	($109.41)	($74.48)	($84.38)	($82.57)	
126									
127	Cash Flow From Financing Activities								
128	+ Increase in Long-term Debt		$5.90	$5.60	$19.31	$7.24	$9.20	$15.41	
129	+ Increase in Short-term Debt		$12.17	$21.82	$14.64	$6.04	$11.12	$10.63	
130	+ Increase in Paid in Capital		$40.00	$30.00	$60.00	$40.00	$40.00	$30.00	
131	- Dividends Paid		($3.17)	($3.63)	($4.36)	($4.92)	($5.69)	($6.32)	
132	Cash Flow From Financing Activities		$54.90	$53.79	$89.59	$48.37	$54.63	$49.72	
133									
134	Change in Cash and Equivalents		$2.11	$1.24	$1.21	$1.78	$1.38	$1.32	
135	Cash and Equivalents at Begin. of Year		$4.27	$6.38	$7.62	$8.83	$10.61	$11.99	
136	Cash and Equivalents at End of Year		$6.38	$7.62	$8.83	$10.61	$11.99	$13.31	

How To Build Your Own Spreadsheet Model.

1. **Open the Basics Spreadsheet.** Open the spreadsheet that you created for Corporate Financial Planning - Basics and immediately save the spreadsheet under a new name using the **File | Save As** command.

2. **Cash Flow from Operating Activities.** Start Net Income, then add or subtract year-to-year changes in other Operating Activities items.

   o   Net Income = Net Income from the Income Statement. Enter =**C23** in cell **C116** and copy it across.

   o   + Depreciation = Accumulated Depreciation (t) - Accumulated Depreciation (t-1). Enter =**C40-B40** in cell **C117** and copy it across.

   o   - Increase in Accounts Receivable = -(Receivables (t) - Receivables (t-1)). Enter =**-(C35-B35)** in cell **C118** and copy it across.

   o   - Increase in Inventories = -(Inventories (t) - Inventories (t-1)). Enter =**-(C36-B36)** in cell **C119** and copy it across.

   o   + Increase in Accounts Payable = Accounts Payable (t) - Accounts Payable (t-1). Enter =**C47-B47** in cell **C120** and copy it across.

   o   Cash Flow From Operating Activity = Sum of the Operating Activity items. Enter =**SUM(C116:C120)** in cell **C121** and copy it across.

3. **Cash Flow from Investing Activities.** Add or subtract year-to-year changes in Investing Activities.

   o   - Investment in Plant and Equipment = -(PPE (t) - PPE (t-1)). Enter =**-(C39-B39)** in cell **C124** and copy it across.

   o   Cash Flow From Investing Activity = Sum of the Investing Activity items. Enter =**C124** in cell **C125** and copy it across.

4. **Cash Flow from Financing Activities.** Add or subtract year-to-year changes in Financing Activities items.

   o   + Increase in Long-term Debt = Long-term Debt (t) - Long-term Debt (t-1). Enter =**C51-B51** in cell **C128** and copy it across.

   o   + Increase in Short-term Debt = Short-term Debt (t) - Short-term Debt (t-1). Enter =**C48-B48** in cell **C129** and copy it across.

   o   + Increase in Paid-In Capital = Paid-In Capital (t) - Paid-In Capital (t-1). Enter =**C55-B55** in cell **C130** and copy it across.

   o   - Dividends Paid = - Dividends from the Income Statement. Enter =**-C28** in cell **C131** and copy it across.

   o   Cash Flow From Financing Activity = Sum of the Financing Activity items. Enter =**SUM(C128:C131)** in cell **C132** and copy it across.

5. **Cash and Equivalents.** The last category sums up the cash flows from operations, investments, and financing and "balances" the Cash Flow Statement by tying the sum of the cash flows to the Change in Cash and Equivalents.

- o Change in Cash and Equivalents = Cash Flow From Operating Activity + Cash Flow From Investing Activity + Cash Flow From Financing Activity. Enter =C121+C125+C132 in cell C134 and copy it across.

- o Cash and Equivalents at the Beginning of the Year = Cash and Equivalents (t-1). Enter =B34 in cell C135 and copy it across.

- o Cash and Equivalents at the End of the Year = Change in Cash and Equivalents + Cash and Equivalents at the Beginning of the Year. Enter =C134+C135 in cell C136 and copy it across.

Notice that the $6.38 Cash and Equivalents at the End of Year 1998, which was obtained by summing all of the cash flows from operations, investments, and financing together with the Beginning of the Year balance for 1998, does indeed equal the $6.38 Cash and Equivalents at the Beginning of Year 1999. Thus, the sum of the cash flows from operations, investments, and financing does equal the Change in Cash and Equivalents. This balancing of the Cash Flow Statement is a direct consequence of the balancing of the Balance Sheet. It is also a good way to check for possible errors in your spreadsheet.

14.4 Ratios

Problem. Given historical and forecasted financial statements for **Cutting Edge B2B Inc.**, create the historical and forecasted financial ratios.

Solution Strategy. Calculate the financial ratios by referencing the appropriate items on the Income Statement or Balance Sheet.

FIGURE 14.7 Historical and Forecasted Financial Ratios for Cutting Edge B2B Inc.

	A	B	C	D	E	F	G	H	I
1	CORPORATE FINANCIAL PLANNING				Ratios				
2	Cutting Edge B2B Inc.	1997	1998	1999	2000	2001	2002	2003	Ave Hist.
3	Financial Plan	Actual	Actual	Actual	Actual	Forecast	Forecast	Forecast	% of Sales
138	Financial Ratios								
139	Profitability								
140	Return On Sales (ROS)		22.8%	21.2%	20.8%	21.0%	21.6%	21.6%	
141	Return On Assets (ROA)		6.4%	5.8%	5.6%	5.6%	5.6%	5.6%	
142	Return On Equity (ROE)		4.4%	4.2%	4.2%	3.9%	4.0%	4.0%	
143									
144	Asset Turnover								
145	Receivables Turnover		414.9%	436.2%	441.6%	431.4%	421.4%	417.9%	
146	Inventory Turnover		204.2%	224.7%	224.5%	218.5%	213.8%	212.0%	
147	Asset Turnover		28.1%	27.5%	26.7%	26.1%	26.0%	25.8%	
148									
149	Financial Leverage								
150	Debt		23.4%	25.0%	26.0%	24.9%	24.8%	25.5%	
151	Times Interest Earned		406.1%	367.3%	325.9%	306.0%	321.6%	322.0%	
152									
153	Liquidity								
154	Current		57.5%	49.2%	49.6%	51.9%	51.9%	51.9%	
155	Quick		28.9%	24.5%	24.7%	25.9%	25.9%	25.9%	
156									
157	Market Value								
158	Price to Earnings		29.30	28.97	29.03	29.40	29.40	29.40	
159	Market to Book		116.5%	113.5%	108.8%	108.3%	110.6%	112.0%	

How To Build Your Own Spreadsheet Model.

1. **Open the Cash Flow Spreadsheet.** Open the spreadsheet that you created for Corporate Financial Planning - Cash Flow and immediately save the spreadsheet under a new name using the **File | Save As** command.

2. **Profitability.** These three ratios indicate the ability of the firm to use its assets productively in generating revenues.

   o Return on Sales (ROS) = EBIT / Sales. Enter **=C19/C13** in cell **C140** and copy it across.

   o Return on Assets (ROA) = EBIT / Average Total Assets = EBIT / ((Total Assets (t-1) + Total Assets (t)) / 2). Enter **=C19/((B43+C43)/2)** in cell **C141** and copy it across.

   o Return on Equity (ROE) = Net Income / Average Total Shareholders Equity = Net Income / ((Total Shareholders Equity (t-1) + Total Shareholders Equity (t)) / 2). Enter **=C23/((B57+C57)/2)** in cell **C142** and copy it across.

3. **Asset Turnover.** These three ratios indicate the degree of profitability of the company.

   o Receivables Turnover = Sales / Average Receivables = Sales / ((Receivables (t-1) + Receivables (t)) / 2). Enter **=C13/((B35+C35)/2)** in cell **C145** and copy it across.

   o Inventory Turnover = Cost of Goods Sold / Average Inventories = Sales / ((Inventories (t-1) + Inventories (t)) / 2). Enter **=C14/((B36+C36)/2)** in cell **C146** and copy it across.

   o Asset Turnover = Sales / Average Total Assets = Sales / ((Total Assets (t-1) + Total Assets (t)) / 2). Enter **=C13/((B43+C43)/2)** in cell **C147** and copy it across.

4. **Financial Leverage.** These two ratios indicate the degree of burden of the company's debt.

   o Debt = Total Debt / Total Assets = (Short-term Debt + Long-term Debt) / Total Assets. Enter **=(C48+C51)/C43** in cell **C150** and copy it across.

   o Times Interest Earned = EBIT / Interest Expense. Enter **=C19/C21** in cell **C151** and copy it across.

5. **Liquidity.** These two ratios indicate the ability of the company to pay its bills and remain solvent.

   o Current = Total Current Assets / Total Current Liabilities. Enter **=C37/C49** in cell **C154** and copy it across.

   o Quick = (Cash and Equivalents + Receivables) / Total Current Liabilities. Enter **=(C34+C35)/C49** in cell **C155** and copy it across.

6. **Market Value.** These two ratios indicate the market value of the firm relative to accounting measures of firm value.

   o Price To Earnings = (Market Price / Share) / Earnings Per Shares. Enter **=C62/C25** in cell **C158** and copy it across.

o Market To Book = (Market Price / Share) / (Total Shareholders Equity / Shares Outstanding). Enter **=C62/(C57/C24)** in cell **C159** and copy it across.

The financial ratios are very useful in interpreting the financial condition of the firm.

14.5 Sensitivity

Problem. Given historical and forecasted financial statements for **Cutting Edge B2B Inc.**, analyze the sensitivity of the 2001 External Funds Needed to the assumed 2001 Sales Growth Rate.

Solution Strategy. Create a Data Table using Sales Growth Rate as the input variable and External Funds Needed as the output variable. Then graph the relationship.

FIGURE 14.8 Sensitivity Analysis for Cutting Edge B2B Inc.

	A	B	C	D	E	F	G	H	I
1	CORPORATE FINANCIAL PLANNING				Sensitivity				
2	Cutting Edge B2B Inc.	1997	1998	1999	2000	2001	2002	2003	Ave Hist.
3	Financial Plan	Actual	Actual	Actual	Actual	Forecast	Forecast	Forecast	% of Sales
161	Data Table: Sensitivity of the External Funds Needed to the Sales Growth Rate								
162			Input Values for Sales Growth Rate						
163	Output Formula:		0.0%	4.0%	8.0%	12.0%	16.0%	20.0%	24.0%
164	External Funds Needed	$53.28	($20.05)	($1.72)	$16.62	$34.95	$53.28	$71.62	$89.95
165									
166									
167				**External Funds Needed by the Sales Growth Rate**					
168									
...									
182									

How To Build Your Own Spreadsheet Model.

1. **Open the Ratios Spreadsheet.** Open the spreadsheet that you created for Corporate Financial Planning - Ratios and immediately save the spreadsheet under a new name using the **File | Save As** command.

2. **Data Table.** Create a list of input values for the 2001 Sales Growth Rate (0.0%, 4.0%, 8.0%, etc.) in the range **C163:I163**. Create an output formula that references the 2001 External Funds Needed by entering the formula **=F63** in cell **B164**. Select the range **B163:I164** for the One-Variable Data Table. This range includes both the input values on the top of the range and the output formula on the left side of the range. Then choose **Data | Table** from the main menu and a

Table dialog box pops up. Enter the cell address **F5** (2001 Sales Growth Rate) in the **Row Input Cell** and click on **OK**.

3. **Graph.** Highlight the input values and the results of the data table (excluding the side) in the range **C163:I164** and then choose **Insert | Chart** from the main menu. Select the **XY (Scatter)** chart type and make other selections to complete the Chart Wizard.

The sensitivity analysis indicates that 2001 External Funds Needed is very sensitive to the assumption about 2001 Sales Growth Rate. Further, there is a linear relationship between 2001 Sales Growth Rate and 2001 External Funds Needed.

14.6 Full-Scale Real Data

Problem. Given historical 10K financial statements for **Nike, Inc.**, forecast their financial statements over the next three years.

Solution Strategy. Modify the financial statement spreadsheet developed for the fictional firm **Cutting Edge B2B Inc.** by adding an additional level of detail found in the actual 10K financial statements of **Nike, Inc.** Then forecast the financial statements in the same way as before.

FIGURE 14.9 Historical and Forecasted Assumptions and Income Statement for Nike, Inc.

	A	B	C	D	E	F	G	H	I
1	CORPORATE FINANCIAL PLANNING				Full-Scale, Real Data				
2	Nike, Inc.	1997	1998	1999	2000	2001	2002	2003	Ave. %
3	Financial Plan	Actual	Actual	Actual	Actual	Forecast	Forecast	Forecast	of Sales
4	Key Assumptions								
5	Sales Growth Rate			-8.1%	2.5%	5.0%	7.0%	9.0%	
6	Tax Rate		38.8%	39.5%	37.0%	38.4%	38.4%	38.4%	38.4%
7	Int Rate on Short-Term Debt		5.6%	5.1%	6.4%	6.5%	6.6%	6.7%	
8	Int Rate on Long-Term Debt		6.5%	6.5%	6.5%	6.7%	6.9%	7.0%	
9	Dividend Payout Rate		31.9%	30.2%	23.0%	25.0%	28.0%	30.0%	
10	Price / Earnings		33.0	38.1	20.0	22.0	25.0	28.0	
11									
12	Income Statement (Mil.$)								
13	Sales		$9,553.1	$8,776.9	$8,995.1	$9,444.9	$10,106.0	$11,015.5	
14	Cost of Goods Sold		$5,881.0	$5,295.3	$5,215.8	$5,663.1	$6,059.5	$6,604.9	60.0%
15	Gross Margin		$3,672.1	$3,481.6	$3,779.3	$3,781.8	$4,046.5	$4,410.7	
16									
17	Selling, Gen & Adm Expenses		$2,623.8	$2,426.6	$2,606.4	$2,647.4	$2,832.7	$3,087.6	28.0%
18	Other Income/Expense, Net		$20.9	$21.5	$23.2	$22.7	$24.3	$26.5	0.2%
19	Restructuring Charge, Net		$129.9	$45.1	($2.5)	$58.1	$62.2	$67.8	0.6%
20	Depreciation		$184.5	$198.2	$188.0	$197.7	$211.5	$230.6	2.1%
21	EBIT		$713.0	$790.2	$964.2	$855.9	$915.8	$998.2	
22									
23	Interest Expense		$60.0	$44.1	$45.0	$91.6	$60.2	$56.5	
24	Taxes		$253.4	$294.7	$340.1	$293.5	$328.5	$361.6	
25	Net Income		$399.6	$451.4	$579.1	$470.8	$527.0	$580.1	
26	Shares Outstanding (Millions)		287.0	282.3	269.6	269.6	269.6	269.6	
27	Earnings Per Share		$1.39	$1.60	$2.15	$1.75	$1.95	$2.15	
28									
29	Allocation of Net Income:								
30	Dividends		$127.3	$136.2	$133.1	$117.7	$147.6	$174.0	
31	Change in Equity		$272.3	$315.2	$446.0	$353.1	$379.5	$406.1	

How To Build Your Own Spreadsheet Model.

1. **Open the Ratios Spreadsheet.** Open the spreadsheet that you created for Corporate Financial Planning - Ratios and immediately save the spreadsheet under a new name using the **File | Save As** command.

FIGURE 14.10 Historical and Forecasted Balance Sheet for Nike, Inc.

	A	B	C	D	E	F	G	H	I
1	CORPORATE FINANCIAL PLANNING				Full-Scale, Real Data				
2	Nike, Inc.	1997	1998	1999	2000	2001	2002	2003	Ave. %
3	Financial Plan	Actual	Actual	Actual	Actual	Forecast	Forecast	Forecast	of Sales
33	Balance Sheet (Mil.$)								
34	Assets								
35	Current Assets								
36	Cash & Equivalents	$445.4	$108.6	$190.1	$254.3	$195.9	$209.6	$228.4	2.1%
37	Receivables	$1,754.1	$1,674.4	$1,540.1	$1,567.2	$1,652.0	$1,768.5	$1,927.6	17.5%
38	Inventories	$1,338.6	$1,396.6	$1,170.6	$1,446.0	$1,386.3	$1,483.3	$1,616.8	14.7%
39	Deferred Income Taxes	$135.7	$156.8	$120.6	$111.5	$134.0	$143.3	$156.2	1.4%
40	Income Taxes Receivable	$0.0	$0.0	$15.9	$2.2	$6.5	$6.9	$7.5	0.1%
41	Prepaid Expenses	$157.1	$196.2	$219.6	$215.2	$218.7	$234.1	$255.1	2.3%
42	Total Current Assets	$3,830.9	$3,532.6	$3,264.9	$3,596.4	$3,594.1	$3,845.6	$4,191.7	
43									
44	Property, Plant & Equip., Net	$922.4	$1,153.1	$1,265.8	$1,583.4	$1,388.2	$1,485.4	$1,619.1	14.7%
45	Intangible Asset & Goodwill	$464.2	$435.8	$426.6	$410.9	$440.5	$471.3	$513.7	4.7%
46	Deferred Inc. Taxes & Other	$143.7	$275.9	$290.4	$266.2	$288.3	$308.4	$336.2	3.1%
47	Total Assets	$5,361.2	$5,397.4	$5,247.7	$5,856.9	$5,711.0	$6,110.8	$6,660.8	60.5%
48									
49	Liabilities and Shareholders' Equity								
50	Current Liabilities								
51	Current Portion of L.T. Debt	$2.2	$1.6	$1.0	$50.1	$18.4	$19.7	$21.5	0.2%
52	Notes Payable	$553.2	$480.2	$419.1	$924.2	$632.1	$676.3	$737.2	6.7%
53	Accounts Payable	$687.1	$584.6	$473.6	$543.8	$552.9	$591.6	$644.8	5.9%
54	Accrued Liabilities	$570.5	$608.5	$553.2	$621.9	$616.6	$659.8	$719.2	6.5%
55	Income Taxes Payable	$53.9	$28.9	$0.0	$0.0	$9.5	$10.2	$11.1	0.1%
56	Total Current Liabilities	$1,866.9	$1,703.8	$1,446.9	$2,140.0	$1,829.5	$1,957.6	$2,133.7	
57									
58	Long-term Debt	$296.0	$379.4	$386.1	$470.3	$268.1	$160.2	$127.8	4.5%
59	Deferred Inc. Taxes & Other	$42.1	$52.3	$79.8	$110.3	$84.5	$90.4	$98.5	0.9%
60	Redeemable Preferred Stock	$0.3	$0.3	$0.3	$0.3	$0.3	$0.3	$0.4	0.0%
61	Total Liabilities	$2,205.3	$2,135.8	$1,913.1	$2,720.9	$2,182.4	$2,208.5	$2,360.4	
62									
63	Shareholders' Equity								
64	Common Stock Class A	$0.2	$0.2	$0.2	$0.2	$0.2	$0.2	$0.2	0.0%
65	Common Stock Class B	$2.7	$2.7	$2.7	$2.6	$2.6	$2.6	$2.6	0.0%
66	Capital in Excess of Stated	$210.6	$262.5	$334.1	$369.0	$369.0	$369.0	$369.0	3.6%
67	Unearned Stock Compen.	$0.0	$0.0	$0.0	($11.7)	($4.1)	($4.4)	($4.8)	0.0%
68	Accum. Other Comp. Inc.	($31.3)	($47.2)	($68.9)	($111.1)	($79.2)	($84.7)	($92.3)	-0.8%
69	Retained Earnings	$2,973.7	$3,043.4	$3,066.5	$2,887.0	$3,240.1	$3,619.6	$4,025.6	33.0%
70	Total Shareholders' Equity	$3,155.9	$3,261.6	$3,334.6	$3,136.0	$3,528.7	$3,902.3	$4,300.3	
71									
72	Total Liab. & Share. Equity	$5,361.2	$5,397.4	$5,247.7	$5,856.9	$5,711.0	$6,110.8	$6,660.8	
73									
74	Debt / (Debt + Equity)	21.2%	20.9%	19.5%	31.5%	20.7%	18.0%	17.1%	
75	Market Price / Share	$57.500	$46.000	$60.938	$42.875	$38.419	$48.873	$60.246	
76	External Funds Needed		$69.0	($61.0)	$718.5	($508)	($18.4)	$90.7	

2. **Add and Delete Rows.** Add rows using the **Insert | Rows** command and delete rows using the **Edit | Delete | Entire Row | OK** command.

   o Add two rows below **Selling, Gen & Adm Expenses** and label them **Other Income/Expense, Net** and **Restructuring Charge, Net**.

   o Add three rows below **Inventories** and label them **Deferred Income Taxes**, **Income Taxes Receivable**, and **Prepaid Expenses**.

   o Delete the rows for **Property Plant & Equip. (PPE)** and **Accumulated Depreciation**.

   o Add one row below **Net PPE** and, on the two blank rows below **Net PPE**, label them **Intangible Asset & Goodwill** and **Deferred Inc. Taxes & Other**.

   o Move the **Accounts Payable** row by selecting the entire row, clicking on **Edit | Cut**, then selecting the cell under **Short-term Debt** and clicking on **Edit | Paste**. Label the row where **Accounts Payble** used to be as **Current Portion of L.T. Debt**. Relabel **Short-term Debt** as **Notes Payable**.

   o Add two rows below **Accounts Payable** and label them **Accrued Liabilities**, and **Income Taxes Payable**.

   o Add four rows below **Paid-in Capital** and label them **Common Stock Class B** , **Capital in Excess of Stated Value**, **Unearned Stock Compen.**, and **Accum. Other Comp. Inc.** Relabel **Paid-in Capital** as **Common Stock Class A**.

3. **Update The Summary Lines.**

   o **EBIT:** Enter =C15-SUM(C17:C20) in cell **C21** and copy it across.

   o **Total Current Assets:** Enter =SUM(B36:B41) in cell **B42** and copy it across.

   o **Total Assets:** Enter =B42+SUM(B44:B46) in cell **B47** and copy it across.

   o **Total Current Liabilities:** Enter =SUM(B51:B55) in cell **B56** and copy it across.

   o **Long-term Debt:** Enter =B61-B56-B59-B60 in cell **B58** and copy it across.

   o **Total Shareholders' Equity:** Enter =SUM(B64:B69) in cell **B70** and copy it across.

4. **Enter Historical Data.** Enter the historical financial statements for **Nike, Inc.** Enter three years of historical Income Statements into the yellow input sections of the range **C13:E24** (see Figure 14.1). Enter the shares outstanding into the range **C26:E26**. Enter dividends into the range **C30:E30**. Enter four years of historical Balance Sheets into the yellow input sections of the range **B36:E69** (see Figure 14.2). Enter the observed market price / share into the range **B75:E75**. All of the data shown in Figures 14.1 and 14.2 come from Nike's 10K financial statement, which is available on the web. To obtain Nike's 10K financial statement, go to **Yahoo! Finance** at quote.yahoo.com, enter Nike's symbol **NKE** in the input box, click on the **Get Quotes** button, in the **More Info** part of the table click on **Research**, then click on **Financials**, then at the very bottom of the page click on **EDGAR Online**, then scroll down the list of financial statements, click on **10K**, and next to **Online HTML Version** click on the **Click Here** button. The 10K statement that you get has a table of contents window on the left. Scroll down this window and

you will see the Income Statement, Balance Sheet, Cash Flow Statement, etc. Click on the item that you want to look at.

5. **Income Statement Percent of Sales.** Given the rows that have been added to the Income Statement, the Percent of Sales section needs to be updated. Add 2 rows to the Income Statement Percent of Sales section someplace below row **79** using the the **Insert | Rows** command. To carry the updated labels down, enter **=A13** in cell **A79**. Then copy all of the formulas down by selecting the range **A79:I79** and copy it to the range **A80:I97**. Delete ranges that correspond to blank sections of the Income Statement.

FIGURE 14.11 Historical and Forecasted Income Statement Percent of Sales for Nike, Inc.

	A	B	C	D	E	F	G	H	I
1	CORPORATE FINANCIAL PLANNING				Full-Scale, Real Data				
2	Nike, Inc.	1997	1998	1999	2000	2001	2002	2003	Ave. %
3	Financial Plan	Actual	Actual	Actual	Actual	Forecast	Forecast	Forecast	of Sales
78	Income Statement (% of Sales)								
79	Sales		100.0%	100.0%	100.0%	100.0%	100.0%	100.0%	100.0%
80	Cost of Goods Sold		61.6%	60.3%	58.0%	60.0%	60.0%	60.0%	60.0%
81	Gross Margin		38.4%	39.7%	42.0%	40.0%	40.0%	40.0%	40.0%
82									
83	Selling, Gen & Adm Expenses		27.5%	27.6%	29.0%	28.0%	28.0%	28.0%	28.0%
84	Other Income/Expense, Net		0.2%	0.2%	0.3%	0.2%	0.2%	0.2%	0.2%
85	Restructuring Charge, Net		1.4%	0.5%	0.0%	0.6%	0.6%	0.6%	0.6%
86	Depreciation		1.9%	2.3%	2.1%	2.1%	2.1%	2.1%	2.1%
87	EBIT		7.5%	9.0%	10.7%	9.1%	9.1%	9.1%	9.1%
88									
89	Interest Expense		0.6%	0.5%	0.5%	1.0%	0.6%	0.5%	0.5%
90	Taxes		2.7%	3.4%	3.8%	3.1%	3.3%	3.3%	3.3%
91	Net Income		4.2%	5.1%	6.4%	5.0%	5.2%	5.3%	5.3%
92	Shares Outstanding (Millions)		3.0%	3.2%	3.0%	2.9%	2.7%	2.4%	3.1%
93	Earnings Per Share		0.0%	0.0%	0.0%	0.0%	0.0%	0.0%	0.0%
94									
95	Allocation of Net Income:		0.0%	0.0%	0.0%	0.0%	0.0%	0.0%	0.0%
96	Dividends		1.3%	1.6%	1.5%	1.2%	1.5%	1.6%	1.5%
97	Change in Equity		2.9%	3.6%	5.0%	3.7%	3.8%	3.7%	3.8%

6. **Balance Sheet Percent of Sales.** Given the rows that have been added and subtracted from the Balance Sheet, the Percent of Sales section needs to be updated. Add 8 rows to the Balance Sheet Percent of Sales section someplace below row **102** using the the **Insert | Rows** command. To carry the updated labels down, copy the cell **A97** to the range **A100:A102**. Then copy all of the formulas down by selecting the range **A102:I102** and copy it to the range **A103:I138**. Delete ranges that correspond to blank sections of the Balance Sheet.

FIGURE 14.12 Historical and Forecasted Balance Sheet Percent of Sales for Nike, Inc.

	A	B	C	D	E	F	G	H	I
1	**CORPORATE FINANCIAL PLANNING**				**Full-Scale, Real Data**				
2	**Nike, Inc.**	1997	1998	1999	2000	2001	2002	2003	Ave. %
3	**Financial Plan**	Actual	Actual	Actual	Actual	Forecast	Forecast	Forecast	of Sales
99	**Balance Sheet (% of Sales)**								
100	**Assets**								
101	Current Assets								
102	Cash & Equivalents		1.1%	2.3%	2.8%	2.1%	2.1%	2.1%	2.1%
103	Receivables		17.5%	17.5%	17.4%	17.5%	17.5%	17.5%	17.5%
104	Inventories		14.6%	13.3%	16.1%	14.7%	14.7%	14.7%	14.7%
105	Deferred Income Taxes		1.6%	1.4%	1.2%	1.4%	1.4%	1.4%	1.4%
106	Income Taxes Receivable		0.0%	0.2%	0.0%	0.1%	0.1%	0.1%	0.1%
107	Prepaid Expenses		2.1%	2.5%	2.4%	2.3%	2.3%	2.3%	2.3%
108	Total Current Assets		37.0%	37.2%	40.0%	38.1%	38.1%	38.1%	38.1%
109									
110	Property, Plant & Equip., Net		12.1%	14.4%	17.6%	14.7%	14.7%	14.7%	14.7%
111	Intangible Asset & Goodwill		4.6%	4.9%	4.6%	4.7%	4.7%	4.7%	4.7%
112	Deferred Inc. Taxes & Other		2.9%	3.3%	3.0%	3.1%	3.1%	3.1%	3.1%
113	Total Assets		56.5%	59.8%	65.1%	60.5%	60.5%	60.5%	60.5%
114									
115	**Liabilities and Shareholders' Equity**								
116	Current Liabilities								
117	Current Portion of L.T. Debt		0.0%	0.0%	0.6%	0.2%	0.2%	0.2%	0.2%
118	Notes Payable		5.0%	4.8%	10.3%	6.7%	6.7%	6.7%	6.7%
119	Accounts Payable		6.1%	5.4%	6.0%	5.9%	5.9%	5.9%	5.9%
120	Accrued Liabilities		6.4%	6.3%	6.9%	6.5%	6.5%	6.5%	6.5%
121	Income Taxes Payable		0.3%	0.0%	0.0%	0.1%	0.1%	0.1%	0.1%
122	Total Current Liabilities		17.8%	16.5%	23.8%	19.4%	19.4%	19.4%	19.4%
123									
124	Long-term Debt		4.0%	4.4%	5.2%	2.8%	1.6%	1.2%	4.5%
125	Deferred Inc. Taxes & Other		0.5%	0.9%	1.2%	0.9%	0.9%	0.9%	0.9%
126	Redeemable Preferred Stock		0.0%	0.0%	0.0%	0.0%	0.0%	0.0%	0.0%
127	Total Liabilities		22.4%	21.8%	30.2%	23.1%	21.9%	21.4%	24.8%
128									
129	Shareholders' Equity								
130	Common Stock Class A		0.0%	0.0%	0.0%	0.0%	0.0%	0.0%	0.0%
131	Common Stock Class B		0.0%	0.0%	0.0%	0.0%	0.0%	0.0%	0.0%
132	Capital in Excess of Stated		2.7%	3.8%	4.1%	3.9%	3.7%	3.3%	3.6%
133	Unearned Stock Compen.		0.0%	0.0%	-0.1%	0.0%	0.0%	0.0%	0.0%
134	Accum. Other Comp. Inc.		-0.5%	-0.8%	-1.2%	-0.8%	-0.8%	-0.8%	-0.8%
135	Retained Earnings		31.9%	34.9%	32.1%	34.3%	35.8%	36.5%	33.0%
136	Total Shareholders' Equity		34.1%	38.0%	34.9%	37.4%	38.6%	39.0%	35.7%
137									
138	Total Liab. & Share. Equity		56.5%	59.8%	65.1%	60.5%	60.5%	60.5%	60.5%

7. **Update The Forecast.** Start with the Assumptions section. The Sales Growth Rate (which is a key driver of the entire model) is a subjective category. One possible forecast is continued recovery from the recent downturn with growth of 5.0%, 7.0%, and 9.0%. The tax rate, which in reality reflects a variety of credits, exemptions, and adjustments, is forecast based on the average realized tax rate in recent years. Enter **=AVERAGE(C6:E6)** in cell **I6** and enter the average realized rate 38.4% as the forecast. Interest rates are forecast to rise slightly over time. The dividend payout rate is forecast to return to its previous level over time. The price/earnings ratios is forecast to recover over time. All of the new lines added will be forecast using he "percent of sales" method, so the "percent of sales" formulas from one row can be copied to the added rows.

98

Select the range **F17:I17** and copy it to the ranges **F18:I19, F39:I41, F45:I46, F51:I51, F54:I55, F59:I60,** and **F67:I68.** Turning to the Shares Outstanding on row 26, Nike's 10K is a little unclear what about what corporate policy is. One possible forecast is flat at the current level of 269.6 million shares. Choose values for the equity choice variables: Common Stock A, Common Stock B, and Capital in Excess of Stated. Enter values in the range **F64:I66,** which maintain a "reasonable" debt / (debt + equity) proportion.

8. **Cash Flow Statement.** Theoretically, the cash flow statement is strictly determined by changes in the balance sheet. As a practical matter, Nike's 10K cash flow statement has added a lot of detail not directly observable from the balance sheet. Therefore, many rows must be added and renamed in order to model the cash flow statement. Add rows using the **Insert | Rows** command.

   o   Add a row below **Net Income** and label it **Income Charges (Credits) Not Affecting Cash.**

   o   Add three rows below **Depreciation** and label them **Non-cash port. of restructuring charge, Deferred Income Taxes,** and **Amortization and other.**

   o   Add four rows below **Inventories.** Then move the **Increase in Accounts Receivable** row by selecting the entire row, clicking on **Edit | Cut,** then selecting the cell under **Inventories** and clicking on **Edit | Past.** Label the row where **Increase in Accounts Receivable** used to be as **Changes in Certain Working Capital Components.** Label the three blank rows below **Increase in Accounts Receivable** as **Decrease (inc.) in Other Current, Assets and Income Taxes Rec.,** and **Increase (dec.) in Accounts Payable,.** Relabel **Increase in Accounts Payable** as **Accrued Liab., & Income Taxes Pay.**

   o   Relabel **Investment in Plant and Equipment** as **Additions to Prop, Plant, and & Equipment.** Then add three row below **Additions to Prop, Plant, and & Equipment** and label them as **Disposals of Prop., Plant, & Equipment, Increase in Other Assets,** and **Increase (dec.) in Other Liabilities.**

   o   Relabel **Increase in Long-term Debt** as **Additions to Long-term Debt.** Then add a row below **Additions to Long-term Debt** and label it **Reductions in Long-term Debt.**

   o   Relabel **Increase in Short-term Debt** as **Increase (dec.) in Notes Payable.** Relabel **Increase in Paid in Capital** as **Proceeds from Exercise of Options.** Then add a row below **Proceeds from Exercise of Options** and label it **Repurchase of Stock.**

   o   Add a row above **Change in Cash and Equivalents** and label it **Effect of Exch. Rate Changes on Cash.** Relabel **Change in Cash and Equivalents** and label it **Net Increase (Dec) in Cash and Equiv.** Add a row below **Net Increase (Dec) in Cash and Equiv.**

FIGURE 14.13 Historical and Forecasted Cash Flow Statement for Nike, Inc.

	A	B	C	D	E	F	G	H	I
1	CORPORATE FINANCIAL PLANNING				Full-Scale, Real Data				
2	Nike, Inc.	1997	1998	1999	2000	2001	2002	2003	Ave. %
3	Financial Plan	Actual	Actual	Actual	Actual	Forecast	Forecast	Forecast	of Sales
140	Cash Flow Statement (Mil.$)								
141	Cash Provided (Used) By Operating Activities								
142	Net Income		$399.6	$451.4	$579.1	$470.8	$527.0	$580.1	
143	Income Charges (Credits) Not Affecting Cash:								
144	Depreciation		$184.5	$198.2	$188.0	$197.7	$211.5	$230.6	2.1%
145	Non-cash port. of restructuring charge		$59.3	$28.0	$0.0	$29.6	$31.7	$34.5	0.3%
146	Deffered Income Taxes		($113.9)	$37.9	$36.8	($11.1)	($11.8)	($12.9)	-0.1%
147	Amortization and other		$49.0	$30.6	$35.6	$39.6	$42.4	$46.2	0.4%
148	Changes in Certain Working Capital Components:								
149	(Increase) decrease in Inventories		($58.0)	$226.0	($275.4)	$59.7	($97.0)	($133.5)	
150	(Increase) dec. in Accounts Receiv.		$79.7	$134.3	($27.1)	($85.6)	($115.7)	($159.2)	
151	Decrease (inc.) in Other Current								
152	Assets and Income Taxes Rec.		($12.6)	$25.0	$65.6	$27.8	$29.7	$32.4	0.3%
153	Increase (dec.) in Accounts Payable,								
154	Accrued Liab., & Income Taxes Pay.		($70.1)	($170.4)	$157.3	($29.2)	($31.2)	($34.0)	-0.3%
155	Cash Provided By Operations		$517.5	$961.0	$759.9	$699.4	$586.5	$584.1	
156									
157	Cash Provided (Used) By Investing Activities								
158	Additions to Prop, Plant, & Equipment		($505.9)	($384.1)	($419.9)	($451.5)	($483.1)	($526.5)	-4.8%
159	Disposals of Prop., Plant, & Equipment		$16.8	$27.2	$25.3	$24.1	$25.8	$28.2	0.3%
160	Increase in Other Assets		($87.4)	($60.8)	($51.3)	($68.6)	($73.4)	($80.0)	-0.7%
161	Increase (dec.) in Other Liabilities		($18.5)	$1.2	$5.9	($3.6)	($3.9)	($4.2)	0.0%
162	Cash Used By Investing Activities		($595.0)	($416.5)	($440.0)	($499.5)	($534.4)	($582.5)	
163									
164	Cash Provided (Used) By Financing Activities								
165	Additions to Long-term Debt		$101.5	$0.0	$0.1	$33.5	$35.8	$39.1	0.4%
166	Reductions in Long-term Debt, Incl. Cur		($2.5)	($1.5)	($1.8)	($2.0)	($2.1)	($2.3)	0.0%
167	Increase (dec.) in Notes Payable		($73.0)	($61.0)	$505.1	($292.1)	$44.2	$60.9	
168	Proceeds from Exercise of Options		$32.2	$54.4	$23.9	$38.5	$41.2	$44.9	0.4%
169	Repurchase of stock		($202.3)	($299.8)	($646.3)	($400.4)	($428.4)	($467.0)	-4.2%
170	Dividends -- common and preferred		($127.3)	($136.2)	($133.1)	($117.7)	($147.6)	($174.0)	-1.5%
171	Cash Used By Financing Activities		($271.4)	($444.1)	($252.1)	($740.3)	($456.9)	($498.5)	
172									
173	Effect of Exch. Rate Changes on Cash		$12.1	($10.9)	($11.6)	($4.0)	($4.3)	($4.6)	0.0%
174	Net Increase (Dec.) in Cash and Equiv.		($336.8)	$89.5	$56.2	($544.3)	($409.1)	($501.6)	
175									
176	Cash and Equvalents, Beg of Year		$445.4	$108.6	$198.1	$255.1	$272.9	$297.5	2.7%
177	Cash and Equvalents, End of Year		$108.6	$198.1	$254.3	($289.3)	($136.1)	($204.1)	

9. **Update The Summary Lines of the Cash Flow Statement.**

   o **Cash Provided By Operations:** Enter =SUM(C142:C154) in cell **C155** and copy it across.

   o **Cash Used By Investing Activities:** Enter =SUM(C158:C161) in cell **C162** and copy it across.

   o **Cash Used By Financing Activities:** Enter =SUM(C165:C170) in cell **C171** and copy it across.

- o **Cash Provided By Operations:** Enter =**C155+C162+C171+C173** in cell **C174** and copy it across.

10. **Enter Historical Data of the Cash Flow Statement.** Enter three years of historical Cash Flow Statements into the yellow input sections of the range **C144:E173** (see Figure 14.5).

11. **Cash Flow Statement Percent of Sales.** Given the rows that have been added to the Income Statement, the Percent of Sales section needs to be updated. Add 15 rows to the Cash Flow Statement Percent of Sales section someplace below row **181** using the the **Insert | Rows** command. To carry the updated labels down, copy **A138** to the range **A180:A181**. Then copy all of the formulas down by selecting the range **A181:I181** and copy it to the range **A182:I216**. Delete ranges that correspond to blank sections of the Cash Flow Statement.

FIGURE 14.14 Historical and Forecasted Cash Flow Statement Percent of Sales for Nike, Inc.

	A	B	C	D	E	F	G	H	I
1	CORPORATE FINANCIAL PLANNING				Full-Scale, Real Data				
2	Nike, Inc.	1997	1998	1999	2000	2001	2002	2003	Ave. %
3	Financial Plan	Actual	Actual	Actual	Actual	Forecast	Forecast	Forecast	of Sales
179	Cash Flow Statement (% of Sales)								
180	Cash Provided (Used) By Operating Activities								
181	Net Income		4.2%	5.1%	6.4%	5.0%	5.2%	5.3%	5.3%
182	Income Charges (Credits) Not Affecting Cash:								
183	Depreciation		1.9%	2.3%	2.1%	2.1%	2.1%	2.1%	2.1%
184	Non-cash port. of restructuring charge		0.6%	0.3%	0.0%	0.3%	0.3%	0.3%	0.3%
185	Deffered Income Taxes		-1.2%	0.4%	0.4%	-0.1%	-0.1%	-0.1%	-0.1%
186	Amortization and other		0.5%	0.3%	0.4%	0.4%	0.4%	0.4%	0.4%
187	Changes in Certain Working Capital Components:								
188	(Increase) decrease in Inventories		-0.6%	2.6%	-3.1%	0.6%	-1.0%	-1.2%	-0.4%
189	(Increase) dec. in Accounts Receiv.		0.8%	1.5%	-0.3%	-0.9%	-1.1%	-1.4%	0.7%
190	Decrease (inc.) in Other Current		0.0%	0.0%	0.0%	0.0%	0.0%	0.0%	0.0%
191	Assets and Income Taxes Rec.		-0.1%	0.3%	0.7%	0.3%	0.3%	0.3%	0.3%
192	Increase (dec.) in Accounts Payable,		0.0%	0.0%	0.0%	0.0%	0.0%	0.0%	0.0%
193	Accrued Liab., & Income Taxes Pay.		-0.7%	-1.9%	1.7%	-0.3%	-0.3%	-0.3%	-0.3%
194	Cash Provided By Operations		5.4%	10.9%	8.4%	7.4%	5.8%	5.3%	8.3%
195									
196	Cash Provided (Used) By Investing Activities								
197	Additions to Prop, Plant, & Equipment		-5.3%	-4.4%	-4.7%	-4.8%	-4.8%	-4.8%	-4.8%
198	Disposals of Prop., Plant, & Equipment		0.2%	0.3%	0.3%	0.3%	0.3%	0.3%	0.3%
199	Increase in Other Assets		-0.9%	-0.7%	-0.6%	-0.7%	-0.7%	-0.7%	-0.7%
200	Increase (dec.) in Other Liabilities		-0.2%	0.0%	0.1%	0.0%	0.0%	0.0%	0.0%
201	Cash Used By Investing Activities		-6.2%	-4.7%	-4.9%	-5.3%	-5.3%	-5.3%	-5.3%
202									
203	Cash Provided (Used) By Financing Activities								
204	Additions to Long-term Debt		1.1%	0.0%	0.0%	0.4%	0.4%	0.4%	0.4%
205	Reductions in Long-term Debt, Incl. Cur		0.0%	0.0%	0.0%	0.0%	0.0%	0.0%	0.0%
206	Increase (dec.) in Notes Payable		-0.8%	-0.7%	5.6%	-3.1%	0.4%	0.6%	1.4%
207	Proceeds from Exercise of Options		0.3%	0.6%	0.3%	0.4%	0.4%	0.4%	0.4%
208	Repurchase of stock		-2.1%	-3.4%	-7.2%	-4.2%	-4.2%	-4.2%	-4.2%
209	Dividends -- common and preferred		-1.3%	-1.6%	-1.5%	-1.2%	-1.5%	-1.6%	-1.5%
210	Cash Used By Financing Activities		-2.8%	-5.1%	-2.8%	-7.8%	-4.5%	-4.5%	-3.6%
211									
212	Effect of Exch. Rate Changes on Cash		0.1%	-0.1%	-0.1%	0.0%	0.0%	0.0%	0.0%
213	Net Increase (Dec.) in Cash and Equiv.		-3.5%	1.0%	0.6%	-5.8%	-4.0%	-4.6%	-0.6%
214									
215	Cash and Equvalents, Beg of Year		4.7%	1.2%	2.2%	2.7%	2.7%	2.7%	2.7%
216	Cash and Equvalents, End of Year		1.1%	2.3%	2.8%	-3.1%	-1.3%	-1.9%	2.1%

12. **Update The Cash Flow Forecast.** All of the new lines added to the Cash Flow Statement will be forecast using he "percent of sales" method, so the "percent of sales" formulas from one row can be copied to the added rows. Select the range **F144:I144** and copy it to the ranges **F145:I147**, **F152:I152, F154:I154, F158:I161, F165:I166, F168:I169,** and **F173:I173**.

13. **Financial Ratios.** Most of the financial ratios carry over without adjustment. The only change that is needed is the Debt percentage where an addition category of debt, Current Portion of L.T. Debt, was added. Enter **=(C51+C52+C58)/C47** in cell **C230** and copy it across.

FIGURE 14.15 Historical and Forecasted Financial Ratios for Nike, Inc.

	A	B	C	D	E	F	G	H	I
1	CORPORATE FINANCIAL PLANNING				Full-Scale, Real Data				
2	Nike, Inc.	1997	1998	1999	2000	2001	2002	2003	Ave. %
3	Financial Plan	Actual	Actual	Actual	Actual	Forecast	Forecast	Forecast	of Sales
217									
218	Financial Ratios								
219	Profitability								
220	Return On Sales (ROS)		7.5%	9.0%	10.7%	9.1%	9.1%	9.1%	
221	Return On Assets (ROA)		13.3%	14.8%	17.4%	14.8%	15.5%	15.6%	
222	Return On Equity (ROE)		12.5%	13.7%	17.9%	14.1%	14.2%	14.1%	
223									
224	Asset Turnover								
225	Receivables Turnover		5.6	5.5	5.8	5.9	5.9	6.0	
226	Inventory Turnover		4.3	4.1	4.0	4.0	4.2	4.3	
227	Asset Turnover		1.8	1.6	1.6	1.6	1.7	1.7	
228									
229	Financial Leverage								
230	Debt		16.0%	15.4%	24.7%	16.1%	14.0%	13.3%	
231	Times Interest Earned		11.9	17.9	21.4	9.3	15.2	17.7	
232									
233	Liquidity								
234	Current		207.3%	225.6%	168.1%	196.4%	196.4%	196.4%	
235	Quick		104.6%	120.1%	85.1%	101.0%	101.0%	101.0%	
236									
237	Market Value								
238	Price to Earnings		33.0	38.1	20.0	22.00	25.00	28.00	
239	Market to Book		404.8%	515.9%	368.6%	293.5%	337.6%	377.7%	

The percentage of sales method does a good job for most purposes. Additional refinements would increase accuracy of the forecast. For example, some items may be better projected as a trend, rather than an average. Other items, such as the Restructuring Charge, may be one time events. The bottom line of this forecast is a gradual recovery in Earnings Per Share from $1.75 to $1.95 to $2.15.

Problems

Skill-Building Problems.

1. Given historical financial statements for **Global Impact P2P** in the Excel file Fplanpro.xls or shown below, forecast their financial statements for the next three years. Explore the company's needs for additional financing as expressed by the following *choice variables*: debt and equity (paid-in capital under shareholder's equity).

2. Given historical and forecasted Income Statements and Balance Sheets for **Global Impact P2P**, create the historical and forecasted Cash Flow Statement.

3. Given historical and forecasted financial statements for **Global Impact P2P**, create the historical and forecasted financial ratios.

Skill-Extending Problems.

4. Select a company with publically traded stock. Locate the historical 10K financial statements for that company over the past few years. This data is available from Yahoo! Finance and EDGAR

On-line and can be obtained by following the procedure described in Step 4 of Corporate Financial Planning - Basics. Forecast your company's financial statements over the next three years.

Live In-class Problems.

5. Given the partial Actual spreadsheet **FplanacZ.xls**, do step **3 The Income Statement and Earnings Per Share**.

6. Given the partial Forecast spreadsheet **FplanfoZ.xls**, do step **4 The Income Statement**.

7. Given the partial Cash Flow spreadsheet **FplancaZ.xls**, do step **5 Cash and Equivalents**.

8. Given the partial Ratios spreadsheet **FplanraZ.xls**, do step **2 Profitability**.

9. Given the partial Sensitivity spreadsheet **FplanseZ.xls**, do step **2 Data Table**.

10. Given the partial Full-scale Real Data spreadsheet **FplanfuZ.xls**, do Key Assumptions part of step **7 Update the Forecast**.

FIGURE 14.16 Historical Assumptions and Income Statement for Global Impact P2P

	A	B	C	D	E	F
1	CORPORATE FINANCIAL PLANNING				Problems	
2	Global Impact P2P	1997	1998	1999	2000	
3	Financial Plan	Actual	Actual	Actual	Actual	
4	**Key Assumptions**					
5	Sales Growth Rate			21.4%	19.3%	
6	Tax Rate		38.8%	38.2%	36.0%	
7	Int Rate on Short-Term Debt		6.3%	6.4%	6.5%	
8	Int Rate on Long-Term Debt		7.4%	7.5%	7.6%	
9	Dividend Payout Rate		25.9%	26.8%	24.4%	
10	Price / Earnings		8.4	8.7	9.3	
11						
12	**Income Statement (Mil.$)**					
13	Sales		$194.29	$235.84	$281.38	
14	Cost of Goods Sold		$112.25	$138.97	$171.57	
15	Gross Margin		$82.04	$96.87	$109.81	
16						
17	Selling, Gen & Adm Expenses		$13.54	$16.87	$19.94	
18	Depreciation		$12.39	$14.58	$18.37	
19	EBIT		$56.11	$65.42	$71.50	
20						
21	Interest Expense		$15.69	$23.88	$24.55	
22	Taxes		$15.68	$15.87	$16.92	
23	Net Income		$24.74	$25.67	$30.03	
24	Shares Outstanding (Millions)		2.10	2.15	2.44	
25	Earnings Per Share		$11.78	$11.94	$12.31	
26						
27	Allocation of Net Income:					
28	Dividends		$6.41	$6.87	$7.33	
29	Change in Equity		$18.33	$18.80	$22.70	

FIGURE 14.17 Historical Balance Sheet for Global Impact P2P

	A	B	C	D	E	F
1	**CORPORATE FINANCIAL PLANNING**				Problems	
2	**Global Impact P2P**	1997	1998	1999	2000	
3	**Financial Plan**	Actual	Actual	Actual	Actual	
31	**Balance Sheet (Mil.$)**					
32	**Assets**					
33	Current Assets					
34	Cash & Equivalents	$8.56	$13.97	$15.34	$17.75	
35	Receivables	$41.63	$49.52	$57.37	$68.91	
36	Inventories	$52.11	$60.94	$73.49	$86.32	
37	Total Current Assets	$102.30	$124.43	$146.20	$172.98	
38						
39	Property, Plant & Equip. (PPE)	$663.29	$846.39	$910.34	$958.31	
40	Accumulated Depreciation	$189.20	$201.59	$216.17	$234.54	
41	Net PPE	$474.09	$644.80	$694.17	$723.77	
42						
43	Total Assets	$576.39	$769.23	$840.37	$896.75	
44						
45	**Liabilities and Shareholders' Equity**					
46	Current Liabilities					
47	Accounts Payable	$62.46	$90.48	$134.32	$174.57	
48	Short-term Debt	$202.12	$307.87	$304.96	$312.85	
49	Total Current Liabilities	$264.58	$398.35	$439.28	$487.42	
50						
51	Long-term Debt	$40.00	$55.74	$62.15	$17.69	
52	Total Liabilities	$304.58	$454.09	$501.43	$505.11	
53						
54	Shareholders' Equity					
55	Paid-in Capital	$180.00	$205.00	$210.00	$240.00	
56	Retained Earnings	$91.81	$110.14	$128.94	$151.64	
57	Total Shareholders' Equity	$271.81	$315.14	$338.94	$391.64	
58						
59	Total Liab. & Share. Equity	$576.39	$769.23	$840.37	$896.75	
60						
61	Debt / (Debt + Equity)	47.1%	53.6%	52.0%	45.8%	
62	Market Price / Share	$94.58	$99.12	$103.47	$114.95	
63	External Funds Needed		$140.49	$8.50	($6.57)	

105

15 Du Pont System Of Ratio Analysis

15.1 Basics

Problem. A company's Net Profit is $170, Pretax Profit is $260, EBIT is $470, Sales is $4,590, Assets is $4,190, and Equity is $4,340. Calculate the company's ROE and decompose the ROE into its components using the Du Pont System.

FIGURE 15.1 Spreadsheet Model of Du Pont System of Ratio Analysis - Basics.

	A	B	C	D	E	F	G
1	Du Pont System of Ratio Analysis					Basics	
2							
3	Inputs						
4	Net Profit	$170					
5	Pretax Profit	$260					
6	EBIT	$470					
7	Sales	$4,590					
8	Assets	$4,190					
9	Equity	$4,340					
10							
11	Outputs						
12	ROE = Net Profit / Equity	3.9%					
13	Components of ROE:						
14	Net Profit / Pretax Profit	65.4%					
15	Pretax Profit / EBIT	55.3%					
16	EBIT / Sales	10.2%					
17	Sales / Assets	109.5%					
18	Assets / Equity	96.5%					

How To Build This Spreadsheet Model.

1. **Enter The Inputs.** Enter the inputs into the range **B4:B9**.

2. **ROE = Net Profit / Equity.** Return on Equity is defined as Net Profit / Equity. Enter **=B4/B9** in the cell **B12**.

3. **Components of ROE.** The essence of the Du Pont System is decomposing Return On Equity into five components:

   • **Net Profit / Pretax Profit.** Enter **=B4/B5** in the cell **B14**.

   • **Rest of the Components.** Copy the cell **B14** to the range **B15:B18**.

The ROE = 3.9%. The decomposition helps us see where this comes from. Here is an intuitive interpretation of the components:

   • Net Profit / Pretax = 65.4% is a tax-burden ratio.

   • Pretax Profits / EBIT = 55.3% is an interest-burden ratio.

- EBIT / Sales = 10.2% is the profit margin.

- Sales / Assets = 109.5% is the asset turnover.

- Asset / Equity = 96.5% is the leverage ratio.

Problems

Skill-Building Problems.

1. A company's Net Profit is $82, Pretax Profit is $153, EBIT is $583, Sales is $3,740, Assets is $5,460, and Equity is $7,230. Calculate the company's ROE and decompose the ROE into its components using the Du Pont System.

2. A company's Net Profit is $265, Pretax Profit is $832, EBIT is $1,045, Sales is $5,680, Assets is $7,620, and Equity is $9,730. Calculate the company's ROE and decompose the ROE into its components using the Du Pont System.

Live In-class Problems.

3. Given the partial Basics spreadsheet **DupontbZ.xls**, do steps **2 ROE = Net Profit / Equity** and **3 Components of ROE**.

16 Life-Cycle Financial Planning

16.1 Basics

Problem. Develop a financial plan for investment and consumption over your life-cycle (from the present until your death). Suppose the inflation rate is 2.0% and the real return on a riskfree money market fund is 3.5%. Suppose that a risky diversified fund offers an average real return of 8.0% and a standard deviation of 17.0%, which is equivalent to the post-World War II average real return and standard deviation on a well-diversified portfolio of US stocks. Suppose that federal income taxes have five brackets with the following rates: 15.0%, 28.0%, 31.0%, 36.0%, and 39.6%. For current year, the upper cutoff on the first four brackets are $43,050, $104,050, $158,550, and $283,150 and these cutoffs are indexed to inflation. The state tax rate = 3.0%, federal FICA-SSI tax rate on salary up to $72,600 is 6.2%, and the federal FICA-Medicare tax rate on any level of salary is 1.45%. Suppose you are currently 25 years old and you expect to earn a salary next year of $70,000. You currently have $0 in a retirement account and plan to work through age 65. You will start receiving social security benefits at age 66. The current level of social security benefits is $15, 480 per year and this is indexed to inflation. Explore the investment and consumption impacts over the life-cycle of the following *choice variables*:

- **Savings Percentage.** The percentage of your annual salary that you contribute to your retirement fund during your working years.
- **Risky Diversified Fund Percentage.** The percentage of your retirement fund that you put in the risky diversified fund (vs. the riskfree money market fund).
- **Withdrawal Percentage.** The percentage of your retirement fund that you withdraw each year to live on during your retirement years.
- **Real Growth Rate in Salary.** The real portion of the annual growth in your salary. You salary also increases with inflation.

FIGURE 16.1 Spreadsheet Model for Life-Cycle Financial Planning - Basics.

	A	B	C	D	E	F	G
1	**LIFE-CYCLE FINANCIAL PLANNING**			**Basics**			
2							
3	**Inputs**						
4	Inflation Rate	2.0%					
5	Real Ret on Riskfree Money Market Fund	3.5%					
6	Ave Real Ret on Risky Diversified Fund	8.0%					
7	Std Dev of Risky Diversified Fund	0.0001%					
8	Federal Income Bracket 1 Tax Rate	15.0%					
9	Federal Income Bracket 2 Tax Rate	28.0%					
10	Federal Income Bracket 3 Tax Rate	31.0%					
11	Federal Income Bracket 4 Tax Rate	36.0%					
12	Federal Income Bracket 5 Tax Rate	39.6%					
13	Federal FICA-SSI Tax Rate on Salary	6.2%					
14	Federal FICA-Medicare Tax on Salary	1.45%					
15	State Income Tax Rate	3.0%					
16							
17	Date	0	1	2	3	4	5
18	Age	25	26	27	28	29	30
19	**Choice Variables**						
20	Savings Percentage		8.1%	8.1%	8.1%	8.1%	8.1%
21	Risky Diversified Fund Percentage		100.0%	100.0%	100.0%	100.0%	100.0%
22	Withdrawal Percentage		0.0%	0.0%	0.0%	0.0%	0.0%
23	Real Growth Rate in Salary			2.0%	2.0%	2.0%	2.0%
24							
25	**Random Variables**						
26	Real Return on Risky Diversified Fund		8.00%	8.00%	8.00%	8.00%	8.00%
27	Real Return on Your Retirement Fund		8.00%	8.00%	8.00%	8.00%	8.00%
28							
29	**Outputs**						
30	Salary		$70,000	$72,828	$75,770	$78,831	$82,016
31	Less Contribution To Retirement Fund		$5,670	$5,899	$6,137	$6,385	$6,643
32	Plus Withdrawal From Retirement Fund		$0	$0	$0	$0	$0
33	Taxable Income		$64,330	$66,929	$69,633	$72,446	$75,373
34	Less Taxes		$19,589	$20,497	$21,444	$22,416	$23,346
35	After-Tax Income		$44,741	$46,432	$48,189	$50,030	$52,027
36	Plus Social Security Benefits		$0	$0	$0	$0	$0
37	Consumption		$44,741	$46,432	$48,189	$50,030	$52,027
38							
39	Retirement Fund	$0	$5,670	$12,145	$19,516	$27,885	$37,361
40	Real Consumption in Current Dollars		$43,864	$44,629	$45,410	$46,220	$47,123
41	Difference in Real Consump (Post-Pre)	$340					
42	Social Security Benefit Level		$15,480	$15,790	$16,105	$16,427	$16,756
43	Federal Income Tax Bracket 1 Cutoff	$43,050	$43,911	$44,789	$45,685	$46,599	$47,531
44	Federal Income Tax Bracket 2 Cutoff	$104,050	$106,131	$108,254	$110,419	$112,627	$114,880
45	Federal Income Tax Bracket 3 Cutoff	$158,550	$161,721	$164,955	$168,255	$171,620	$175,052
46	Federal Income Tax Bracket 4 Cutoff	$283,150	$288,813	$294,589	$300,481	$306,491	$312,620
47	Federal FICA-SSI Wage Cap	$72,600	$74,052	$75,533	$77,044	$78,585	$80,156

Real Consumption Over The Life-Cycle (chart, y-axis "Real Consump" $0–$200,000, x-axis "Age" 25–85)

Solution Strategy. Develop a spreadsheet model of investment and consumption on a year-by-year basis over an entire lifetime. You need to choose how to divide your salary between providing consumption now vs. savings (to provide for consumption in the future). Your savings are put in a tax-deferred retirement account and each year you need to decide what percentage to contribute to it (or withdraw from it). You avoid paying taxes on contributions to the retirement fund, but you suffer paying taxes when you withdraw from it. Salary less contributions plus withdraws gives you taxable income upon which you pay taxes. The after-tax income plus social security benefits provide for consumption each year. You need to choose what percentage of your retirement funds to invest in the risky diversified fund. The rest of your retirement funds will be invested in the riskfree money market fund and will grow at the riskfree rate. Investing in the risky diversified fund will give you a higher average returns than the riskfree money market fund, but also more risk. You also need to choose how fast to withdraw funds from your retirement account during your retirement years. A steady state withdraw policy is one that withdraws the average real increase in the retirement fund each year. This avoids touching the principal amount and allows it to grow at the rate of inflation. A steady state withdraw policy can be sustained indefinitely (i.e., no matter how long you live). For convenience, the spreadsheet analysis is carried out to age 90. How long will you live? Well, for today's US population of 65 year olds, average life expectancy is 82. To determine your individual life expectancy, add to (or subtract from) 82 based your individual health-conscious practices. Not smoking adds nine years. Aerobic exercising and getting seven to eight hours of sleep per night adds three years. A healthy diet and maintaining a desirable weight based on your height adds three years. A thorough annual medical exam to catch cancer and other health problems early adds two years. The following six items add one year each: (1) daily aspirin to reduce fatal heart attacks, (2) preventing high blood pressure, (3) avoiding accidents, (4) getting immunized against pneumonia and influenza, (5) avoiding suicide and AIDS, and (6) avoiding heavy alcohol consumption. For the subset of today's US 65 year olds who follow all of these health-conscious practices, life expectancy is 105! These life expectancy figures are conservative in the sense that they do not take into account future scientific/medical progress. For more information on the factors effecting longevity and the long-run impact of scientific and medical progress, read "Hello Methuselah! Living to 100 and Beyond" by George Webster, Ph.D.

How To Build This Spreadsheet Model.

1. **Inputs.** Enter the *inputs* described in the problem into the range **B4:B15**, the cells **B18**, **C30**, **B39**, **C42**, and the range **B43:B47**. For the time being, enter **0.0001%** in cell **B7** as the standard deviation rather than 17%. Lock in the left column of titles by selecting the cell **B1** and clicking on **Window | Freeze Panes**.

2. **Date and Age.** For the Date row, enter **0, 1, 2,..., 65** in the range **B17:BO17**. The easy way to do this is enter **0** in cell **B17**, **1** in cell **C17**, highlight the range **B17:C17**, put the cursor over the lower right corner of cell **C17** until it becomes a "plus" icon, and drag the cursor all the way across to cell **BO17**. For the Age row, enter **=B18+1** in cell **C18** and copy the cell to the range **D18:BO18**.

3. **Choice Variables.** Each year, starting with age 26 (column C) and continuing through age 90 (column BO), you need to make certain decisions. Each decision is called a choice variable. Enter initial values for the choice variables into the ranges **C20:BO22** and **D23:BO23**. **Figure 2** below shows the two steps involved in implementing retirement. (1) Enter **-100.0%** in cell **AQ23**, which is the age 66 (first retirement year) Real Growth Rate in Salary. This causes the age 66 Salary in cell **AQ30** to drop to zero. (2) Given that you have no salary, you need to withdraw a percentage of the money in your retirement fund to live on. A Steady State Withdrawal Percentage = Average Real Return on the Retirement Fund * (1 + Inflation Rate) = (Risky Diversified Fund Percentage * Average Real Return on the Risk Diversified Fund + (1 - Risky Diversified Fund Percentage) * Real Return on the Riskfree Money Market Fund) * (1 + Inflation Rate). Enter **=(AQ21*$B$6+(1-AQ21)*$B$5)*(1+$B$4)** in cell **AQ22** and copy it across. By the way, the last term "(1 + Inflation Rate)" takes care of the cross-product between (1 + real return) and (1 + inflation rate), so that the retirement fund can grow at the inflation rate.

FIGURE 16.2 Working Years vs. Retirement Years.

A	AO	AP	AQ	AR	AS
17 Date	39	40	41	42	43
18 Age	64	65	66	67	68
19 **Choice Variables**					
20 Savings Percentage	8.1%	8.1%	0.0%	0.0%	0.0%
21 Risky Diversified Fund Percentage	100.0%	100.0%	50.0%	50.0%	50.0%
22 Withdrawal Percentage	0.0%	0.0%	5.9%	5.9%	5.9%
23 Real Growth Rate in Salary	2.0%	2.0%	-100.0%	0.0%	0.0%
24					
25 **Random Variables**					
26 Real Return on Risky Diversified Fund	8.00%	8.00%	8.00%	8.00%	8.00%
27 Real Return on Your Retirement Fund	8.00%	8.00%	5.75%	5.75%	5.75%
28					
29 **Outputs**					
30 Salary	$315,291	$328,028	$0	$0	$0
31 Less Contribution To Retirement Fund	$25,539	$26,570	$0	$0	$0
32 Plus Withdrawal From Retirement Fund	$0	$0	$234,156	$238,840	$243,616
33 Taxable Income	$289,752	$301,458	$234,150	$238,840	$243,616
34 Less Taxes	$93,959	$97,941	$59,984	$61,184	$62,407
35 After-Tax Income	$195,793	$203,517	$174,172	$177,656	$181,209
36 Plus Social Security Benefits	$0	$0	$34,180	$34,864	$35,561
37 Consumption	$195,793	$203,517	$208,353	$212,520	$216,770
38					
39 Retirement Fund	$3,600,092	$3,992,431	$4,072,285	$4,153,729	$4,236,810
40 Real Consumption in Current Dollars	$90,446	$92,171	$92,511	$92,511	$92,511
41 Difference in Real Consump (Post-Pre)					
42 Social Security Benefit Level	$32,853	$33,510	$34,180	$34,864	$35,561
43 Federal Income Tax Bracket 1 Cutoff	$93,192	$95,056	$96,957	$98,896	$100,874
44 Federal Income Tax Bracket 2 Cutoff	$225,242	$229,747	$234,341	$239,028	$243,809
45 Federal Income Tax Bracket 3 Cutoff	$343,220	$350,085	$357,086	$364,228	$371,513
46 Federal Income Tax Bracket 4 Cutoff	$612,947	$625,206	$637,711	$650,465	$663,474
47 Federal FICA-SSI Wage Cap	$157,160	$160,304	$163,510	$166,780	$170,116

As you adapt this model to your own situation, it is not necessary to go from full-time work to zero work. You could consider retiring to part-time work and then gradually tapering off. For example, you could drop to half-time work by entering -50% in your first retirement year and then enter -100.0% in the year that you stop working entirely.

4. **Random Variables.** Assume that the Real Return on the Risky Diversified Fund is normally distributed with the mean given in cell **B6** and the standard deviation given in cell **B7**. The Excel function **RAND()** generates a random variable with a uniform distribution over the interval from 0 to 1 (that is, an equal chance of getting any number between 0 and 1). To transform this uniformly distributed random variable into a normally distributed one, just place it inside the Excel function **NORMINV**.[1] Enter **=NORMINV(RAND(),$B$6,$B$7)** in cell **C26** and copy it across. The real return that you get depends on how much you have placed in risky vs. riskfree

---

[1] The "Transformation Method" for converting a uniform random variable x into some other random variable y based on a cumulative distribution F is $y(x) = F^{-1}(x)$. See Press, W., B. Flannery, S. Teukolsky, and W. Vetterling, 1987, Numerical Recopies: The Art of Scientific Computing, Cambridge University Press, chapter on Random Numbers, subsection on the Transformation Method, page 201.

funds. Real Return on Your Retirement Fund = (Risky Diversified Fund Percentage) * (Real Return on Risky Diversified Fund) + (1 - Risky Diversified Fund Percentage) * (Real Return on Riskfree Money Market Fund). Enter **=C21*C26+(1-C21)*$B$5** in cell **C27** and copy it across.

FIGURE 16.3 Old Age Years.

	A	BK	BL	BM	BN	BO
17	Date	61	62	63	64	65
18	Age	86	87	88	89	90
19	**Choice Variables**					
20	Savings Percentage	0.0%	0.0%	0.0%	0.0%	0.0%
21	Risky Diversified Fund Percentage	50.0%	50.0%	50.0%	50.0%	50.0%
22	Withdrawal Percentage	5.9%	5.9%	5.9%	5.9%	5.9%
23	Real Growth Rate in Salary	0.0%	0.0%	0.0%	0.0%	0.0%
24						
25	**Random Variables**					
26	Real Return on Risky Diversified Fund	8.00%	8.00%	8.00%	8.00%	8.00%
27	Real Return on Your Retirement Fund	5.75%	5.75%	5.75%	5.75%	5.75%
28						
29	**Outputs**					
30	Salary	$0	$0	$0	$0	$0
31	Less Contribution To Retirement Fund	$0	$0	$0	$0	$0
32	Plus Withdrawal From Retirement Fund	$347,944	$354,903	$362,001	$369,241	$376,625
33	Taxable Income	$347,944	$354,903	$362,001	$369,241	$376,625
34	Less Taxes	$89,133	$90,916	$92,734	$94,589	$96,480
35	After-Tax Income	$258,811	$263,987	$269,267	$274,652	$280,145
36	Plus Social Security Benefits	$50,790	$51,806	$52,842	$53,899	$54,977
37	Consumption	$309,601	$315,793	$322,109	$328,551	$335,122
38						
39	Retirement Fund	$6,051,201	$6,172,222	$6,295,662	$6,421,572	$6,550,000
40	Real Consumption in Current Dollars	$92,511	$92,511	$92,511	$92,511	$92,511
41	Difference in Real Consump (Post-Pre)					
42	Social Security Benefit Level	$50,790	$51,806	$52,842	$53,899	$54,977
43	Federal Income Tax Bracket 1 Cutoff	$144,073	$146,955	$149,894	$152,892	$155,950
44	Federal Income Tax Bracket 2 Cutoff	$348,219	$355,183	$362,287	$369,533	$376,924
45	Federal Income Tax Bracket 3 Cutoff	$530,612	$541,224	$552,048	$563,089	$574,351
46	Federal Income Tax Bracket 4 Cutoff	$947,604	$966,556	$985,888	$1,005,605	$1,025,717
47	Federal FICA-SSI Wage Cap	$242,967	$247,826	$252,783	$257,838	$262,995

5. **Outputs.** Here are the formulas for each row:

- **Salary** = Last Year's Salary * (1 + Inflation Rate) * (1 + Real Growth Rate in Salary) in working years   Enter **=C30*(1+$B$4)*(1+D23)** in cell **D30** and copy it across.
- **Less Contribution To Retirement Fund** = (Savings Percentage) * (Salary). Enter **=C20*C30** in cell **C31** and copy it across.
- **Plus Withdrawal From Retirement Fund** = (Withdrawal Percentage) * (Last Period's Retirement Fund). Enter **=C22*B39** in cell **C32** and copy it across.
- **Taxable Income** = Salary - (Contribution To Retirement Fund) + (Withdrawal From Retirement Fund).
  Enter **=C30-C31+C32** in cell **C33** and copy it across.
- **Taxes** = (Bracket 1 Tax Rate) * MIN(Taxable Income, Bracket 1 Cutoff)
  + (Bracket 2 Tax Rate) * MAX(MIN(Taxable Income, Bracket 2 Cutoff)
     - Bracket 1 Cutoff, 0)
  + (Bracket 3 Tax Rate) * MAX(MIN(Taxable Income, Bracket 3 Cutoff)
     - Bracket 2 Cutoff, 0)
  + (Bracket 4 Tax Rate) * MAX(MIN(Taxable Income, Bracket 4 Cutoff)

               - Bracket 3 Cutoff, 0)

            + (Bracket 5 Tax Rate) * MAX(Taxable Income - Bracket 4 Cutoff, 0)

            + (Federal FICA-SSI Tax Rate) * MIN(Salary, Federal FICA-SSI Wage Cap)

            + (Federal FICA-Medicare Tax Rate) * Salary

            + (State Income Tax Rate) * Taxable Income

Enter =$B$8*MIN(C33,C43)

        +$B$9*MAX(MIN(C33,C44)-C43,0)

        +$B$10*MAX(MIN(C33,C45)-C44,0)

        +$B$11*MAX(MIN(C33,C46)-C45,0)

        +$B$12*MAX(C33-C46,0)

        +$B$13*MIN(C30,C47)

        +$B$14*C30

        +$B$15*C33 in cell C34 and copy it across.

o **After-Tax Income** = Taxable Income - Taxes. Enter =C33-C34 in cell C35 and copy it across.

o **Plus Social Security Benefits** = 0 in working years

                         = Social Security Benefit Level in retirement year

o Enter **0** in cell **C36** and copy the cell to the range **D36:AP36**. Enter **=AQ42** in cell **AQ36** and copy it across.

o **Consumption** = After-Tax Income + Social Security Benefits. Enter =C35+C36 in cell C37 and copy it across.

o **Retirement Fund** = Last Year's Retirement Fund * (1 + Inflation Rate) * (1 + Real Return on Your Retirement Fund) + Contribution to the Retirement Fund - Withdrawal from the Retirement Fund. Enter =B39*(1+$B$4)*(1+C27)+C31-C32 in cell C39 and copy it across.

o **Real Consumption** = (Nominal Consumption) / ((1 + Inflation Rate) ^ Number of periods)
Enter =C37/((1+$B$4)^C17) in cell C40 and copy it across.

o **Difference in Real Consumption (Post-Pre)** = Real Consumption in Post-Retirement - Real Consumption in Pre-Retirement. Enter =AQ40-AP40 in cell B41.

o **Social Security Benefit Level** = Last Year's Social Security Benefit Level * (1 + Inflation Rate).
Enter =C42*(1+$B$4) in cell D42 and copy it across. To check your social security eligibility and benefit level, surf the Social Security Administration's web site http://www.ssa.gov/OACT/ANYPIA/.

o **Federal Income Tax Bracket Cutoffs.** = Last Year's Federal Income Tax Bracket Cutoff * (1 + Inflation Rate). Enter =B43*(1+$B$4) in cell C43 and copy the cell to the range **C43:BO46**.

o **Federal FICA-SSI Wage Cap.** = Last Year's Federal FICA-SSI Wage Cap * (1 + Inflation Rate).
Enter =B47*(1+$B$4) in cell C47 and copy it across.

6. **Graph Real Consumption Over The Life-Cycle.** Highlight the range **B18:BO18**, then hold down the Control button and (while still holding it down) select the range **B40:BO40**. Next choose **Insert | Chart** from the main menu. Select an **XY(Scatter)** chart type and make other selections to complete the Chart Wizard. Place the graph in the range **C2:G16**.

7. **Adjust Savings Percentage To Smooth Real Consumption Over The Life-Cycle.** It doesn't make any sense to live like a king in your working years and the live in poverty in your retirement years. Similarly, it doesn't make sense to live in poverty in your working years and live like a king in your retirement years. The key idea is that you want to have a smooth pattern of real consumption over the life-cycle. The easiest way to get a smooth consumption pattern is to adjust the savings percentage. The easiest way to do this is to have a constant savings percentage during your working years by tying this savings percentage to a single cell and then manually adjust this cell. Enter **=C20** in cell **D20** and copy it across. Then manually adjust cell **C20** up or down in small increments until the Difference in Real Consumption (Post-Pre) in cell **B41** is reasonably close to zero.

Looking at the big picture, the retirement fund starts at $0 and rises smoothly to $4,072,321 in the first retirement year and then increases at the rate of inflation each year after that. Focusing on the graph of real consumption over the life-cycle, we see that real consumption (in current dollars) starts out at $43,864 and rises smoothly to $92,511 at retirement and then stays constant at that level throughout retirement -- a comfortable lifestyle!

8. **Adjust The Standard Deviation and View The Risk Involved.** Now change the standard deviation to a realistic figure. Enter **17.0000%** in cell **B7**. The random variables in rows **26** and **27** will spring to life and the graph of real consumption over the life-cycle will reflect the high or low realizations of the risky diversified fund. Press the **F9** Recalculation key several times and you will see the real consumption rate dance all over the graph. **Figure 4** shows a low consumption case due to low real returns. **Figure 5** shows a medium consumption case due to medium real returns **Figure 6** shows a high consumption case due to high real returns.

FIGURE 16.4 A Low Consumption Case Due To Low Real Returns in the Risky Diversified Fund.

	A	B	C	D	E	F	G
1	**LIFE-CYCLE FINANCIAL PLANNING**			Basics			
2							
3	**Inputs**						
4	Inflation Rate	2.0%					
5	Real Ret on Riskfree Money Market Fund	3.5%					
6	Ave Real Ret on Risky Diversified Fund	8.0%					
7	Std Dev of Risky Diversified Fund	17.0000%					
8	Federal Income Bracket 1 Tax Rate	15.0%					
9	Federal Income Bracket 2 Tax Rate	28.0%					
10	Federal Income Bracket 3 Tax Rate	31.0%					
11	Federal Income Bracket 4 Tax Rate	36.0%					
12	Federal Income Bracket 5 Tax Rate	39.6%					
13	Federal FICA-SSI Tax Rate on Salary	6.2%					
14	Federal FICA-Medicare Tax on Salary	1.45%					
15	State Income Tax Rate	3.0%					
16							
17	Date	0	1	2	3	4	5
18	Age	25	26	27	28	29	30
19	**Choice Variables**						
20	Savings Percentage		8.1%	8.1%	8.1%	8.1%	8.1%
21	Risky Diversified Fund Percentage		100.0%	100.0%	100.0%	100.0%	100.0%
22	Withdrawal Percentage		0.0%	0.0%	0.0%	0.0%	0.0%
23	Real Growth Rate in Salary			2.0%	2.0%	2.0%	2.0%
24							
25	**Random Variables**						
26	Real Return on Risky Diversified Fund		-0.44%	22.99%	-20.34%	5.52%	6.95%
27	Real Return on Your Retirement Fund		-0.44%	22.99%	-20.34%	5.52%	6.95%
28							
29	**Outputs**						
30	Salary		$70,000	$72,828	$75,770	$78,831	$82,016
31	Less Contribution To Retirement Fund		$5,670	$5,899	$6,137	$6,385	$6,643
32	Plus Withdrawal From Retirement Fund		$0	$0	$0	$0	$0
33	Taxable Income		$64,330	$66,929	$69,633	$72,446	$75,373
34	Less Taxes		$19,589	$20,497	$21,444	$22,416	$23,346
35	After-Tax Income		$44,741	$46,432	$48,189	$50,030	$52,027
36	Plus Social Security Benefits		$0	$0	$0	$0	$0
37	Consumption		$44,741	$46,432	$48,189	$50,030	$52,027
38							
39	Retirement Fund	$0	$5,670	$13,012	$16,711	$24,371	$33,230
40	Real Consumption in Current Dollars		$43,864	$44,629	$45,410	$46,220	$47,123

Chart (rows 2–16, columns C–G): **Real Consumption Over The Life-Cycle** — Real Consumption (vertical axis, $0 to $200,000) versus Age (horizontal axis, 25 to 85).

FIGURE 16.5 A Medium Consumption Case Due To Medium Real Returns in the Risky Diversified Fund.

	A	B	C	D	E	F	G
1	**LIFE-CYCLE FINANCIAL PLANNING**			Basics			
2							
3	**Inputs**						
4	Inflation Rate	2.0%					
5	Real Ret on Riskfree Money Market Fund	3.5%					
6	Ave Real Ret on Risky Diversified Fund	8.0%					
7	Std Dev of Risky Diversified Fund	17.0000%					
8	Federal Income Bracket 1 Tax Rate	15.0%					
9	Federal Income Bracket 2 Tax Rate	28.0%					
10	Federal Income Bracket 3 Tax Rate	31.0%					
11	Federal Income Bracket 4 Tax Rate	36.0%					
12	Federal Income Bracket 5 Tax Rate	39.6%					
13	Federal FICA-SSI Tax Rate on Salary	6.2%					
14	Federal FICA-Medicare Tax on Salary	1.45%					
15	State Income Tax Rate	3.0%					
16							
17	Date	0	1	2	3	4	5
18	Age	25	26	27	28	29	30
19	**Choice Variables**						
20	Savings Percentage		8.1%	8.1%	8.1%	8.1%	8.1%
21	Risky Diversified Fund Percentage		100.0%	100.0%	100.0%	100.0%	100.0%
22	Withdrawal Percentage		0.0%	0.0%	0.0%	0.0%	0.0%
23	Real Growth Rate in Salary		2.0%	2.0%	2.0%	2.0%
24							
25	**Random Variables**						
26	Real Return on Risky Diversified Fund		-1.32%	10.17%	29.24%	17.03%	0.59%
27	Real Return on Your Retirement Fund		-1.32%	10.17%	29.24%	17.03%	0.59%
28							
29	**Outputs**						
30	Salary		$70,000	$72,828	$75,770	$78,831	$82,016
31	Less Contribution To Retirement Fund		$5,670	$5,899	$6,137	$6,385	$6,643
32	Plus Withdrawal From Retirement Fund		$0	$0	$0	$0	$0
33	Taxable Income		$64,330	$66,929	$69,633	$72,446	$75,373
34	Less Taxes		$19,589	$20,497	$21,444	$22,416	$23,346
35	After-Tax Income		$44,741	$46,432	$48,189	$50,030	$52,027
36	Plus Social Security Benefits		$0	$0	$0	$0	$0
37	Consumption		$44,741	$46,432	$48,189	$50,030	$52,027
38							
39	Retirement Fund	$0	$5,670	$12,271	$22,313	$33,021	$40,524
40	Real Consumption in Current Dollars		$43,864	$44,629	$45,410	$46,220	$47,123

Real Consumption Over The Life-Cycle

116

FIGURE 16.6 A High Consumption Case Due To High Real Returns in the Risky Diversified Fund.

	A	B	C	D	E	F	G
1	LIFE-CYCLE FINANCIAL PLANNING		Basics				
2							
3	**Inputs**						
4	Inflation Rate	2.0%					
5	Real Ret on Riskfree Money Market Fund	3.5%					
6	Ave Real Ret on Risky Diversified Fund	8.0%					
7	Std Dev of Risky Diversified Fund	17.0000%					
8	Federal Income Bracket 1 Tax Rate	15.0%					
9	Federal Income Bracket 2 Tax Rate	28.0%					
10	Federal Income Bracket 3 Tax Rate	31.0%					
11	Federal Income Bracket 4 Tax Rate	36.0%					
12	Federal Income Bracket 5 Tax Rate	39.6%					
13	Federal FICA-SSI Tax Rate on Salary	6.2%					
14	Federal FICA-Medicare Tax on Salary	1.45%					
15	State Income Tax Rate	3.0%					
16							
17	Date	0	1	2	3	4	5
18	Age	25	26	27	28	29	30
19	**Choice Variables**						
20	Savings Percentage		8.1%	8.1%	8.1%	8.1%	8.1%
21	Risky Diversified Fund Percentage		100.0%	100.0%	100.0%	100.0%	100.0%
22	Withdrawal Percentage		0.0%	0.0%	0.0%	0.0%	0.0%
23	Real Growth Rate in Salary			2.0%	2.0%	2.0%	2.0%
24							
25	**Random Variables**						
26	Real Return on Risky Diversified Fund		16.46%	-12.99%	8.71%	-1.67%	4.79%
27	Real Return on Your Retirement Fund		16.46%	-12.99%	8.71%	-1.67%	4.79%
28							
29	**Outputs**						
30	Salary		$70,000	$72,828	$75,770	$78,831	$82,016
31	Less Contribution To Retirement Fund		$5,670	$5,899	$6,137	$6,385	$6,643
32	Plus Withdrawal From Retirement Fund		$0	$0	$0	$0	$0
33	Taxable Income		$64,330	$66,929	$69,633	$72,446	$75,373
34	Less Taxes		$19,589	$20,497	$21,444	$22,416	$23,346
35	After-Tax Income		$44,741	$46,432	$48,189	$50,030	$52,027
36	Plus Social Security Benefits		$0	$0	$0	$0	$0
37	Consumption		$44,741	$46,432	$48,189	$50,030	$52,027
38							
39	Retirement Fund	$0	$5,670	$10,931	$18,258	$24,699	$33,043
40	Real Consumption in Current Dollars		$43,864	$44,629	$45,410	$46,220	$47,123

Real Consumption Over The Life-Cycle

These three graphs are "representative" of the risk you face from investing in the risky diversified fund. In the low case, real consumption drops to about $40,000. In the medium case, real consumption fluctuates between $75,000 and $100,000. In the high case, real consumption fluctuates between $125,000 and $160,000. Clearly, there is substantial risk from being so heavily exposed to the risky diversified fund.

There is a direct connection between risk and return. A high percentage in the risky diversified fund percentage gives you a high average return and high risk. Whereas a low percentage in the risky diversified fund percentage gives you a low average return and low risk. The choice is up to you.

Problems

Skill-Building Problems.

1. Suppose the inflation rate is 2.4% and the real return on a riskfree money market fund is 3.8%. Suppose that a risky diversified fund offers an average real return of 7.2% and a standard deviation of 19.3%. Suppose that federal income taxes have five brackets with the following rates: 15.0%, 28.0%, 31.0%, 36.0%, and 39.6%. For current year, the upper cutoff on the first four brackets are $43,050, $104,050, $158,550, and $283,150 and these cutoffs are indexed to inflation. The state tax rate = 4.5%, federal FICA-SSI tax rate on salary up to $72,600 is 6.2%, and the federal FICA-Medicare tax rate on any level of salary is 1.45%. Suppose you are currently 35 years old and you expect to earn a salary next year of $90,000. You currently have $40,000 in a retirement account and plan to work through age 70. You will start receiving social security benefits at age 71. The current level of social security benefits is $15, 480 per year and this is indexed to inflation. Develop a financial plan for investment and consumption over your life-cycle.

Skill-Extending Problems.

2. Extend the Life-Cycle Financial Planning model by converting the spreadsheet into a Dynamic Chart by adding spinners to drive the inputs. See Black Scholes Option Pricing - Dynamic Chart for details on how to implement spinners. After you click on the spinners to change the inputs, then adjust the Savings Percentage to have a smooth consumption pattern.

Live In-class Problems.

3. Given the partial Basics spreadsheet **LifebasZ.xls**, do step **3 Choice Variables**.

PART 5 OPTIONS AND CORPORATE FINANCE

17 Binomial Option Pricing

17.1 Single Period

Problem. The current stock price of All-Net is $100.00, the potential up movement / period of All-Net's stock price is 30.00%, the potential down movement / period of All-Net's stock price is -20.00%, the riskfree rate is 2.0% per period, the exercise price of an one-period, European call option on All-Net is $90.00, the exercise price of an one-period, European put option on All-Net is $90.00, the time to maturity for both options is 0.75 years (nine months), and the number of periods for both options is 1. What are the current prices of the call and put?

Solution Strategy. First, calculate the date 1, maturity date items: stock up price, stock down price, and the corresponding call and put payoffs. Second, calculate the shares of stock and money borrowed to create a replicating portfolio that replicates the option payoff at maturity. Finally, calculate the price now of the replicating portfolio and, in the absence of arbitrage, this will be the option price now.

FIGURE 17.1 Spreadsheet Model of Binomial Option Pricing - Single Period - Call Option.

	A	B	C	D	E	F	G
1	BINOMIAL OPTION PRICING		Single Period				Call
2							
3	**Inputs**						
4	Option Type: 1=Call, 0=Put	1					
5	Stock Price Now	$100.00					
6	Up Movement / Period	30.00%					
7	Down Movement / Period	-20.00%					
8	Riskfree Rate / Period	2.00%					
9	Exercise Price	$90.00					
10	Time To Maturity (Years)	0.75					
11	Number of Periods	1					
12							
13		**Now**	**Maturity**				
14	**Period**	**0**	**1**				
15	**Time**	**0.000**	**0.750**				
16							
17	**Stock**	$100.00	$130.00				
18			$80.00				
19							
20	**Call**	$17.25	$40.00				
21			$0.00				
22							
23	**Replicating Portfolio**						
24							
25	**Stock Shares Bought (Sold)**						
26		0.800					
27							
28	**Money Lent (Borrowed)**						
29		($62.75)					

How To Build This Spreadsheet Model.

119

1. **Inputs.** Enter **1** in cell **B4**. This will serve as a switch between a call option and a put option. To highlight which type of option is being evaluated, enter **=IF($B$4=1,"Call","Put")** in cell **G1** and copy this cell to cell **A20**. Enter the other inputs into the range **B5:B11**.

2. **Enter Periods and Time.** Enter the periods **0** and **1** in cells **B14** and **C14**. The formula for Time = Time To Maturity * (Period / Number of Periods). Enter **=$B$10*(B14/$B$11)** in cell **B15** and copy it to the cell **C15**.

3. **Stock Prices.** Set the Date 0 Stock Price equal to the Stock Price Now by entering **=B5** in cell **B17**. Calculate the Date 1 Stock Up Price = Stock Price Now * (1 + Up Movement / Period) by entering **=B17*(1+B6)** in cell **C17**. Calculate the Date 1 Stock Down Price = Stock Price Now * (1 + Down Movement / Period) by entering **=B17*(1+B7)** in cell **C18**.

4. **Option Payoffs At Maturity.** The formulas for option payoffs are:
   o   For a Call, the Payoff At Maturity = Max (Stock Price At Maturity – Exercise Price, 0).
   o   For a Put, the Payoff At Maturity = Max (Exercise Price – Stock Price At Maturity, 0). Enter **=IF($B$4=1,MAX(C17-$B$9,0),MAX($B$9-C17,0))** in cell **C20** and copy it to the cell **C21**.

5. **Create A Replicating Portfolio.** For the Replicating Portfolio, calculate the Stock Shares Bought **(Sold)** using the Hedge Ratio = (Option Up Payoff – Option Down Payoff) / (Stock Up Price – Stock Down Price). In cell **B26**, enter **=(C20-C21)/(C17-C18)**. For the Replicating Portfolio, calculate the amount of Money Lent **(Borrowed)** = (Call Down Payoff –Hedge Ratio * Stock Down Price) / (1 + Riskfree Rate / Period). In cell **B29**, enter **=(C21-B26*C18)/(1+B8)**. Notice that replicating a Call option requires **<u>Buying</u>** Shares of Stock and **<u>Borrowing</u>** Money, whereas a Put option requires **<u>Selling</u>** Shares of Stock and **<u>Lending</u>** Money.

6. **Calculate the Option Price Now.** In the absence of arbitrage, the Option Price Now = Replicating Portfolio Price Now = Number of Shares of Stock * Stock Price Now + Money Borrowed. In cell **B20**, enter **=B26*B17+B29**.

We see that the Binomial Option Pricing model predicts a one-period European call price of $17.25. Now let's check the put.

120

FIGURE 17.2 Spreadsheet Model of Binomial Option Pricing - Single Period - Put Option.

	A	B	C	D	E	F	G
1	BINOMIAL OPTION PRICING			Single Period			Put
2							
3	**Inputs**						
4	Option Type: 1=Call, 0=Put	0					
5	Stock Price Now	$100.00					
6	Up Movement / Period	30.00%					
7	Down Movement / Period	-20.00%					
8	Riskfree Rate / Period	2.00%					
9	Exercise Price	$90.00					
10	Time To Maturity (Years)	0.75					
11	Number of Periods	1					
12							
13		**Now**	**Maturity**				
14	**Period**	0	1				
15	**Time**	0.000	0.750				
16							
17	**Stock**	$100.00	$130.00				
18			$80.00				
19							
20	**Put**	$5.49	$0.00				
21			$10.00				
22							
23	**Replicating Portfolio**						
24							
25	**Stock Shares Bought (Sold)**						
26		(0.200)					
27							
28	**Money Lent (Borrowed)**						
29		$25.49					

7. **Put Option.** Enter **0** in cell B4.

We see that the Binomial Option Pricing model predicts a one-period European put price of $5.49.

17.2 Multi-Period

Problem. The current stock price of Energy Systems is $60.00, the potential up movement / period of Energy Systems' stock price is 10.00%, the potential down movement / period of Energy Systems' stock price is -5.00%, the riskfree rate is 0.5% per period, the exercise price of an one-period, European call option on Energy Systems is $65.00, the exercise price of an one-period, European put option on Energy Systems is $65.00, the time to maturity for both options is 2.00 years, and the number of periods for both options is 8. What are the current prices of the call and put?

Solution Strategy. First, build a multi-period tree of stock prices. Second, calculate call and put payoffs at maturity. Third, build the multi-period trees of the shares of stock and money borrowed to create a replicating portfolio that replicates the option period by period. Finally, build a multi-period tree of the value of the replicating portfolio and, in the absence of arbitrage, this will be value of the option.

FIGURE 17.3 Spreadsheet Model of Binomial Option Pricing - Multi-Period - Call Option.

	A	B	C	D	E	F	G	H	I	J
1	BINOMIAL OPTION PRICING		Multi-Period				Call			
2										
3	Inputs									
4	Option Type: 1=Call, 0=Put	1								
5	Stock Price Now	$60.00								
6	Up Movement / Period	10.00%								
7	Down Movement / Period	-5.00%								
8	Riskfree Rate / Period	0.50%								
9	Exercise Price	$65.00								
10	Time To Maturity (Years)	2.00								
11	Number of Periods	8								
12										
13		Now								Maturity
14	Period	0	1	2	3	4	5	6	7	8
15	Time	0.000	0.250	0.500	0.750	1.000	1.250	1.500	1.750	2.000
16										
17	Stock	$60.00	$66.00	$72.60	$79.86	$87.85	$96.63	$106.29	$116.92	$128.62
18			$57.00	$62.70	$68.97	$75.87	$83.45	$91.80	$100.98	$111.08
19				$54.15	$59.57	$65.52	$72.07	$79.28	$87.21	$95.93
20					$51.44	$56.59	$62.25	$68.47	$75.32	$82.85
21						$48.87	$53.76	$59.13	$65.05	$71.55
22							$46.43	$51.07	$56.18	$61.79
23								$44.11	$48.52	$53.37
24									$41.90	$46.09
25										$39.81
26										
27	Call	$3.93	$6.73	$10.94	$16.78	$24.13	$32.60	$41.94	$52.25	$63.62
28			$2.34	$4.34	$7.65	$12.66	$19.42	$27.44	$36.30	$46.08
29				$1.20	$2.46	$4.81	$8.84	$14.93	$22.53	$30.93
30					$0.48	$1.12	$2.52	$5.39	$10.64	$17.85
31						$0.12	$0.32	$0.87	$2.39	$6.55
32							$0.00	$0.00	$0.00	$0.00
33								$0.00	$0.00	$0.00
34									$0.00	$0.00
35										$0.00

How To Build This Spreadsheet Model.

1. **Start with the Single Period Spreadsheet, Enter the Inputs, and Delete Rows.** Open the spreadsheet that you created for Binomial Option Pricing – Single Period and immediately save the spreadsheet under a new name using the **File | Save As** command. Enter the new inputs into the range **B5:B11**. Delete rows **20** through **29** by selecting the range **A20:A29**, clicking on **Edit**, **Delete**, selecting the **Entire Row** radio button on the **Delete** dialog box, and clicking on **OK**.

2. **Enter Periods and Time.** Enter the periods **0, 1, 2, ... , 8** in cells **B14** and **J14**. The formula for Time = Time To Maturity * (Period / Number of Periods). Enter **=$B$10*(B14/$B$11)** in cell **B15** and copy the cell to the range **C15:J15**.

3. **The Stock Price Tree.** As in the single period case, the Period 0 Stock Price is equal to the Stock Price Now. Turning to the rest of the Stock Price Tree, we want to create the entire tree with one copy command to a square range. To do this we have to determine whether a cell in the square area is on the tree or off the tree. Further, there are two different formulas to use on the tree (a Down Price vs. an Up Price). Hence, there are three possibilities:

- When the cell to the left and the cell diagonally to the upper left are both blank, then show a blank.
- When the cell to the left is blank and the cell diagonally to the upper left has a number, then you are on the lower edge of the triangle so calculate the Down Price = (Stock Price in the Upper Left) * (1 + Down Movement / Period)
- When both cells have numbers, then calculate the Up Price = (Stock Price to the Left) * (1 + Up Movement / Period) Enter **=IF(B17="",IF(B16="",""),B16*(1+$B$7)),B17*(1+$B$6))** in cell **C17** and copy this cell to the 9-by-9 square range **C17:J25**. The nested IF statements cause a binomial tree to form in the triangular area from **C17** to **J17** to **J25**. Incidentally, the same procedure could create a binomial tree for any number of periods. For example, if you wished to create a 20 period model, then you would simply copy this cell to a 20-by-21 square range. In the **Binomial Option Pricing Full-Scale Real Data** spreadsheet model, we will exploit this feature to create a 50 period model!

4. **Option Payoffs At Maturity.** Copy the option type indicator from cell **G1** and copy this cell to cell **A27**. The formulas for option payoffs are:
   - For a Call, the Payoff At Maturity = Max (Stock Price At Maturity – Exercise Price, 0).
   - For a Put, the Payoff At Maturity = Max (Exercise Price – Stock Price Maturity, 0). Enter **=IF($B$4=1,MAX(J17-$B$9,0),MAX($B$9-J17,0))** in cell **J27** and copy this cell to the range **J28:J35**.

	A	B	C	D	E	F	G	H	I	J
1	BINOMIAL OPTION PRICING	Multi-Period					Call			
2										
3	Inputs									
4	Option Type: 1=Call, 0=Put	1								
5	Stock Price Now	$60.00								
6	Up Movement / Period	10.00%								
7	Down Movement / Period	-5.00%								
8	Riskfree Rate / Period	0.50%								
9	Exercise Price	$65.00								
10	Time To Maturity (Years)	2.00								
11	Number of Periods	8								
12										
13		Now								Maturity
14	Period	0	1	2	3	4	5	6	7	8
15	Time	0.000	0.250	0.500	0.750	1.000	1.250	1.500	1.750	2.000
37	Replicating Portfolio									
38										
39	Stock Shares Bought (Sold)									
40		0.487	0.667	0.838	0.958	1.000	1.000	1.000	1.000	
41			0.367	0.552	0.758	0.929	1.000	1.000	1.000	
42				0.244	0.413	0.644	0.882	1.000	1.000	
43					0.130	0.259	0.484	0.803	1.000	
44						0.043	0.108	0.269	0.671	
45							0.000	0.000	0.000	
46								0.000	0.000	
47									0.000	
48										
49	Money Lent (Borrowed)									
50		($25.32)	($37.28)	($49.93)	($59.71)	($63.72)	($64.03)	($64.35)	($64.68)	
51			($18.60)	($30.26)	($44.66)	($57.86)	($64.03)	($64.35)	($64.68)	
52				($11.99)	($22.16)	($37.36)	($54.74)	($64.35)	($64.68)	
53					($6.20)	($13.53)	($27.59)	($49.61)	($64.68)	
54						($2.00)	($5.50)	($15.06)	($41.28)	
55							$0.00	$0.00	$0.00	
56								$0.00	$0.00	
57									$0.00	

5. **The Stock Shares Bought (Sold) Tree.** At each point in the 8-by-8 square range, you need to determine if you are on the tree or off the tree. There are two possibilities:
   o When the corresponding cell in the Stock Price area is blank, then show a blank.
   o When the corresponding cell in the Stock Price area has a number, then use the Hedge Ratio = (Option Up Payoff – Option Down Payoff) / (Stock Up Price – Stock Down Price).

   Enter **=IF(C28="","",(C27-C28)/(C17-C18))** in cell **B40** and copy this cell to the 8-by-8 square range **B40:I47**. A binomial tree will form in the triangular area from **B40** to **I40** to **I47**. Again the same procedure could create a binomial tree for any number of periods.

6. **The Money Lent (Borrowed) Tree.** At each point in the 8-by-8 square range, you need to determine if you are on the tree or off the tree. There are two possibilities:
   o When the corresponding cell in the Stock Price area is blank, then show a blank.

- o When the corresponding cell in the Stock Price area has a number, then calculate the amount of Money Lent (**Borrowed**) = (Call Down Payoff – Hedge Ratio * Stock Down Price) / (1 + Riskfree Rate / Period). Enter **=IF(C28="","",(C28-B40*C18)/(1+$B$8))** in cell **B50** and copy this cell to the 8-by-8 square range **B50:I57**. A binomial tree will form in the triangular area from **B50** to **I50** to **I57**. Again the same procedure could create a binomial tree for any number of periods.

7. **The Option Price Tree.** At each point in the 8-by-8 square range (excluding column **J** containing option payoffs at maturity), you need to determine if you are on the tree or off the tree. There are two possibilities:
   - o When the corresponding cell in the Stock Price area is blank, then show a blank.
   - o When the corresponding cell in the Stock Price area has a number, then (in the absence of arbitrage) the Option Price At Each Node = Price Of The Corresponding Replicating Portfolio = Number of Shares of Stock * Stock Price + Money Borrowed.

   Enter **=IF(C28="","",B40*B17+B50)** in cell **B27** and copy this cell to the 8-by-9 range **B27:I34. Be sure not to copy over column J containing option payoffs at maturity.** A binomial tree will form in the triangular area from **B27** to **J27** to **J35**. Again the same procedure could create a binomial tree for any number of periods.

We see that the Binomial Option Pricing model predicts an eight-period European call price of $3.93. Now let's check the put.

125

FIGURE 17.5 Spreadsheet Model of Binomial Option Pricing - Multi-Period - Put.

	A	B	C	D	E	F	G	H	I	J
1	**BINOMIAL OPTION PRICING**			Multi-Period			Put			
2										
3	**Inputs**									
4	Option Type: 1=Call, 0=Put	0								
5	Stock Price Now	$60.00								
6	Up Movement / Period	10.00%								
7	Down Movement / Period	-5.00%								
8	Riskfree Rate / Period	0.50%								
9	Exercise Price	$65.00								
10	Time To Maturity (Years)	2.00								
11	Number of Periods	8								
12										
13			Now							Maturity
14	Period	0	1	2	3	4	5	6	7	8
15	Time	0.000	0.250	0.500	0.750	1.000	1.250	1.500	1.750	2.000
16										
17	**Stock**	$60.00	$66.00	$72.60	$79.86	$87.85	$96.63	$106.29	$116.92	$128.62
18			$57.00	$62.70	$68.97	$75.87	$83.45	$91.80	$100.98	$111.08
19				$54.15	$59.57	$65.52	$72.07	$79.28	$87.21	$95.93
20					$51.44	$56.59	$62.25	$68.47	$75.32	$82.85
21						$48.87	$53.76	$59.13	$65.05	$71.55
22							$46.43	$51.07	$56.18	$61.79
23								$44.11	$48.52	$53.37
24									$41.90	$46.09
25										$39.81
26										
27	**Put**	$6.39	$3.50	$1.43	$0.32	$0.00	$0.00	$0.00	$0.00	$0.00
28			$8.11	$4.72	$2.08	$0.51	$0.00	$0.00	$0.00	$0.00
29				$10.13	$6.29	$3.01	$0.80	$0.00	$0.00	$0.00
30					$12.44	$8.25	$4.30	$1.27	$0.00	$0.00
31						$14.96	$10.60	$6.09	$2.02	$0.00
32							$17.61	$13.29	$8.50	$3.21
33								$20.25	$16.16	$11.63
34									$22.78	$18.91
35										$25.19

8. **Put Option.** Enter **0** in cell **B4**.

We see that the Binomial Option Pricing model predicts an eight-period European put price of $6.39.

FIGURE 17.6 Spreadsheet of Binomial Option Pricing - Multi-Period - Put (Continued).

	A	B	C	D	E	F	G	H	I	J
1	**BINOMIAL OPTION PRICING** Multi-Period						**Put**			
2										
3	**Inputs**									
4	Option Type: 1=Call, 0=Put	0								
5	Stock Price Now	$60.00								
6	Up Movement / Period	10.00%								
7	Down Movement / Period	-5.00%								
8	Riskfree Rate / Period	0.50%								
9	Exercise Price	$65.00								
10	Time To Maturity (Years)	2.00								
11	Number of Periods	8								
12										
13		**Now**								**Maturity**
14	Period	0	1	2	3	4	5	6	7	8
15	Time	0.000	0.250	0.500	0.750	1.000	1.250	1.500	1.750	2.000
37	**Replicating Portfolio**									
38										
39	**Stock Shares Bought (Sold)**									
40		(0.513)	(0.333)	(0.162)	(0.042)	0.000	0.000	0.000	0.000	
41			(0.633)	(0.448)	(0.242)	(0.071)	0.000	0.000	0.000	
42				(0.756)	(0.587)	(0.356)	(0.118)	0.000	0.000	
43					(0.870)	(0.741)	(0.516)	(0.197)	0.000	
44						(0.957)	(0.892)	(0.731)	(0.329)	
45							(1.000)	(1.000)	(1.000)	
46								(1.000)	(1.000)	
47									(1.000)	
48										
49	**Money Lent (Borrowed)**									
50		$37.14	$25.49	$13.16	$3.69	$0.00	$0.00	$0.00	$0.00	
51			$44.17	$32.83	$18.74	$5.85	$0.00	$0.00	$0.00	
52				$51.09	$41.24	$26.35	$9.29	$0.00	$0.00	
53					$57.20	$50.19	$36.44	$14.74	$0.00	
54						$61.71	$58.54	$49.29	$23.39	
55							$64.03	$64.35	$64.68	
56								$64.35	$64.68	
57									$64.68	

As in the single period case, replicating a Call option requires **Buying** Shares of Stock and **Borrowing** Money, whereas a Put option requires **Selling** Shares of Stock and **Lending** Money. Notice that the quantity of Money Borrowed or Lent and the quantity of Shares Bought or Sold changes over time and differs for up nodes vs. down nodes. This process of changing the replicating portfolio every period based on the realized up or down movement in the underlying stock price is called dynamic replication.

Price accuracy can be increased by subdividing the interval into more periods (15, 30, etc.). Typically, from 30 subperiods to 100 periods are required in order to achieve price accuracy to the penny.

17.3 Risk Neutral

The previous spreadsheet model, **Binomial Option Pricing Multi-Period**, determined the price of an option by constructing a replicating portfolio, which combines a stock and a bond to replicate the payoffs of the option. An alternative way to price an option is the Risk Neutral method. Both techniques give you the same answer. The main advantage of the Risk Neutral method is that it is faster and easier to implement. The Replicating Portfolio method required the construction of four trees (stock prices, shares of stock **bought (sold)**, money **lent (borrowed)**, and option prices). The Risk Neutral method will only require two trees (stock prices and option prices).

FIGURE 17.7 Spreadsheet Model of Binomial Option Pricing - Risk Neutral - Call Option.

	A	B	C	D	E	F	G	H	I	J
1	**BINOMIAL OPTION PRICING** Risk Neutral						Call			
2										
3	Inputs					Outputs				
4	Option Type: 1=Call, 0=Put	1		Risk Neutral Probability		36.67%				
5	Stock Price Now	$60.00								
6	Up Movement / Period	10.00%								
7	Down Movement / Period	-5.00%								
8	Riskfree Rate / Period	0.50%								
9	Exercise Price	$65.00								
10	Time To Maturity (Years)	2.00								
11	Number of Periods	8								
12										
13		Now								Maturity
14	Period	0	1	2	3	4	5	6	7	8
15	Time	0.000	0.250	0.500	0.750	1.000	1.250	1.500	1.750	2.000
16										
17	Stock	$60.00	$66.00	$72.60	$79.86	$87.85	$96.63	$106.29	$116.92	$128.62
18			$57.00	$62.70	$68.97	$75.87	$83.45	$91.80	$100.98	$111.08
19				$54.15	$59.57	$65.52	$72.07	$79.28	$87.21	$95.93
20					$51.44	$56.59	$62.25	$68.47	$75.32	$82.85
21						$48.87	$53.76	$59.13	$65.05	$71.55
22							$46.43	$51.07	$56.18	$61.79
23								$44.11	$48.52	$53.37
24									$41.90	$46.09
25										$39.81
26										
27	Call	$3.93	$6.73	$10.94	$16.78	$24.13	$32.60	$41.94	$52.25	$63.62
28			$2.34	$4.34	$7.65	$12.66	$19.42	$27.44	$36.30	$46.08
29				$1.20	$2.46	$4.81	$8.84	$14.93	$22.53	$30.93
30					$0.48	$1.12	$2.52	$5.39	$10.64	$17.85
31						$0.12	$0.32	$0.87	$2.39	$6.55
32							$0.00	$0.00	$0.00	$0.00
33								$0.00	$0.00	$0.00
34									$0.00	$0.00
35										$0.00

How To Build This Spreadsheet Model.

1. **Start with the Multi-Period Spreadsheet.** Open the spreadsheet that you created for Binomial Option Pricing – Multi-Period and immediately save the spreadsheet under a new name using the **File Save As** command.

2. **Risk Neutral Probability.** Calculate the Risk Neutral Probability = (Riskfree Rate / Period - Down Movement / Period) / (Up Movement / Period - Down Movement / Period). Enter **=(B8-B7)/(B6-B7)** in cell **F4**.

3. **The Option Price Tree.** At each point in the 8-by-9 range, you need to determine if you are on the tree or off the tree. There are two possibilities:
   o   When the corresponding cell in the Stock Price area is blank, then show a blank.
   o   When the corresponding cell in the Stock Price area has a number, then (in the absence of arbitrage) the Option Price At Each Node = Expected Value of the Option Price Next

128

Period (using the Risk Neutral Probability) Discounted At The Riskfree Rate = [(Risk Neutral Probability) * (Stock Up Price) + (1 - Risk Neutral Probability) * (Stock Down Price)] / (1+ Riskfree Rate / Period).

Enter =IF(C28="","",($F$4*C27+(1-$F$4)*C28)/(1+$B$8)) in cell **B27** (yielding a blank output at first) and then copy this cell to the 8-by-8 range **B27:I34**. **Be sure not to copy over column J containing option payoffs at maturity.** A binomial tree will form in the triangular area from B27 to J27 to J35. Again the same procedure could create a binominal tree for any number of periods. For appearances, delete rows **37** through **57** by selecting the range **A37:A57**, clicking on **Edit**, **Delete**, selecting the **Entire Row** radio button on the **Delete** dialog box, and clicking on **OK**.

We see that the Risk Neutral method predicts an eight-period European call price of $3.93. This is identical to Replicating Portfolio Price. Now let's check the put.

FIGURE 17.8 Spreadsheet Model of Binomial Option Pricing - Risk Neutral - Put Option.

	A	B	C	D	E	F	G	H	I	J
1	**BINOMIAL OPTION PRICING**			Risk Neutral			Put			
2										
3	**Inputs**				**Outputs**					
4	Option Type: 1=Call, 0=Put	0		Risk Neutral Probability		36.67%				
5	Stock Price Now	$60.00								
6	Up Movement / Period	10.00%								
7	Down Movement / Period	-5.00%								
8	Riskfree Rate / Period	0.50%								
9	Exercise Price	$65.00								
10	Time To Maturity (Years)	2.00								
11	Number of Periods	8								
12										
13		**Now**								**Maturity**
14	**Period**	0	1	2	3	4	5	6	7	8
15	**Time**	0.000	0.250	0.500	0.750	1.000	1.250	1.500	1.750	2.000
16										
17	**Stock**	$60.00	$66.00	$72.60	$79.86	$87.85	$96.63	$106.29	$116.92	$128.62
18			$57.00	$62.70	$68.97	$75.87	$83.45	$91.80	$100.98	$111.08
19				$54.15	$59.57	$65.52	$72.07	$79.28	$87.21	$95.93
20					$51.44	$56.59	$62.25	$68.47	$75.32	$82.85
21						$48.87	$53.76	$59.13	$65.05	$71.55
22							$46.43	$51.07	$56.18	$61.79
23								$44.11	$48.52	$53.37
24									$41.90	$46.09
25										$39.81
26										
27	**Put**	$6.39	$3.50	$1.43	$0.32	$0.00	$0.00	$0.00	$0.00	$0.00
28			$8.11	$4.72	$2.08	$0.51	$0.00	$0.00	$0.00	$0.00
29				$10.13	$6.29	$3.01	$0.80	$0.00	$0.00	$0.00
30					$12.44	$8.25	$4.30	$1.27	$0.00	$0.00
31						$14.96	$10.60	$6.09	$2.02	$0.00
32							$17.61	$13.29	$8.50	$3.21
33								$20.25	$16.16	$11.63
34									$22.78	$18.91
35										$25.19

4. **Put Option.** Enter **0** in cell **B4**.

We see that the Risk Neutral method predicts an eight-period European put price of $6.39. This is identical to Replicating Portfolio Price. Again, we get the same answer either way. The advantage of the Risk Neutral method is that we only have to construct two trees, rather than four trees.

17.4 Full-Scale Real Data

The binomial model can be used to price real-world European calls and puts. Further, the Binomial Tree / Risk Neutral method can be extended to price *any* type of derivative security (European vs. American vs. other, on any underlying asset(s), with any underlying dividends or cash flows, with any derivative payoffs at maturity and/or payoffs before maturity). Indeed, it is one of the most popular techniques on Wall Street for pricing and hedging derivatives.

Problem Using Real Data. On December 13, 1999, the stock price of Amazon.com was $102.50, the yield on a riskfree Treasury Bill maturing on April 20, 2000 was 5.47%, the exercise price of an April 100 European call on Amazon.com was $100.00, the exercise price of an April 100 European put on Amazon.com was $100.00, and the time to maturity for both April 21, 2000 maturity options was 0.3556 years. What is the annual standard deviation of Amazon.com stock? What are the current prices of the call and put under the *continuous* annualization convention? What are the current prices of the call and put under the *discrete* annualization convention?

Solution Strategy. Collect Amazon.com's historical stock prices from Yahoo Finance! and calculate the annual standard deviation. Use the annual standard deviation and the annual riskfree rate to calculate the up movement / period, down movement / period, and riskfree rate / period. Extend the Binomial Option Pricing - Risk Neutral model to full-scale (50 periods) in order to achieve greater price accuracy.

FIGURE 17.9 Spreadsheet Model of Binomial Option Pricing - Estimating Volatility.

	A	B	C	D	E	F	G	H
1	**BINOMIAL OPTION PRICING**					**Estimating Volatility**		
2								
3	Date	Open	High	Low	Close	Volume	Discrete Return	Continuous Return
4	13-Dec-99	106.6250	106.6250	101.5000	102.5000	8,653,700	-3.93%	-4.00%
5	10-Dec-99	111.9375	112.0000	104.4375	106.6875	14,929,000	2.96%	2.91%
6	9-Dec-99	95.5000	113.0000	93.4375	103.6250	41,364,600	17.01%	15.71%
7	8-Dec-99	86.8125	93.0000	86.0000	88.5625	12,867,200	2.90%	2.86%
8	7-Dec-99	88.0000	88.0000	84.3750	86.0625	6,727,100	-1.92%	-1.94%
9	6-Dec-99	86.8750	89.8750	84.6875	87.7500	9,199,200	1.37%	1.36%
10	3-Dec-99	92.5000	93.3750	86.0625	86.5625	11,151,200	-2.81%	-2.85%
11	2-Dec-99	86.0000	91.3125	85.6250	89.0625	9,538,700	4.78%	4.67%
12	1-Dec-99	87.2500	87.8750	81.9688	85.0000	10,663,600	-0.07%	-0.07%
13	30-Nov-99	88.2656	88.8750	83.8125	85.0625	13,465,500	-5.94%	-6.13%
14	29-Nov-99	95.5000	96.8750	90.1250	90.4375	18,053,700	-2.89%	-2.93%
62	22-Sep-99	62.8750	66.5000	60.6875	66.0000	10,037,500	6.02%	5.85%
63	21-Sep-99	61.6250	63.9375	61.0000	62.2500	8,232,500	-0.80%	-0.80%
64	20-Sep-99	63.6875	65.0000	62.6875	62.7500	5,957,100	-1.67%	-1.68%
65	17-Sep-99	65.6250	66.0000	62.7500	63.8125	7,239,500	-2.20%	-2.23%
66	16-Sep-99	64.9375	65.8125	62.7500	65.2500	7,058,900	-0.48%	-0.48%
67	15-Sep-99	67.7500	67.9375	65.0000	65.5625	7,817,300	-0.66%	-0.67%
68	14-Sep-99	62.7500	66.4375	62.7500	66.0000	8,782,800	4.24%	4.16%
69	13-Sep-99	65.6250	66.0000	62.5000	63.3125	7,747,600		
70								
71					Standard Deviation (Daily)		5.68%	5.42%
72					Standard Deviation (Annual)		90.23%	86.07%

130

How To Build This Spreadsheet Model.

1. **Collect Historical Stock Price Data.** Go to <u>**Yahoo Finance!**</u> (<u>**quote.yahoo.com**</u>), enter **AMZN** (the ticker symbol for Amazon.com) in the **Get Quotes** box, click on **Chart**, at the bottom of the page click on **Other: historical quotes**, adjust the start date if you want more than three months of data, click on **Download Spreadsheet Format**, and save the **csv** file. Launch Excel and open the **csv** file.

2. **Calculate Discrete and Continuous Returns.** There are two conventions for calculating stock returns. A simple percent change yields the Discrete Return = [(Price on date t) - (Price on date t-1)] / (Price on date t-1). Enter **=(E4-E5)/E5** in cell **G4** and copy it down. The Continuous Return = LN[(Price on date t) / (Price on date t-1)]. Enter **=LN(E4/E5)** in cell **H4** and copy it down.

3. **Calculate the Daily and Annual Standard Deviation.** Use Excel's function **STDEV** to calculate the sample standard deviation of daily discrete returns and daily continuous returns. Enter **=STDEV(G4:G68)** in cell **G71** and copy the cell to **H71**. Convert the daily standard deviation to annual standard deviation by multiplying by the square root of the number of trading days in the year. By way of explanation, the stock variance is proportion to the units of time. Hence, the stock standard deviation is proportional to the square root of the units of time. The empirical evidence shows that is better to use trading days rather than calendar days, since trading days is a better predictor of stock volatility than calendar days. There are 252 trading days in the year, so we multiply by the square root of 252. Enter **=G71*SQRT(252)** in cell **G72** and copy it to the cell **H72**.

We find that Amazon.com's annual standard deviation is 90.23% based on discrete returns and is 86.07% based on continuous returns.

131

FIGURE 17.10 Spreadsheet Model of Binomial Option Pricing - Full-Scale Real Data - Call.

	A	B	C	D	E	F	AX	AY	AZ
1	**BINOMIAL OPTION PRICING**				Full-Scale Real Data				
2					Call	Continuous			
3	**Inputs**					Outputs			
4	Option Type: 1=Call, 0=Put	1			Time / Period	0.007			
5	Stock Price Now	$102.50			Riskfree Rate / Period	0.04%			
6	Standard Dev (Annual)	86.07%			Up Movement / Period	7.53%			
7	Riskfree Rate (Annual)	5.47%			Down Movement / Period	-7.00%			
8	Exercise Price	$100.00			Risk Neutral Probability	48.45%			
9	Time To Maturity (Years)	0.3556							
10	Number of Periods	50							
11	Annualization Convention: 1=Discrete, 0=Continuous	0							
12									
13			Now						Maturity
14		Period	0	1	2	3	4	48	49	50
15		Time	0.000	0.007	0.014	0.021	0.028	0.341	0.348	0.356
16										
17		Stock	$102.50	$110.22	$118.51	$127.44	$137.03	$3,340.75	$3,592.25	$3,862.69
18				$95.32	$102.50	$110.22	$118.51	$2,889.33	$3,106.85	$3,340.75
19					$88.65	$95.32	$102.50	$2,498.91	$2,687.04	$2,889.33
20						$82.44	$88.65	$2,161.24	$2,323.95	$2,498.91
21							$76.67	$1,869.20	$2,009.93	$2,161.24
22								$1,616.63	$1,738.33	$1,869.20
23								$1,398.18	$1,503.44	$1,616.63
24								$1,209.25	$1,300.29	$1,398.18
25								$1,045.85	$1,124.59	$1,209.25
26								$904.53	$972.63	$1,045.85
27								$782.31	$841.20	$904.53
28								$676.60	$727.53	$782.31
29								$585.17	$629.23	$676.60
30								$506.10	$544.20	$585.17
31								$437.71	$470.67	$506.10
32								$378.57	$407.07	$437.71
33								$327.41	$352.06	$378.57
34								$283.17	$304.49	$327.41
35								$244.91	$263.35	$283.17
36								$211.82	$227.76	$244.91

4. **Start with the Risk Neutral Spreadsheet and Freeze Panes.** Open the spreadsheet that you created for Binomial Option Pricing – Risk Neutral and immediately save the spreadsheet under a new name using the **File | Save As** command. It will be helpful for navigation purposes to lock in both column titles and row titles. Select cell **G16** and click on **Window | Freeze Panes**.

5. **Rearrange the Inputs.** Select the range **A6:B7** and drag the range (hover the cursor over the lower highlighted line, click on the left mouse button, and hold it down while you move it) to cell **E6**. Select the range **A8:B8** and drag the range to cell **E5**. Select the range **A9:B11** and drag the range to cell **A8**. Select the range **E4:F4** and drag the range to cell **E8**.

6. **Enter the New Inputs.** Enter the Full-Scale Real Data inputs in the range **B4:B11** as shown in **Figure 2**. The value in cell **B11** serves as a switch between the Discrete and Continuous Annualization Conventions. To accommodate both annualization conventions, enter

=IF(B11=1,90.23%,86.07%) in cell **B6** for the Annual Standard Deviation. To highlight which annualization convention is in use, enter **=IF($B$11=1,"Discrete","Continuous")** in cell **E2**.

7. **Calculate the New Outputs.** Calculate four new "per period" outputs:
   o **Time / Period** = (Time To Maturity) / (Number of Periods). Enter **=B9/B10** in cell **F4**.
   o **Riskfree Rate / Period** = (Annual Riskfree Rate) * (Time / Period) under the discrete annualization convention or = exp[(Annual Riskfree Rate) * (Time / Period)] -1 under the continuous annualization convention. Enter **=IF($B$11=1,B7*F4,EXP(B7*F4)-1)** in cell **F5**.
   o **Up Movement / Period** = (Annual Standard Deviation) * Square Root (Time / Period) under the discrete annualization convention or = exp[(Annual Standard Deviation) * Square Root (Time / Period)] -1 under the continuous annualization convention. Enter **=IF($B$11=1,B6*SQRT(F4),EXP(B6*SQRT(F4))-1)** in cell **F6**.
   o **Down Movement / Period** = -(Annual Standard Deviation) * Square Root (Time / Period) under the discrete annualization convention or = exp[-(Annual Standard Deviation) * Square Root (Time / Period)] -1 under the continuous annualization convention. Enter **=IF($B$11=1,-B6*SQRT(F4),EXP(-B6^SQRT(F4))-1)** in cell **F7**. The up movement / period and down movement / period are calibrated to correspond to the stock's annual standard deviation. It is not necessary to calibrate them to the stock's expected return.[1]

8. **Extend The Periods and Time to 50 Periods.** Select the range **B14:C14**, grab the fill bar (hover the mouse over the lower-right corner of the selection - when it turns to a "+" sign, click the left mouse button), and fill in the range **D14:AZ14**. Select the cell **B15** and copy it to the range **C15:AZ15**.

9. **Extend The Stock Price Tree to 50 Periods.** Add some rows to make space between the Stock Price Tree and the Option Price Tree. Select the range **A26:A67** and click on **Insert | Rows**. Then, copy cell **C17** to the 50-by-51 range **C17:AZ67**. A binomial tree will form in the triangular area from **C17** to **AZ17** to **AZ67**.

---

[1] At full-scale (50 periods), the binomial option price is very insensitive to the expected return of the stock. For example, suppose that you calibrated this Amazon.com case to an annual expected return of 10%. Just add 10%*F4 to the formulas for the up and down movements / period. So the up movement / period in cell F6 would become =IF($B$11=1,10%*F4+B6*SQRT(F4),EXP(10%*F4+B6*SQRT(F4))-1) and the down movement / period in cell F7 would become =IF($B$11=1,10%*F4-B6*SQRT(F4),EXP(10%*F4-B6*SQRT(F4))-1). This changes the option price by less than 1/100th of one penny! In the (Black Scholes) limit as the number of (sub)periods goes to infinity, the option price becomes totally insensitive to the expected return of the stock. Because of this insensitivity, the conventions for calculating the up movement / period and down movement / period ignore the expected return of the stock.

133

FIGURE 17.11 Spreadsheet of Binomial Option Pricing - Full-Scale Real Data - Call (Continued).

	A	B	C	D	E	F	AX	AY	AZ
1	**BINOMIAL OPTION PRICING**			**Full-Scale Real Data**					
2				Call	Continuous				
3	Inputs				Outputs				
4	Option Type: 1=Call, 0=Put	1			Time / Period	0.007			
5	Stock Price Now	$102.50			Riskfree Rate / Period	0.04%			
6	Standard Dev (Annual)	86.07%			Up Movement / Period	7.53%			
7	Riskfree Rate (Annual)	5.47%			Down Movement / Period	-7.00%			
8	Exercise Price	$100.00			Risk Neutral Probability	48.45%			
9	Time To Maturity (Years)	0.3556							
10	Number of Periods	50							
11	Annualization Convention: 1=Discrete, 0=Continuous	0							
12									
13			Now						Maturity
14	Period	0	1	2	3	4	48	49	50
15	Time	0.000	0.007	0.014	0.021	0.028	0.341	0.348	0.356
68									
69	Call	$22.61	$27.48	$33.15	$39.68	$47.15	$3,240.82	$3,492.29	$3,762.69
70			$18.04	$22.17	$27.04	$32.70	$2,789.40	$3,006.89	$3,240.75
71				$14.17	$17.62	$21.73	$2,398.98	$2,587.07	$2,789.33
72					$10.94	$13.77	$2,061.32	$2,223.99	$2,398.91
73						$8.28	$1,769.28	$1,909.97	$2,061.24
74							$1,516.71	$1,638.37	$1,769.20
75							$1,298.26	$1,403.48	$1,516.63
76							$1,109.33	$1,200.33	$1,298.18
77							$945.93	$1,024.63	$1,109.25
78							$804.61	$872.67	$945.85
79							$682.38	$741.24	$804.53
80							$576.68	$627.57	$682.31
81							$485.25	$529.27	$576.60
82							$406.18	$444.24	$485.17
83							$337.79	$370.71	$406.10
84							$278.65	$307.11	$337.71
85							$227.49	$252.10	$278.57
86							$183.25	$204.53	$227.41
87							$144.99	$163.39	$183.17
88							$111.89	$127.80	$144.91

10. **Extend The Option Payoffs At Maturity to 50 Periods.** Copy the old payoffs at maturity starting in cell **J69** and to the new payoffs at maturity range **AZ69:AZ119**.

11. **Extend The Option Price Tree to 50 Periods.** Copy cell **B69** to the range **B69:AY118**. A binomial tree will form in the triangular area from **B69** to **AZ69** to **AZ119**.

We see that the Full-Scale Real Data model predicts an European call price of $22.61. This is only one cent different that what the Black-Scholes model predicts given identical inputs! Now let's check the put.

FIGURE 17.12 Spreadsheet Model of Binomial Option Pricing - Full-Scale Real Data - Put Option.

	A	B	C	D	E	F	AX	AY	AZ
1	**BINOMIAL OPTION PRICING**			**Full-Scale Real Data**					
2				Put	Continuous				
3	**Inputs**				**Outputs**				
4	Option Type: 1=Call, 0=Put	0		Time / Period		0.007			
5	Stock Price Now	$102.50		Riskfree Rate / Period		0.04%			
6	Standard Dev (Annual)	86.07%		Up Movement / Period		7.53%			
7	Riskfree Rate (Annual)	5.47%		Down Movement / Period		-7.00%			
8	Exercise Price	$100.00		Risk Neutral Probability		48.45%			
9	Time To Maturity (Years)	0.3556							
10	Number of Periods	50							
11	Annualization Convention: 1=Discrete, 0=Continuous	0							
12									
13		Now							Maturity
14	Period	0	1	2	3	4	48	49	50
15	Time	0.000	0.007	0.014	0.021	0.028	0.341	0.348	0.356
16									
17	Stock	$102.50	$110.22	$118.51	$127.44	$137.03	$3,340.75	$3,592.25	$3,862.69
18			$95.32	$102.50	$110.22	$118.51	$2,889.33	$3,106.85	$3,340.75
19				$88.65	$95.32	$102.50	$2,498.91	$2,687.04	$2,889.33
20					$82.44	$88.65	$2,161.24	$2,323.95	$2,498.91
21						$76.67	$1,869.20	$2,009.93	$2,161.24
22							$1,616.63	$1,738.33	$1,869.20
23							$1,398.18	$1,503.44	$1,616.63
24							$1,209.25	$1,300.29	$1,398.18
25							$1,045.85	$1,124.59	$1,209.25
26							$904.53	$972.63	$1,045.85
27							$782.31	$841.20	$904.53
28							$676.60	$727.53	$782.31
29							$585.17	$629.23	$676.60
30							$506.10	$544.20	$585.17
31							$437.71	$470.67	$506.10
32							$378.57	$407.07	$437.71
33							$327.41	$352.06	$378.57
34							$283.17	$304.49	$327.41
35							$244.91	$263.35	$283.17
36							$211.82	$227.76	$244.91

12. **Put Option.** Enter **0** in cell **B4**.

	A	B	C	D	E	F	AX	AY	AZ
1	**BINOMIAL OPTION PRICING**			Full-Scale Real Data					
2				Put	Continuous				
3	**Inputs**				Outputs				
4	Option Type: 1=Call, 0=Put	0		Time / Period		0.007			
5	Stock Price Now	$102.50		Riskfree Rate / Period		0.04%			
6	Standard Dev (Annual)	86.07%		Up Movement / Period		7.53%			
7	Riskfree Rate (Annual)	5.47%		Down Movement / Period		-7.00%			
8	Exercise Price	$100.00		Risk Neutral Probability		48.45%			
9	Time To Maturity (Years)	0.3556							
10	Number of Periods	50							
11	Annualization Convention: 1=Discrete, 0=Continuous	0							
12									
13			Now						Maturity
14		Period	0	1	2	3	4	48	49	50
15		Time	0.000	0.007	0.014	0.021	0.028	0.341	0.348	0.356
68										
69		Put	$18.18	$15.38	$12.79	$10.44	$8.35	$0.00	$0.00	$0.00
70				$20.83	$17.82	$15.01	$12.41	$0.00	$0.00	$0.00
71					$23.67	$20.49	$17.46	$0.00	$0.00	$0.00
72						$26.68	$23.35	$0.00	$0.00	$0.00
73							$29.84	$0.00	$0.00	$0.00
74								$0.00	$0.00	$0.00
75								$0.00	$0.00	$0.00
76								$0.00	$0.00	$0.00
77								$0.00	$0.00	$0.00
78								$0.00	$0.00	$0.00
79								$0.00	$0.00	$0.00
80								$0.00	$0.00	$0.00
81								$0.00	$0.00	$0.00
82								$0.00	$0.00	$0.00
83								$0.00	$0.00	$0.00
84								$0.00	$0.00	$0.00
85								$0.00	$0.00	$0.00
86								$0.00	$0.00	$0.00
87								$0.00	$0.00	$0.00
88								$0.00	$0.00	$0.00

We see that the Full-Scale Real Data model predicts an European put price of $18.18. This is only one cent different that what the Black-Scholes model predicts given identical inputs! The accuracy of the binomial model can be increased to any desired degree by increasing the number of periods. Whereas the Black Scholes model (and its natural extensions) is limited to a narrow range of derivatives, the Binomial Option Pricing model can be extended to price *any* derivative security (any type, any underlying asset(s), any underlying cash flows, any derivative payoffs).

Problems

Skill-Building Problems.

1. The current stock price of a company is $37.50, the potential up movement / period of the stock price is 22.0%, the potential down movement / period of the stock price is -13.00%, the riskfree rate is 4.0% per period, the exercise price of an one-period, European call option on the stock is $39.00, the exercise price of an one-period, European put option on the stock is $39.00, the time

to maturity for both options is 0.58 years, and the number of periods for both options is 1. Determine the replicating portfolio and the current prices of the call and put.

2. The current stock price of a company is $23.75, the potential up movement / period of the stock price is 27.0%, the potential down movement / period of the stock price is -9.00%, the riskfree rate is 5.0% per period, the exercise price of an European call option on the stock is $22.00, the exercise price of an European put option on the stock is $22.00, the time to maturity for both options is 0.39 years, and the number of periods for both options is 8. Determine the replicating portfolio on each date and the current prices of the call and put.

3. The current stock price of a company is $43.25, the potential up movement / period of the stock price is 19.0%, the potential down movement / period of the stock price is -14.00%, the riskfree rate is 4.0% per period, the exercise price of an European call option on the stock is $45.00, the exercise price of an European put option on the stock is $45.00, the time to maturity for both options is 0.83 years, and the number of periods for both options is 8. Determine the risk neutral proability and the current prices of the call and put.

4. Collect Cisco Systems' historical stock prices from Yahoo Finance! From the financial media, collect the current stock price of Cisco Systems, the exercise price of an European call option on Cisco Systems, the exercise price of an European put option on Cisco Systems, the time to maturity for both options, and the yield on a riskfree Treasury Bill maturing as close as possible to the maturity date of the options. Determine:

(a.) What is the annual standard deviation of Cisco Systems stock?

(b.) What is the risk neutral probability and the current prices of the call and put under the *continuous* annualization convention?

(c.) What is the risk neutral probability and the current prices of the call and put under the *discrete* annualization convention?

Skill-Extending Problems.

5. Extend the Binomial Option Pricing model to incorporate a $2.00 / share dividend that will be paid out in period 5. In other words, all of the period 5 stock prices will be reduced by $2.00. Determine the current prices of the call and put.

6. Extend the Binomial Option Pricing model to analyze Digital Options. The only thing which needs   to   be   changed   is   the   option's   payoff   at   maturity.
(a.) For a Digital Call, the Payoff At Maturity = $1.00 When Stock Price At Mat > Exercise Price
Or $0.00   Otherwise.
(b.) For a Digital Put, the Payoff At Maturity = $1.00 When Stock Price At Mat < Exercise Price
Or $0.00 Otherwise.

7. Extend the Binomial Option Pricing model to determine how fast the binomial option price converges to the price in the Black Scholes Option Pricing model. Reduce the Full-Scale model to a 10 period model and to a 20 period model. Increase the 50 period model to a 100 period model. Then for the same inputs, compare call and put prices of the 10 period, 20 period, 50 period, 100 period, and Black-Scholes models.

8. Extend the Binomial Option Pricing model to determine how fast the binomial option price with averaging of adjacent odd and even numbers of periods converges to the price in the Black Scholes Option Pricing. As you increase the number of periods in the binomial model, it oscillates between overshooting and undershooting the true price. A simple technique to increase price efficiency is to average adjacent odd and even numbers of periods. For example, average the 10 period call price and the 11 period call price. Reduce the Full-Scale model to a 10 period, 11 period, 20 period, and 21 period model. Increase the 50 period model to a 51 period, 100 period, and 101 period model. Then for the same inputs, compare call and put prices of the average of the 10 and 11 period models, 20 and 21 period models, 50 and 51 period models, 100 and 101 period models, and Black-Scholes model.

Live In-class Problems.

9. Given the partial Single Period spreadsheet **BinosinZ.xls**, do steps **4 Option Payoffs at Maturity, 5 Create a Replicating Portfolio,** and **6 Calculate the Option Price Now**.

10. Given the partial Multi-Period spreadsheet **BinomulZ.xls**, do step **7 The Option Price Tree**.

11. Given the partial Risk Neutral spreadsheet **BinoneuZ.xls**, do step **2 Risk Neutral Probability** and **3 The Option Price Tree**.

12. Given the partial Full-Scale Real Data spreadsheet **BinofulZ.xls**, do step **7 Calculate the New Outputs**.

18 Black Scholes Option Pricing

18.1 Basics

Problem. On December 13, 1999, the stock price of Amazon.com was $102.50, the continuous annual standard deviation was 86.07%, the yield on a riskfree Treasury Bill maturing on April 20th was 5.47%, the exercise price of an April 100 European call on Amazon.com was $100.00, the exercise price of an April 100 European put on Amazon.com was $100.00, and the time to maturity for both April 21st maturity options was 0.3556 years. What are the current prices of the call and put?

FIGURE 18.1 Spreadsheet for Black Scholes Option Pricing - Basics.

	A	B	C	D	E	F
1	BLACK SCHOLES OPTION PRICING				Basics	
2						
3	**Inputs**					
4	Stock Price Now (P)	$102.50				
5	Standard Dev - Annual (σ)	86.07%				
6	Riskfree Rate - Annual (k_{RF})	5.47%				
7	Exercise Price (X)	$100.00				
8	Time To Maturity - Years (t)	0.3556				
9						
10	**Outputs**					
11	d1	0.343				
12	d2	-0.171				
13	N(d1)	0.634				
14	N(d2)	0.432				
15	Call Price (V)	$22.68				
16						
17	-d1	-0.343				
18	-d2	0.171				
19	N(-d1)	0.366				
20	N(-d2)	0.568				
21	Put Price	$18.17				

How To Build This Spreadsheet Model.

1. **Inputs.** Enter the inputs described above into the range **B4:B8**.

2. **d1 and d2 Formulas.** The d_1 formula is $\left(\ln\left(P/X\right)+\left(k_{RF}+\sigma^2/2\right)\cdot t\right)/\left(\sigma\cdot\sqrt{t}\right)$. In cell **B11**, enter

   =(LN(B4/B7)+(B6+B5^2/2)*B8)/(B5*SQRT(B8)).

   The d_2 formula is $d_1-\sigma\sqrt{t}$. In cell **B12**, enter
   =B11-B5*SQRT(B8).

3. **Cumulative Normal Formulas.** Enter $N(d_1)$ using the cumulative normal function **NORMSDIST** in cell **B13** =NORMSDIST(B11). Copy the cell **B13** to cell **B14** or enter $N(d_2)$ using the cumulative normal function **NORMSDIST** in cell **B14** =NORMSDIST(B12).

139

4. **European Call Price Formula.** The Black-Scholes call formula is $V = PN(d_1) - Xe^{-k_{RF}t}N(d_2)$. In cell **B15**, enter

   =B4*B13-B7*EXP(-B6*B8)*B14

   We see that the Black-Scholes model predicts an European call price of $22.60. This is only one cent different that what the Binomial Option Pricing - Full-Scale Real Data model predicts given identical inputs! Now let's do the put.

5. **-d1 and -d2 Formulas.** For the labels, enter '-d1 in A17 and '-d2 A18. The ' tells Excel that it is a label, not a formula. For the two put formula terms, they are just opposite in sign from their call formula counterparts. Enter =-B11 in B17 and =-B12 in B18.

6. **Cumulative Normal Formulas.** Enter $N(-d_1)$ using the cumulative normal function **NORMSDIST** in cell **B19**

   =NORMSDIST(B17)

   Copy the cell **B19** to cell **B20** or enter $N(-d_2)$ using the cumulative normal function **NORMSDIST** in cell **B20**

   =NORMSDIST(B18)

7. **European Put Price Formula.** The Black-Scholes put formula is $Put = -PN(-d_1) + Xe^{-k_{RF}t}N(-d_2)$. In cell **B21**, enter

   =-B4*B19+B7*EXP(-B6*B8)*B20

We see that the Black-Scholes model predicts an European put price of $18.17. This is only one cent different that what the Binomial Option Pricing - Full-Scale Real Data model predicts given identical inputs! The advantage of the Black Scholes model (and its natural extensions) is that it is quick and easy to calculate, but the disadvantage is that it is limited to a narrow range of derivatives.

18.2 Continuous Dividend

Problem. Amazon.com doesn't pay a dividend, but suppose that it did. Specifically, suppose that Amazon.com paid dividends in tiny amounts on a continuous basis throughout the year at a 3.00% / year rate. What would be the new price of the April 100 European call and April 100 European put?

Solution Strategy. Modify the Basics spreadsheet to incorporate the continuous dividend version of the Black Scholes model.

FIGURE 18.2 Spreadsheet for Black Scholes Option Pricing - Continuous Dividend.

	A	B	C	D	E	F	G	H
1	**BLACK SCHOLES OPTION PRICING**				**Continuous Dividend**			
2								
3	**Inputs**							
4	Stock Price Now (P)	$102.50						
5	Standard Dev - Annual (σ)	86.07%						
6	Riskfree Rate - Annual (k$_{RF}$)	5.47%						
7	Exercise Price (X)	$100.00						
8	Time To Maturity - Years (t)	0.3556						
9	Dividend yield (d)	3.00%						
10								
11	**Outputs**							
12	d1	0.322						
13	d2	-0.191						
14	N(d1)	0.626						
15	N(d2)	0.424						
16	Call Price (V)	$21.91						
17								
18	-d1	-0.322						
19	-d2	0.191						
20	N(-d1)	0.374						
21	N(-d2)	0.576						
22	Put Price	$16.57						

How To Build This Spreadsheet Model.

1. **Start with the Basics Spreadsheet, Add A Row, and Enter The Dividend Yield.** Open the spreadsheet that you created for Black Scholes Option Pricing – Basics and immediately save the spreadsheet under a new name using the **File | Save As** command. Add a row by selecting the cell **A9** and clicking on **Insert | Rows.** Enter the dividend yield in cell **A9.**

2. **Modify the d1 Formula.** In the continuous dividend version, the d_1 formula is modified by subtracting the continuous dividend yield d in the numerator. The new d_1 formula is $\left(\ln\left(P/X\right)+\left(k_{RF}-d+\sigma^2/2\right)\cdot t\right)/\left(\sigma\cdot\sqrt{t}\right)$. In cell **B12,** enter

$$=(LN(B4/B7)+(B6-B9+B5^2/2)*B8)/(B5*SQRT(B8))$$

3. **Modify the Call Price Formula.** The modified call formula is $V = Pe^{-dt}N\left(d_1\right)-Xe^{-k_{RF}t}N\left(d_2\right)$, where d is the continuous dividend yield. In cell **B16,** enter

$$=B4*EXP(-B9*B8)*B14-B7*EXP(-B6*B8)*B15$$

We see that the Black-Scholes Option Pricing - Continuous Dividend model predicts an European call price of $21.91. This is a drop of 69 cents from the no dividend version. Now let's do the put.

4. **Modify the Put Price Formula.** The modified put formula is $Put = -Pe^{-dt}N\left(-d_1\right)+Xe^{-k_{RF}t}N\left(-d_2\right)$. In cell **B22,** enter

$$=-B4*EXP(-B9*B8)*B20+B7*EXP(-B6*B8)*B21$$

We see that the Black-Scholes model predicts an European put price of $18.57. This is a rise of 40 cents from the no dividend version.

18.3 Dynamic Chart

If you increased the standard deviation of the stock, what would happen to the price of the call option? If you increased the time to maturity, what would happen to the price of the call? You can answer these questions and more by creating an *Dynamic Chart* using "spinners." Spinners are up-arrow / down-arrow buttons that allow you to easily change the inputs to the model with the click of a mouse. Then the spreadsheet recalculates the model and instantly redraws the model outputs on the graph.

FIGURE 18.3 Spreadsheet model for Black Scholes Option Pricing - Dynamic Chart - Call Option.

	A	B	C	D	E	F	G	H	I	J
1	BLACK SCHOLES OPTION PRICING					Dynamic Chart			Call	
2										
3	Inputs									
4	Option Type: 1=Call, 0=Put	1	▲ ▼	1						
5	Standard Dev - Annual (σ)	90%	▲ ▼	9						
6	Riskfree Rate - Annual (k_RF)	6.0%	▲ ▼	6						
7	Exercise Price (X)	$100.00	▲ ▼	100						
8	Time To Maturity - Yrs (t)	0.40	▲ ▼	4						
9										
10										
11										
12	Dynamic Chart Outputs									
13	Stock Price Now (P)	$0.01	$20.00	$40.00	$60.00	$80.00	$100.00	$120.00	$140.00	$160.00
14	Option Price	$0.00	$0.02	$0.88	$4.66	$12.30	$23.40	$37.16	$52.82	$69.81
15	Intrinsic Value									
16										
17	d1	-15.815	-2.493	-1.279	-0.568	-0.064	0.327	0.647	0.917	1.151
18	d2	-16.386	-3.064	-1.849	-1.138	-0.634	-0.243	0.076	0.347	0.581
19	N(d1)	0.000	0.006	0.101	0.285	0.475	0.628	0.741	0.820	0.875
20	N(d2)	0.000	0.001	0.032	0.127	0.263	0.404	0.530	0.636	0.719
21	Call Price (V)	$0.00	$0.02	$0.88	$4.66	$12.30	$23.40	$37.16	$52.82	$69.81
22										
23	-d1	15.815	2.493	1.279	0.568	0.064	-0.327	-0.647	-0.917	-1.151
24	-d2	16.386	3.064	1.849	1.138	0.634	0.243	-0.076	-0.347	-0.581
25	N(-d1)	1.000	0.994	0.899	0.715	0.525	0.372	0.259	0.180	0.125
26	N(-d2)	1.000	0.999	0.968	0.873	0.737	0.596	0.470	0.364	0.281
27	Put Price	$97.61	$77.64	$58.50	$42.28	$29.92	$21.02	$14.78	$10.44	$7.43

How To Build This Spreadsheet Model.

1. **Start with the Basics Spreadsheet, Rearrange the Rows, and Add A Switch.** Open the spreadsheet that you created for Black Scholes Option Pricing – Basics and immediately save the spreadsheet under a new name using the **File | Save As** command. Add six rows by selecting the range **A11:A16**, clicking on **Insert | Rows**. Select the range **A4:B4** and drag the range (hover the cursor over the lower highlighted line, click on the left mouse button, and hold it down while you move it) to cell **A13**. Enter **1** in cell **B4**. This will serve as a switch between a call option and a

put option. To highlight which type of option is being graphed, enter =IF($B$4=1,"Call","Put") in cell **I1**.

2. **Increase Row Height for the Spinners.** Select the range **A4:A8**. Then click on **Format | Row | Height** from the main menu. Enter a height of **30** and click on **OK**.

3. **Display the Forms Toolbar.** Select **View | Toolbars | Forms** from the main menu.

4. **Create the Spinners.** Look for the up-arrow / down-arrow button on the **Forms** toolbar (which will display the word "**Spinner**" if you hover the cursor over it) and click on it. Then draw the box for a spinner from the upper left corner of cell **C4** down to the lower right corner of the cell. Then a spinner appears in the cell **C4**. Right click on the spinner (press the right mouse button while the cursor is above the spinner) and a small menu pops up. Click on **Copy**. Then select the cell **C5** and click on **Paste**. This creates an identical spinner in the cell **C5**. Repeat the process three times more. Select cell **C6** and click on **Paste**. Select cell **C7** and click on **Paste**. Select cell **C8** and click on **Paste**. You now have five spinners down column C.

5. **Create The Cell Links.** Right click on the first spinner in the cell **C4** and a small menu pops up. Click on **Format Control** and a dialog box pops up. Click on the **Control** tab, then enter the cell link **D4** in the **Cell link** edit box and click on **OK**. Repeat this procedure for the other four spinners. Link the spinner in cell **C5** to cell **D5**. Link the spinner in cell **C6** to cell **D6**. Link the spinner in cell **C7** to cell **D7**. Link the spinner in cell **C8** to cell **D8**. Test your spinners by clicking on the up-arrows and down-arrows of the spinners to see how they change the values in the linked cells.

6. **Create Scaled Inputs.** The values in the linked cells are always integers, but they can be scaled appropriately to the problem at hand. Restrict the value in cell **B4** to be either 1 or 0 by entering =IF(D4>1,1,D4). In cell **B5**, enter =D5/10+0.001. In cell **B6**, enter =D6/100. In cell **B7**, enter =D7. In cell **B8**, enter =D8/10+0.001. The additional terms **+0.001** in cells **B5** and **B8**, prevent the scaled value from going to zero when the linked cell goes to zero. When the standard deviation or a time to maturity literally became zero, then the Black Scholes call and put formulas blow-up.

7. **Create Stock Price Inputs.** In the range **B13:L13**, enter the values **0.01, 20, 40, 60, ..., 200**. In cell **M13**, enter **0.01**. In cell **N13**, enter **=B7**. In cell **O13**, enter **=L13**.

8. **Convert The Input Cell References To Absolute References.** In order to convert the input cell references contained in the formulas in cells **B17**, **B18**, **B21**, and **B27** to absolute references. That is, put $s in front of any references to the *input cells* in the range **B4:B8**. When you are done, the formula in cell **B17** will look like =(LN(B13/$B$7)+($B$6+$B$5^2/2)*$B$8)/($B$5*SQRT($B$8)). Cell **B18** will look like =B17-$B$5*SQRT($B$8). Cell **B21** will look like =B13*B19-$B$7*EXP(-$B$6*$B$8)*B20. Cell **B27** will look like =-B13*B25+$B$7*EXP(-$B$6*$B$8)*B26.

9. **Copy The Formulas.** Select the formulas in the range **B17:B27** and copy them to the range **C17:O27**.

10. **Option Price.** Reference the Call Price or the Put Price depending on which type of option is selected in cell **B4**. Enter =IF($B$4=1,B21,B27) in cell **B14** and copy the cell to the range **C14:L14**.

11. **Add The Intrinsic Value.** If the option was maturing now, rather than later, its payoff would be: For a call, **Max (Stock Price Now - Exercise Price, 0)**. For a put, **Max (Exercise Price - Stock Price Now, 0)**. This is the so-called "Intrinsic Value" of the option. In cell **M15**, enter the formula **=IF(B4=1,MAX(M13-$B$7,0),MAX($B$7-M13,0))** and copy this cell to the range **N15:O15**.

FIGURE 18.4 Option Price and Intrinsic Value.

	A	K	L	M	N	O
12	**Dynamic Chart Outputs**					
13	Stock Price Now (P)	$180.00	$200.00	$0.01	$100.00	$200.00
14	Option Price	$87.71	$106.24			
15	Intrinsic Value			$0.00	$0.00	$100.00

12. **Graph the Option Price and Intrinsic Value.** Select the range B13:O15. Next choose **Insert | Chart** from the main menu. Select an **XY(Scatter)** chart type and make other selections to complete the Chart Wizard. Place the graph in the range **E2:J11**.

FIGURE 18.5 Spreadsheet model for Black Scholes Option Pricing - Dynamic Chart - Put Option.

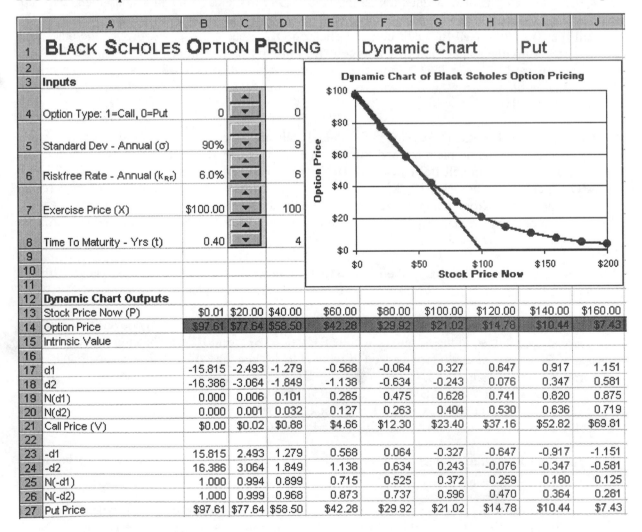

	A	B	C	D	E	F	G	H	I	J
1	**BLACK SCHOLES OPTION PRICING**					**Dynamic Chart**			**Put**	
3	**Inputs**									
4	Option Type: 1=Call, 0=Put	0		0						
5	Standard Dev - Annual (σ)	90%		9						
6	Riskfree Rate - Annual (k_{RF})	6.0%		6						
7	Exercise Price (X)	$100.00		100						
8	Time To Maturity - Yrs (t)	0.40		4						
12	**Dynamic Chart Outputs**									
13	Stock Price Now (P)	$0.01	$20.00	$40.00	$60.00	$80.00	$100.00	$120.00	$140.00	$160.00
14	Option Price	$97.61	$77.64	$58.50	$42.28	$29.92	$21.02	$14.78	$10.44	$7.43
15	Intrinsic Value									
17	d1	-15.815	-2.493	-1.279	-0.568	-0.064	0.327	0.647	0.917	1.151
18	d2	-16.386	-3.064	-1.849	-1.138	-0.634	-0.243	0.076	0.347	0.581
19	N(d1)	0.000	0.006	0.101	0.285	0.475	0.628	0.741	0.820	0.875
20	N(d2)	0.000	0.001	0.032	0.127	0.263	0.404	0.530	0.636	0.719
21	Call Price (V)	$0.00	$0.02	$0.88	$4.66	$12.30	$23.40	$37.16	$52.82	$69.81
23	-d1	15.815	2.493	1.279	0.568	0.064	-0.327	-0.647	-0.917	-1.151
24	-d2	16.386	3.064	1.849	1.138	0.634	0.243	-0.076	-0.347	-0.581
25	N(-d1)	1.000	0.994	0.899	0.715	0.525	0.372	0.259	0.180	0.125
26	N(-d2)	1.000	0.999	0.968	0.873	0.737	0.596	0.470	0.364	0.281
27	Put Price	$97.61	$77.64	$58.50	$42.28	$29.92	$21.02	$14.78	$10.44	$7.43

Your *Dynamic Chart* allows you to change Black-Scholes inputs and instantly see the impact on a graph of the option price and intrinsic value. This allows you to perform instant experiments on the Black-Scholes option pricing model. Below is a list of experiments that you might want to perform:

- What happens when the standard deviation is increased?
- What happens when the time to maturity is increased?
- What happens when the exercise price is increased?
- What happens when the riskfree rate is increased?
- What happens when the dividend yield is increased?
- What happens when the standard deviation is really close to zero?
- What happens when the time to maturity is really close to zero?

Notice that the Black-Scholes option price is usually greater than the payoff you would obtain if the option was maturing today (the "intrinsic value"). This extra value is called the "Time Value" of the option. Given your result in the last experiment above, can you explain *why* the extra value is called the "Time Value"?

18.4 Implied Volatility

Problem. On December 14, 1999, the S&P 500 index closed at 1,403. European call and put options on the S&P 500 index with the exercise prices show below traded for the following prices:

Exercise price	1,350	1,375	1,400	1,425	1,450
Call price	$81	$66 1/4	$46	$31	$19 1/4
Put price	$18	$23 5/8	$30 1/2	$41 1/2	$55

These call options mature on January 21, 2000 (the third Friday of January). The S&P 500 portfolio pays a continuous dividend yield of 1.18% per year and the annual yield on a Treasury Bill which matures on January 20th is 5.34% per year. What is the implied volatility of each of these calls and puts? What pattern do these implied volatilities follow across exercise prices and between calls vs. puts?

Solution Strategy. Calculate the difference between the observed option price and the option price predicted by the continuous dividend yield version of the Black-Scholes model using a dummy value for the stock volatility. Have the Excel Solver tool adjust the stock volatility by trial and error until the difference between the observed price and the model price is equal to zero (within a very small error tolerance).

FIGURE 18.6 Spreadsheet for Black Scholes Option Pricing - Implied Volatility.

	A	B	C	D	E	F	G	H	I	J	K
1	**BLACK SCHOLES OPTION PRICING**					**Implied Volatility**					
2											
3	**Inputs**										
4	Option Type: 1=Call, 0=Put	1	1	1	1	1	0	0	0	0	0
5	Stock Price Now (P)	$1,403	$1,403	$1,403	$1,403	$1,403	$1,403	$1,403	$1,403	$1,403	$1,403
6	Standard Dev - Annual (σ)	5.34%	5.34%	5.34%	5.34%	5.34%	5.34%	5.34%	5.34%	5.34%	5.34%
7	Riskfree Rate - Annual (k_{RF})	$1,350	$1,375	$1,400	$1,425	$1,450	$1,350	$1,375	$1,400	$1,425	$1,450
8	Exercise Price (X)	0.1028	0.1028	0.1028	0.1028	0.1028	0.1028	0.1028	0.1028	0.1028	0.1028
9	Dividend yield (d)	1.18%	1.18%	1.18%	1.18%	1.18%	1.18%	1.18%	1.18%	1.18%	1.18%
10	Observed Option Price	$81.00	$66.25	$46.00	$31.00	$19.25	$18.00	$23.63	$30.50	$41.50	$55.00
11											
12	**Outputs**										
13	d1	0.556	0.329	0.125	-0.129	-0.419	0.612	0.389	0.136	-0.161	-0.504
14	d2	0.472	0.244	0.051	-0.198	-0.482	0.537	0.320	0.073	-0.219	-0.558
15	N(d1)	0.711	0.629	0.550	0.448	0.338	0.730	0.651	0.554	0.436	0.307
16	N(d2)	0.682	0.596	0.520	0.422	0.315	0.704	0.625	0.529	0.413	0.288
17	Call Price (V)	$81.00	$66.25	$46.00	$31.00	$19.25	$76.86	$57.62	$39.63	$25.77	$14.41
18											
19	-d1	-0.556	-0.329	-0.125	0.129	0.419	-0.612	-0.389	-0.136	0.161	0.504
20	-d2	-0.472	-0.244	-0.051	0.198	0.482	-0.537	-0.320	-0.073	0.219	0.558
21	N(-d1)	0.289	0.371	0.450	0.552	0.662	0.270	0.349	0.446	0.564	0.693
22	N(-d2)	0.318	0.404	0.480	0.578	0.685	0.296	0.375	0.471	0.587	0.712
23	Put Price	$22.14	$32.25	$36.87	$46.73	$59.84	$18.00	$23.62	$30.50	$41.50	$55.00
24											
25	**Solver**										
26	Differ (observed - model)	4E-07	3E-08	9E-07	2E-08	1E-07	7E-08	7E-08	1E-08	8E-07	1E-07
27	Implied Volatility from Calls	26.03%	26.73%	23.11%	21.28%	19.78%					
28	Implied Volatility from Puts						23.30%	21.60%	19.52%	18.33%	16.78%

How To Build This Spreadsheet Model.

1. **Start with the Continuous Dividend Spreadsheet, Rearrange The Rows, and Add A Switch.** Open the spreadsheet that you created for Black Scholes Option Pricing – Continuous Dividend and immediately save the spreadsheet under a new name using the **File | Save As** command. Add a row by selecting the cell **A4** and clicking on **Insert | Rows**. Select the range **A6:B6** and drag the range (hover the cursor over the lower highlighted line, click on the left mouse button, and hold it down while you move it) to cell **A27**. Select the range **A7:B10** and drag the range to cell **A6**. Enter **1** in cell **B4**. This will serve as a switch between a call option and a put option.

2. **Enter the January 1,350 Call Inputs.** Enter the inputs for the January 1,350 Call in the range **B4:B9** and enter the observed option price for the January 1,350 Call the in cell **B10**.

3. **Difference (Observed – Model).** The Difference (Observed - Model) is:
   Observed Option Price - Model Call Price for a Call Option
   Observed Option Price - Model Put Price for a Put Option.
   Enter **=IF(B4=1,B10-B17,B10-B23)** in cell **B26**.

4. **Copy the Entire Column over Nine More Columns**. Select the range **B4:B27** and copy it to the range **C4:K27**.

146

5. **Enter the Options Inputs.** In the range **B4:F27**, enter the inputs for the five call options. In the range **G4:K27**, enter the inputs for the five put options. Select the put volatilities in the range **G27:K27** and drag the range down to cell **G28**.

6. **Call Up Excel Solver.** From Excel's main menu, click on **Tools** and then **Solver**. (If you don't see **Solver** on the **Tools** Menu, then click on **Tools | Add-Ins**, check the **Solver Add-In** box, and click on **OK**.)

7. **Set-up Solver.** In the Solver dialog box, enter cell **B26** as the <u>Set Target Cell</u>. In the <u>Equal to</u> row, click on the option button for <u>Value of</u> and enter **0** in the adjacent box. Enter cell **B27** as the <u>By Changing Cell</u>. See figure below.

FIGURE 18.7 Solver dialog box.

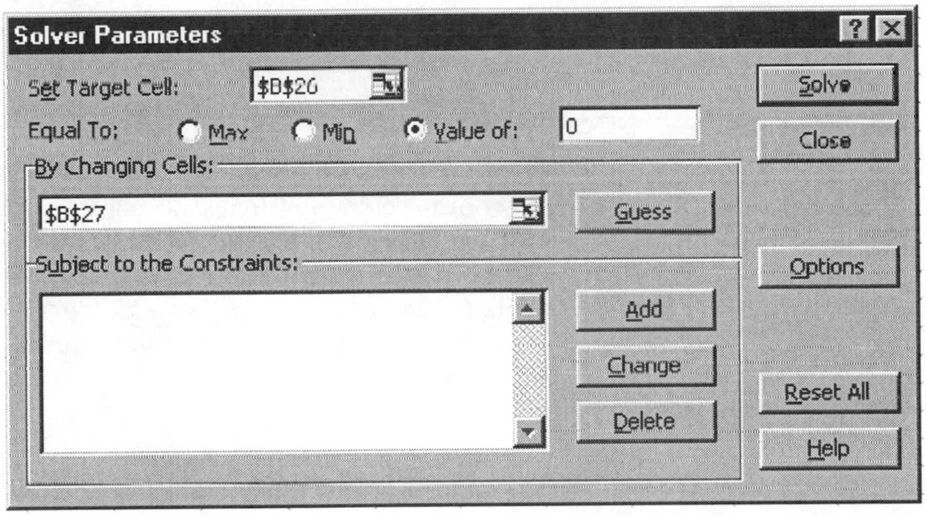

8. **Run Solver.** Click on the <u>Solve</u> button.

By trial and error, the Solver adjusts the value of the Implied Volatility in cell **B27** until the Difference (Observed – Model) in cell **B26** equals zero (within a very small error tolerance). This results in an implied volatility of 26.03%. Your results may differ by a slight amount (usually only in the second decimal) depending on Solver's error tolerance.

9. **Repeat.** Repeat steps **7** and **8** to solve the problems in columns **D, E, ..., K**.

10. **Graph the Implied Volatilities Across Exercise Prices and Option Types.** Highlight the range **B7:K7**, then hold down the Control button and (while still holding it down) select the range **B27:K28**. Next choose **Insert | Chart** from the main menu. Select an **XY(Scatter)** chart type and make other selections to complete the Chart Wizard.

FIGURE 18.8. Graph of the "Scowl" Pattern of Implied Volatilities.

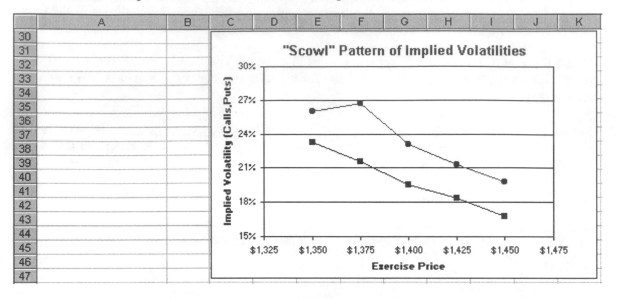

If the market's beliefs about the distribution of returns of the S&P 500 Index matched the theoretical distribution of returns assumed by the Black-Scholes model, then all of the implied volatilities would be the same. From the graph we see this is not the case. The implied volatility pattern declines sharply with the exercise price and puts have lower implied volatilities than calls. In the '70s and '80s, the typical implied volatility pattern was a U-shaped, "Smile" pattern. Since the '90s, it is more typical to see a downward-sloping, "Scowl" pattern.

Problems

Skill-Building Problems.

1. The current stock price of a company is $54.50, the continuous annual standard deviation was 53.00%, the exercise price of an European call on the stock is $58.00, the exercise price of an European put on the stock is $58.00, the time to maturity for both options is 0.43 years, and the yield on a riskfree Treasury Bill maturing on the same date at the options is 6.72%. Determine the current prices of the call and put.

2. Perform instant experiments on whether changing various inputs causes an increase or decrease in the Call Price and in the Put Price and by how much.
   (a.) What happens when the standard deviation is increased?
   (b.) What happens when the time to maturity is increased?
   (c.) What happens when the exercise price is increased?
   (d.) What happens when the riskfree rate is increased?
   (e.) What happens when the dividend yield is increased?
   (f.) What happens when the standard deviation is really close to zero?
   (g.) What happens when the time to maturity is really close to zero?

3. The current stock price of a company is $39.25, the continuous annual standard deviation was 47.00%, the exercise price of an European call on the stock is $36.00, the exercise price of an European put on the stock is $36.00, the time to maturity for both options is 0.82 years, the yield on a riskfree Treasury Bill maturing on the same date at the options is 4.23%, and the continuous

dividend paid throughout the year at the rate of 2.40% / year rate. Determine the current prices of the call and put.

4. The S&P 500 index closes at 2000. European call and put options on the S&P 500 index with the exercise prices show below trade for the following prices:

Exercise price	1,950	1,975	2,000	2,025	2,050
Call price	$88	$66	$47	$33	$21
Put price	$25	$26	$32	$44	$58

All options mature in 88 days. The S&P 500 portfolio pays a continuous dividend yield of 1.56% per year and the annual yield on a Treasury Bill which matures on the same day as the options is 4.63% per year. Determine what is the implied volatility of each of these calls and puts. What pattern do these implied volatilities follow across exercise prices and between calls vs. puts?

Live In-class Problems.

5. Given the partial Basics spreadsheet **BsoptbaZ.xls**, complete step **2 d1 and d2 Formulas, 3 Cumulative Normal Formulas**, and **4 European Call Price Formula**.

6. Given the partial Continuous Dividend spreadsheet **BsoptdiZ.xls**, do steps **2 Modify the d1 Formula, 3 Modify the Call Price Formula**, and **4 Modify the Put Price Formula**.

7. Given the partial Dynamic Chart spreadsheet **BsoptdyZ.xls**, do steps **10 Option Price** and **11 Add the Intrinsic Value**.

8. Given the partial Implied Volatility spreadsheet **BsoptimZ.xls**, do steps **6 Call Up Excel Solver, 7 Set-up Solver, 8 Run Solver**, and **9 Repeat**.

19 Debt And Equity Valuation

19.1 Two Methods

Problem. The Value of the Firm (V) is $340 million, the Face Value of the Debt (B) is $160 million, the time to maturity of the debt (t) is 2.00 years, the riskfree rate (k_{RF}) is 5.0%, and the standard deviation of the return on the firm's assets (σ) is 50.0%. There are two different methods for valuing the firm's equity and risky debt based in an option pricing framework. Using both methods, what the firm's Equity Value (E) and Risky Debt Value (D)? Do both methods produce the same result?

Solution Strategy. In the first method, equity is considered to be a call option. Thus, E = Call Price. For this call option, the underlying asset is the Value of the Firm (V) and the exercise price is the face value of the debt (B). Hence, the call price is calculated from the Black-Scholes call formula by substituting V for P and B for X. The rational is that if V > B, then the equityholders gain the net profit V-B. However, if V < B, then the equityholders avoid the loss by declaring bankruptcy, turning V over to the debtholders, and walking away with zero rather than owing money. Thus, the payoff to equityholders is Max (V - B, 0), which has the same payoff form as a call option. Further, we can use the fact that Debt plus Equity equals Total Value of Firm (D + E = V) and obtain the value of debt D = V - E = V - Call.

In the second method, Risky Debt is considered to be Riskfree Debt minus a Put option. Thus, D = Riskfree Debt - Put. For this put option, the underlying asset is also the Value of the Firm (V) and the exercise price is also the face value of the debt (B). Hence, the put price is calculated from the Black-Scholes put formula by substituting V for P and B for X. The rational is that the put option is a *Guarantee* against default in repaying the face value of the debt (B). Specifically, if V > B, then the equityholders repay the face value B in full and the value of the guarantee is zero. However, if V < B, then the equityholders only pay V and default on the rest, so the guarantee must pay the balance B - V. Thus, the payoff on the guarantee is Max (B - V, 0), which has the same payoff form as a put option. Further, we can use the fact that Debt plus Equity equals Total Value of Firm (D + E = V) and obtain E = V - Risky Debt = V - (Riskfree Debt - Put).

FIGURE 19.1 Spreadsheet for Stocks and Risky Bonds.

	A	B	C	D	E	F	G
1	**DEBT AND EQUITY VALUATION**				**Two Methods**		
2							
3	**Inputs**						
4	Value of Firm (V)	$340.00					
5	Firm Asset Std Dev (σ)	50.0%					
6	Risk-free Rate (k_{RF})	5.0%					
7	Face Value of Debt (B)	$160.00					
8	Time to Maturity (t)	2.00					
9							
10	**Outputs**						
11	d1	1.561					
12	d2	0.854					
13	N(d1)	0.941					
14	N(d2)	0.803					
15	Call Price	$203.54					
16							
17	-d1	-1.561					
18	-d2	-0.854					
19	N(-d1)	0.059					
20	N(-d2)	0.197					
21	Put Price	$8.31					
22	Riskfree Debt Value	$144.77					
23							
24		**Method One:**			**Method Two:**		
25		**Equity is a Call**			**Risky Debt is Riskfree Debt minus Put**		
26							
27	Equity Value (E)	= Call	$203.54		= V - Riskfree Debt + Put	$203.54	
28							
29	Risky Debt Value (D)	= V - Call	$136.46		= Riskfree Debt - Put	$136.46	
30							
31	Total Value of Firm (V)	= V	$340.00		= V	$340.00	

How To Build Your Own Spreadsheet Model.

1. **Start with the Black Scholes Option Pricing - Basics Spreadsheet and Change the Inputs.** Open the spreadsheet that you created for Black Scholes Option Pricing – Basics and immediately save the spreadsheet under a new name using the **File | Save As** command. Relabel the inputs in the range **A4:A8** and enter the new inputs values into the range **B4:B8**.

2. **Riskfree Debt Value.** The present value of riskfree debt paying B at maturity is $Be^{-k_{RF}t}$. Enter **=B7*EXP(-B6*B8)** in cell **B22**.

3. **Method One.** Based on the first method:

   o Equity = Call Price. Enter **=B15** in cell **C27**.

   o Risky Debt = V – Call Price. Enter **=B4-B15** in cell **C29**.

   o Total Value = Equity + Risky Debt. Enter **=C27+C29** in cell **C31**.

4. **Method Two.** Based on the second method:

- o Equity = V – Riskfree Debt Value + Put Price. Enter **=B4-B22+B21** in cell **F27**.

- o Risky Debt = Riskfree Debt Value – Put Price. Enter **=B22-B21** in cell **F29**.

- o Total Value = Equity + Risky Debt. Enter **=F27+F29** in cell **F31**.

Both methods of doing the calculation find that the Equity Value (E) = $203.54 and the Risky Debt Value (D) = $136.46. We can verify that both methods should always generate the same results. Consider what we get if we equate the Method One and Method Two expressions for the Equity Value (E): **Call Price = V – Riskfree Bond Value + Put Price**. You may recognize this as a alternative version of Put-Call Parity. The standard version of Put-Call Parity is: **Call Price = Stock Price - Bond Price + Put Price**. To get the alternative version, just substitute V for the Stock Price and substitute the Riskfree Bond Value for the Bond Price. Consider what we get if we equate the Method One and Method Two expressions for the Risky Debt Value (D): **V - Call Price = Riskfree Bond - Put Price**. This is simply a rearrangement of the alternative version of Put-Call Parity. Since Put-Call Parity is always true, then both methods of valuing debt and equity will always yield the same results!

19.2 Impact of Risk

Problem. What impact does the firm's risk have upon the firm's Debt and Equity valuation? Specifically, if you increased Firm Asset Standard Deviation, then what would happen to the firm's Equity Value and Risky Debt Value?

Solution Strategy. Create a **Data Table** of Equity Value and Risky Debt Value for different input values for the Firm's Asset Standard Deviation. Then graph the results and interpret it.

FIGURE 19.2 Spreadsheet of the Sensitivity of Equity Value and Risky Debt Value.

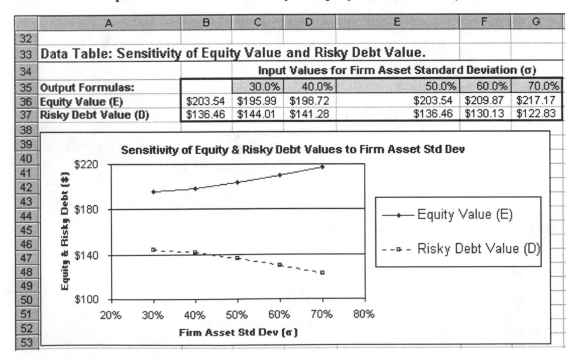

	A	B	C	D	E	F	G
32							
33	**Data Table: Sensitivity of Equity Value and Risky Debt Value.**						
34			**Input Values for Firm Asset Standard Deviation (σ)**				
35	**Output Formulas:**		30.0%	40.0%	50.0%	60.0%	70.0%
36	**Equity Value (E)**	$203.54	$195.99	$198.72	$203.54	$209.87	$217.17
37	**Risky Debt Value (D)**	$136.46	$144.01	$141.28	$136.46	$130.13	$122.83

How To Build This Spreadsheet Model.

1. **Start with the Debt and Equity Valuation - Two Methods Spreadsheet and Change the Inputs.** Open the spreadsheet that you created for Debt and Equity Valuation – Two Methods and immediately save the spreadsheet under a new name using the **File | Save As** command.

2. **Create A List of Input Values and Add Two More Output Formulas.** Create a list of input values for the Firm Asset Standard Deviation (30.0%, 40.0%, 50.0%, etc.) in the range **C35:G35**. Add two more output formulas. One that references the firm's Equity Value (E) by entering the formula **=C27** in cell **B36**. Another that references the firm's Risky Debt Value (D) by entering the formula **=C29** in cell **B37**.

3. **Data Table.** Select the range **B35:G37** for the Data Table. This range includes both the list of input values at the top of the data table and the two output formulas on the side of the data table. Then choose **Data | Table** from the main menu and a **Table** dialog box pops up. Enter the Firm Asset Standard Deviation cell **B5** in the **Row Input Cell** and click on **OK**.

4. **Graph the Sensitivity Analysis.** Highlight the range **C36:G37** and then choose **Insert | Chart** from the main menu. Select an **XY(Scatter)** chart type and make other selections to complete the Chart Wizard.

Looking at the chart, we see that increasing the firm's asset standard deviation causes a wealth transfer from debtholders to equityholders. This may seem surprising, but this is a direct consequence equity being a call option and debt being V *minus* a call option. We know that increasing the standard deviation makes a call more valuable, so equivalently increases the firm's asset standard deviation makes the firm's Equity Value more valuable and reduces the Risky Debt Value by the same amount.

The intuitive rational for this is that an increase in standard deviation allows equityholders to benefit from more frequent and bigger increases in V, while not being hurt by more frequent and bigger decreases in V. In the later case, the equityholders are going to declare bankruptcy anyway so they don't care how much V drops. Debtholders are the mirror image. They do *not* benefit from more frequent and bigger increases in V since repayment is capped at B, but they are *hurt* by more frequent and bigger decreases in V. In the latter case, the size of the repayment default (B – V) increases as V drops more.

The possibility of transferring wealth from debtholders to equityholders (or visa versa) illustrates the potential for conflict between equityholders and debtholders. Equityholders would like the firm to take on riskier projects, but debtholders would like the firm to focus on safer projects. Whether the firm ultimately decides to take on risky or safe projects will determine how wealth is divided between the two groups.

Problems

Skill-Building Problems.

1. The Value of the Firm (V) is $780 million, the Face Value of the Debt (B) is $410 million, the time to maturity of the debt (t) is 1.37 years, the riskfree rate (k_{RF}) is 3.2%, and the standard deviation of the return on the firm's assets (σ) is 43.0%. Using both methods of debt and equity valuation, what the firm's Equity Value (E) and Risky Debt Value (D)? Do both methods produce the same result?

2. Determine what impact an increase in the Firm Asset Standard Deviation has on the firm's Equity Value and Risky Debt Value.

Live In-class Problems.

3. Given the partial Two Methods spreadsheet **DevaltwZ.xls**, do step **3 Method One** and **4 Method Two**.

4. Given the partial Impact of Risk spreadsheet **DevalimZ.xls**, complete step **2 Create A List of Input Values and Add Two More Output Formulas** and **3 Data Table**.

20 Real Options

20.1 Using Black Scholes

Problem. You have the opportunity to purchase a piece of land for $0.4 million which has known reserves of 200,000 barrels of oil. The reserves are worth $5.3 million based on the current crude oil price of $26.50 per barrel. The cost of building the plant and equipment to develop the oil is $5.7 million, so it is not profitable to develop these reserves right now. However, development may become profitable in the future if the price of crude oil goes up. For simplicity, assume there is a single date in 1.0 years when you can decide whether to develop the oil or not. Further assume that all of the oil can be produced immediately. Using historical data on crude oil prices, you determine that the mean value of the reserves is $6.0 million based on a mean value of the one-year ahead oil price of $30.00 per barrel and the standard deviation 30.0%. The riskfree rate is 6.0% and cost of capital for a project of this type is 13.80%. What is the project's NPV using the Black-Scholes call formula? What would the NPV be if you committed to develop it today no matter what and thus, (incorrectly) ignored the option to develop the oil only if it is profitable?

Solution Strategy. One year from now, you will develop the oil if it is profitable and won't develop it if it is not. Thus, the payoff is Max (Value of the Reserves - Cost of Development, 0). This is identical to the payoff of a call option, where the Cost of Development is the Exercise Price and the Value of the Reserves Now is the Asset Price Now. Calculate the NPV using the Black-Scholes call formula. Calculate the NPV Ignoring Option projecting expected cash flows from developing the oil no matter whether it is profitable or not and discounting these expected cash flows back to the present.

FIGURE 20.1 Spreadsheet for Real Options Using Black-Scholes.

	A	B	C	D	E
1	**REAL OPTIONS**	**Using Black-Scholes**			
2					
3	**Inputs**				
4	Asset Value Now (V)	$5.30			
5	Asset Value Std Dev - Annual (σ)	30.0%			
6	Riskfree Rate - Annual (k_{RF})	6.0%			
7	Exercise Price (X)	$5.70			
8	Time To Maturity - Years (t)	1.00			
9	Land Cost = Cost of Real Option	$0.40			
10	Date 1 Expected Asset Value	$6.00			
11	Discount Rate	13.80%			
12					
13	**NPV Using Black-Scholes**				
14	d1	0.11			
15	d2	-0.19			
16	N(d1)	0.543			
17	N(d2)	0.424			
18	Black-Scholes Value	$0.60			
19	NPV Using Black-Scholes	$0.20			
20					
21	**NPV Ignoring Option**				
22	Date	0	1		
23	Expected Cash Flows ($ Millions)	($0.40)	$0.30		
24	Present Value of Exp Cash Flows	($0.40)	$0.26		
25	NPV Ignoring Option	($0.14)			

How To Build Your Own Spreadsheet Model.

<u>NPV Using Black-Scholes</u>

1. **Start with the Black Scholes Option Pricing - Basics Spreadsheet and Change the Inputs.** Open the spreadsheet that you created for Black Scholes Option Pricing – Basics and immediately save the spreadsheet under a new name using the **File | Save As** command. Add three rows by selecting the range **A9:A11** and clicking on **Insert | Rows**. Then delete five rows by selecting **A20:A24**, clicking on **Edit | Delete...**, selecting **Entire Row**, and click on **OK**. Relabel the input labels in the range **A4:A11** and enter the new inputs values into the range **B4:B11**. Lock in the first eleven rows as titles by selecting cell **A12** and clicking on **Window | Freeze Panes**.

2. **NPV Using Black-Scholes.** The NPV of the proposal to purchase the land is the difference between the Value of the Real Option (as calculated by the Black-Scholes call formula) and the Cost of the Real Option (equal to the cost of the land). Enter **=B18-B9** in cell **B19**.

<u>NPV Ignoring Option</u>

3. **Expected Cash Flows.** The Date 0 Expected Cash Flow is a (negative) payment for the cost of the land. Enter **=-B9** in cell **B23**. The Date 1 Expected Cash Flow is Date 1 Expected Asset Value minus Exercise Price (Cost of Development). Enter **=B10-B7** in cell **C23**.

4. **Present Value of Expected Cash Flows.** Calculate the Present Value of the Expected Cash Flow = (Expected Cash Flow) / ((1 + Discount Rate)^Date Number). Enter **=B23/((1+$B$11)^B22)** in cell **B24** and copy it to cell **C24**. The Discount Rate $B$11 uses an absolute reference because it stays constant from date to date.

5. **NPV Ignoring Option.** Calculate the NPV Ignoring Option by summing all of the present value of cash flow terms. Enter **=SUM(B24:C24)** in cell **B25**.

We obtain opposite results from the two approaches. The NPV Using Black-Scholes is positive $0.20 million, whereas the Ignore Option NPV is negative ($0.14) million. NPV Ignoring Option incorrectly concludes that the project should be rejected. This mistake happened precisely because it ignores the option to develop oil only when profitable and avoid the cost of development when it is not. NPV Using Black-Scholes correctly demonstrates that the project should be accepted. This is because the *value of the option* to develop the oil when profitable is greater than the *cost of the option* (i.e., the cost of the land).

20.2 Using The Binomial Model

Problem. Given the same real options project as was analyzed using the Black-Scholes technique, calculate the project's NPV using the binomial model. Compare this result to the Black-Scholes result.

Solution Strategy. The project can be viewed as a call option, where the Cost of Development is the Exercise Price and the Value of the Reserves Now is the Asset Price Now. This call option can be valued using the Binomial Option Pricing model. Open the spreadsheet that you created for Binomial Option Pricing - Risk Neutral. Make some changes so that the standard deviation and other inputs can be translated into corresponding up and down movements of the binomial model. Calculate the NPV Using Binomial by taking the Binomial Option Value and subtracting the cost of the option (i.e., cost of the land).

FIGURE 20.2 Spreadsheet for Real Options Using The Binomial Model.

	A	B	C	D	E	F	G	H	I	J
1	REAL OPTIONS	Using The Binomial Model								
2					Call	Continuous				
3	Inputs				Outputs					
4	Option Type: 1=Call, 0=Put	1			Time / Period	0.13				
5	Asset Value Now (V)	$5.30			Riskfree Rate / Period	0.75%				
6	Asset Value Std Dev (σ)	30.00%			Up Movement / Period	11.19%				
7	Riskfree Rate - Annual (k_RF)	6.00%			Down Movement / Period	-10.06%				
8	Exercise Price (X)	$5.70			Risk Neutral Probability	50.89%				
9	Time To Maturity - Yrs (t)	1.00								
10	Number of Periods	8								
11	Annualization Convention: 1=Discrete, 0=Continuous	0								
12	Land Cost = Real Opt Cost	$0.40								
13										
14		Now								Maturity
15	Period	0	1	2	3	4	5	6	7	8
16	Time	0.000	0.125	0.250	0.375	0.500	0.625	0.750	0.875	1.000
17										
18	Stock	$5.30	$5.89	$6.55	$7.29	$8.10	$9.01	$10.02	$11.14	$12.38
19			$4.77	$5.30	$5.89	$6.55	$7.29	$8.10	$9.01	$10.02
20				$4.29	$4.77	$5.30	$5.89	$6.55	$7.29	$8.10
21					$3.86	$4.29	$4.77	$5.30	$5.89	$6.55
22						$3.47	$3.86	$4.29	$4.77	$5.30
23							$3.12	$3.47	$3.86	$4.29
24								$2.80	$3.12	$3.47
25									$2.52	$2.80
26										$2.27
27										
28	Call	$0.62	$0.92	$1.34	$1.89	$2.59	$3.43	$4.40	$5.48	$6.68
29			$0.31	$0.50	$0.78	$1.19	$1.76	$2.49	$3.35	$4.32
30				$0.12	$0.21	$0.37	$0.63	$1.03	$1.63	$2.40
31					$0.03	$0.06	$0.11	$0.22	$0.43	$0.85
32						$0.00	$0.00	$0.00	$0.00	$0.00
33							$0.00	$0.00	$0.00	$0.00
34								$0.00	$0.00	$0.00
35									$0.00	$0.00
36										$0.00
37										
38	NPV Using Binomial	$0.22								

How To Build Your Own Spreadsheet Model.

1. **Start with the Risk Neutral Spreadsheet.** Open the spreadsheet that you created for Binomial Option Pricing – Risk Neutral and immediately save the spreadsheet under a new name using the **File | Save As** command.

2. **Rearrange the Inputs.** Select the range **A6:B7** and drag the range (hover the cursor over the lower highlighted line, click on the left mouse button, and hold it down while you move it) to cell **E6**. Select the range **A8:B8** and drag the range to cell **E5**. Select the range **A9:B11** and drag the range to cell **A8**. Select the range **E4:F4** and drag the range to cell **E8**.

3. **Enter the New Inputs.** Enter the Full-Scale Real Data inputs in the range **B4:B11** as shown in **Figure 2**. Enter **30.00%** in cell **B6** for the Annual Standard Deviation. The value in cell **B11**

157

serves as a switch between the Discrete and Continuous Annualization Conventions. To highlight which annualization convention is in use, enter **=IF($B$11=1,"Discrete","Continuous")** in cell **E2**.

4. **Calculate the New Outputs.** Calculate four new "per period" outputs:

   o **Time / Period** = (Time To Maturity) / (Number of Periods). Enter **=B9/B10** in cell **F4**.

   o **Riskfree Rate / Period** = (Annual Riskfree Rate) * (Time / Period) under the discrete annualization convention or = exp[(Annual Riskfree Rate) * (Time / Period)] -1 under the continuous annualization convention. Enter **=IF($B$11=1,B7*F4,EXP(B7*F4)-1)** in cell **F5**.

   o **Up Movement / Period** = (Annual Standard Deviation) * Square Root (Time / Period) under the discrete annualization convention or = exp[(Annual Standard Deviation) * Square Root (Time / Period)] -1 under the continuous annualization convention. Enter **=IF($B$11=1,B6*SQRT(F4),EXP(B6*SQRT(F4))-1)** in cell **F6**.

   o **Down Movement / Period** = -(Annual Standard Deviation) * Square Root (Time / Period) under the discrete annualization convention or = exp[-(Annual Standard Deviation) * Square Root (Time / Period)] -1 under the continuous annualization convention. Enter **=IF($B$11=1,-B6*SQRT(F4),EXP(-B6*SQRT(F4))-1)** in cell **F7**.

5. **NPV Using Binomial.** The formula for NPV Using Binomial = Call Value - Real Option Cost. Enter **=B28-B12** in cell **B38**.

The NPV Using Binomial is $0.22 million. This is very close to the NPV Using Black-Scholes of $0.20 million. If you expanded the number of steps in the binomial model to 50 or 100 steps, then the difference between the two techniques would go away.

Looking at the range **J28:J36**, we see that in 4 of the 9 states of nature the value of the reserves is high enough to lead to oil development and thus profit is positive. In 5 of the 9 states of nature the value of reserves is low enough that the oil is *not* developed and thus the profit is zero.

20.3 Sensitivity to Std Dev

Problem. We know that an increase in the standard deviation of an underlying asset makes regular call and put options more valuable. In the real option setting of the oil development project, what would happen if you increased asset value standard deviation to the NPV Using Black-Scholes, NPV Ignoring Option, and NPV Using Binomial?

FIGURE 20.3 A Spreadsheet of the Sensitivity to Std Dev.

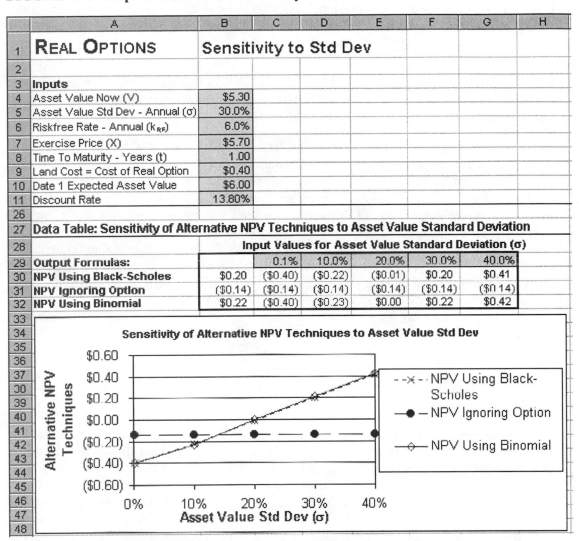

	A	B	C	D	E	F	G	H
1	**REAL OPTIONS**	**Sensitivity to Std Dev**						
2								
3	**Inputs**							
4	Asset Value Now (V)	$5.30						
5	Asset Value Std Dev - Annual (σ)	30.0%						
6	Riskfree Rate - Annual (k_RF)	6.0%						
7	Exercise Price (X)	$5.70						
8	Time To Maturity - Years (t)	1.00						
9	Land Cost = Cost of Real Option	$0.40						
10	Date 1 Expected Asset Value	$6.00						
11	Discount Rate	13.80%						
26								
27	**Data Table: Sensitivity of Alternative NPV Techniques to Asset Value Standard Deviation**							
28			**Input Values for Asset Value Standard Deviation (σ)**					
29	**Output Formulas:**		0.1%	10.0%	20.0%	30.0%	40.0%	
30	**NPV Using Black-Scholes**	$0.20	($0.40)	($0.22)	($0.01)	$0.20	$0.41	
31	**NPV Ignoring Option**	($0.14)	($0.14)	($0.14)	($0.14)	($0.14)	($0.14)	
32	**NPV Using Binomial**	$0.22	($0.40)	($0.23)	$0.00	$0.22	$0.42	

How To Build Your Own Spreadsheet Model.

1. **Start with the Real Options - Using Black Scholes Spreadsheet.** Open the spreadsheet that you created for Real Options - Using Black Scholes and immediately save the spreadsheet under a new name using the **File | Save As** command. Open the spreadsheet that you created for Real Options - Using The Binomial Model and keep it open. You will build a cell link to it and from it.

2. **Create A List of Input Values, Two Output Formulas, And A Standard Deviation Connection.** Create a list of input values for the Asset Value Standard Deviation (0.1%, 10.0%, 20.0%, etc.) in the range **C29:G29**. Create three output formulas. One that references the NPV Using Black Scholes by entering the formula =B19 in cell **B30**. Another that references the NPV Ignoring Option by entering the formula =B25 in cell **B31**. A third that references the NPV Using Binomial by entering the formula =[Realobin.xls]Sheet1!$B$38 in cell **B32**, where the **[Realobin.xls]** is the name of the Excel file which contains the **Real Options - Using The Binomial Model** spreadsheet. We need to connect the standard deviation on the two spreadsheets so that the Data Table will work across both spreadsheets. In the Real Options - Using The Binomial Model spreadsheet, enter =[Realostd.xls]Sheet1!$B$5 in cell **B6**.

159

3. **Data Table.** Select the range **B29:G32** for the Data Table. This range includes both the list of input values at the top of the data table and the three output formulas on the side of the data table. Then choose **Data | Table** from the main menu and a **Table** dialog box pops up. Enter the Asset Value Standard Deviation cell **B5** in the **Row Input Cell** and click on **OK**.

4. **Graph the Sensitivity Analysis.** Highlight the range **C29:G32** and then choose **Insert | Chart** from the main menu. Select an **XY(Scatter)** chart type and make other selections to complete the Chart Wizard.

Both the data table and the graph show that NPV Using Black Scholes and NPV Using Binomial are nearly identical over a wide range of Asset Value Standard Deviations with only a penny or two difference. Figure 1 shows that an increase in Asset Value Standard Deviation causes both the NPV Using Black Scholes and the NPV Using Binomial to increase, but leaves the NPV Ignoring Option unaffected. Why does the increase in Asset Value Standard Deviation have such different effects? Essentially, the two option-based techniques take into account the option to develop the oil *only if it is profitable* and this option ncreases in value as standard deviation goes up. By contrast, the NPV Ignoring Option approach precommits to develop the oil no matter what and thus ignores the option. Indeed, Asset Value Standard Deviation is not even an input in the NPV Ignoring Option calculation. This lack of sensitivity to Asset Value Standard Deviation by the NPV Ignoring Option technique is an error. Both the NPV Using Black Scholes and the NPV Using Binomial show the correct amount of sensitivity to Asset Value Standard Deviation.

Problems

Skill-Building Problems.

1. You have the opportunity to purchase a piece of land for $0.7 million which has known reserves of 375,000 barrels of oil. The reserves are worth $12.6 million based on the current crude oil price of $33.60 per barrel. The cost of building the plant and equipment to develop the oil is $4.5 million, so it is not profitable to develop these reserves right now. However, development may become profitable in the future if the price of crude oil goes up. For simplicity, assume there is a single date in 1.4 years when you can decide whether to develop the oil or not. Further assume that all of the oil can be produced immediately. Using historical data on crude oil prices, you determine that the mean value of the reserves is $13.4 million based on a mean value of the one-year ahead oil price of $35.73 per barrel and the standard deviation 30.0%. The riskfree rate is 4.7% and cost of capital for a project of this type is 12.15%. What is the project's NPV using the Black-Scholes call formula? What would the NPV be if you committed to develop it today no matter what and thus, (incorrectly) ignored the option to develop the oil only if it is profitable?

2. Given the same real options project as problem 1, calculate the project's NPV using the binomial model. Compare this result to the Black-Scholes result.

3. What would happen if you increased asset value standard deviation to the NPV Using Black-Scholes, NPV Ignoring Option, and NPV Using Binomial?

Live In-class Problems.

4. Given the partial Using Black Scholes spreadsheet **RealoblZ.xls**, do steps **2 NPV using Black-Scholes, 3 Expected Cash Flows, 4 Present Value of Expected Cash Flows,** and **5 NPV Ignoring Option**.

5. Given the partial Using The Binomial Model spreadsheet **RealoblZ.xls**, do step **5 NPV using Binomial**.

6. Given the partial Sensitivity to Std Dev spreadsheet **RealostZ.xls**, do steps **2 Create A List of Input Values, Two Output Formulas, And A Standard Deviation Connection** and **3 Data Table**.

SINGLE PC LICENSE AGREEMENT AND LIMITED WARRANTY

READ THIS LICENSE CAREFULLY BEFORE USING THIS PACKAGE. BY USING THIS PACKAGE, YOU ARE AGREEING TO THE TERMS AND CONDITIONS OF THIS LICENSE. IF YOU DO NOT AGREE, DO NOT OPEN THE PACKAGE. PROMPTLY RETURN THE UNOPENED PACKAGE AND ALL ACCOMPANYING ITEMS TO THE PLACE YOU OBTAINED THEM [[FOR A FULL REFUND OF ANY SUMS YOU HAVE PAID FOR THE SOFTWARE]]. *THESE TERMS APPLY TO ALL LICENSED SOFTWARE ON THE DISK EXCEPT THAT THE TERMS FOR USE OF ANY SHAREWARE OR FREEWARE ON THE DISKETTES ARE AS SET FORTH IN THE ELECTRONIC LICENSE LOCATED ON THE DISK:*

1. GRANT OF LICENSE and OWNERSHIP: The enclosed computer programs <<and data>> ("Software") are licensed, not sold, to you by Prentice-Hall, Inc. ("We" or the "Company") and in consideration [[of your payment of the license fee, which is part of the price you paid]] [[of your purchase or adoption of the accompanying Company textbooks and/or other materials,]] and your agreement to these terms. We reserve any rights not granted to you. You own only the disk(s) but we and/or our licensors own the Software itself. This license allows you to use and display your copy of the Software on a single computer (i.e., with a single CPU) at a single location for academic use only, so long as you comply with the terms of this Agreement. You may make one copy for back up, or transfer your copy to another CPU, provided that the Software is usable on only one computer.

2. RESTRICTIONS: You may not transfer or distribute the Software or documentation to anyone else. Except for backup, you may not copy the documentation or the Software. You may not network the Software or otherwise use it on more than one computer or computer terminal at the same time. You may not reverse engineer, disassemble, decompile, modify, adapt, translate, or create derivative works based on the Software or the Documentation. You may be held legally responsible for any copying or copyright infringement which is caused by your failure to abide by the terms of these restrictions.

3. TERMINATION: This license is effective until terminated. This license will terminate automatically without notice from the Company if you fail to comply with any provisions or limitations of this license. Upon termination, you shall destroy the Documentation and all copies of the Software. All provisions of this Agreement as to limitation and disclaimer of warranties, limitation of liability, remedies or damages, and our ownership rights shall survive termination.

4. LIMITED WARRANTY AND DISCLAIMER OF WARRANTY: Company warrants that for a period of 60 days from the date you purchase this SOFTWARE (or purchase or adopt the accompanying textbook), the Software, when properly installed and used in accordance with the Documentation, will operate in substantial conformity with the description of the Software set forth in the Documentation, and that for a period of 30 days the disk(s) on which the Software is delivered shall be free from defects in materials and workmanship under normal use. The Company does not warrant that the Software will meet your requirements or that the operation of the Software will be uninterrupted or error-free. Your only remedy and the Company's only obligation under these limited warranties is, at the Company's option, return of the disk for a refund of any amounts paid for it by you or replacement of the disk. THIS LIMITED WARRANTY IS THE ONLY WARRANTY PROVIDED BY THE COMPANY AND ITS LICENSORS, AND THE COMPANY AND ITS LICENSORS DISCLAIM ALL OTHER WARRANTIES, EXPRESS OR IMPLIED, INCLUDING WITHOUT LIMITATION, THE IMPLIED WARRANTIES OF MERCHANTABILITY AND FITNESS FOR A PARTICULAR PURPOSE. THE COMPANY DOES NOT WARRANT, GUARANTEE OR MAKE ANY REPRESENTATION REGARDING THE ACCURACY, RELIABILITY, CURRENTNESS, USE, OR RESULTS OF USE, OF THE SOFTWARE.

5. LIMITATION OF REMEDIES AND DAMAGES: IN NO EVENT, SHALL THE COMPANY OR ITS EMPLOYEES, AGENTS, LICENSORS, OR CONTRACTORS BE LIABLE FOR ANY INCIDENTAL, INDIRECT, SPECIAL, OR CONSEQUENTIAL DAMAGES ARISING OUT OF OR IN CONNECTION WITH THIS LICENSE OR THE SOFTWARE, INCLUDING FOR LOSS OF USE, LOSS OF DATA, LOSS OF INCOME OR PROFIT, OR OTHER LOSSES, SUSTAINED AS A RESULT OF INJURY TO ANY PERSON, OR LOSS OF OR DAMAGE TO PROPERTY, OR CLAIMS OF THIRD PARTIES, EVEN IF THE COMPANY OR AN AUTHORIZED REPRESENTATIVE OF THE COMPANY HAS BEEN ADVISED OF THE POSSIBILITY OF SUCH DAMAGES. IN NO EVENT SHALL THE LIABILITY OF THE COMPANY FOR DAMAGES WITH RESPECT TO THE SOFTWARE EXCEED THE AMOUNTS ACTUALLY PAID BY YOU, IF ANY, FOR THE SOFTWARE OR THE ACCOMPANYING TEXTBOOK. BECAUSE SOME JURISDICTIONS DO NOT

ALLOW THE LIMITATION OF LIABILITY IN CERTAIN CIRCUMSTANCES, THE ABOVE LIMITATIONS MAY NOT ALWAYS APPLY TO YOU.

6. GENERAL: THIS AGREEMENT SHALL BE CONSTRUED IN ACCORDANCE WITH THE LAWS OF THE UNITED STATES OF AMERICA AND THE STATE OF NEW YORK, APPLICABLE TO CONTRACTS MADE IN NEW YORK, AND SHALL BENEFIT THE COMPANY, ITS AFFILIATES AND ASSIGNEES. HIS AGREEMENT IS THE COMPLETE AND EXCLUSIVE STATEMENT OF THE AGREEMENT BETWEEN YOU AND THE COMPANY AND SUPERSEDES ALL PROPOSALS OR PRIOR AGREEMENTS, ORAL, OR WRITTEN, AND ANY OTHER COMMUNICATIONS BETWEEN YOU AND THE COMPANY OR ANY REPRESENTATIVE OF THE COMPANY RELATING TO THE SUBJECT MATTER OF THIS AGREEMENT. If you are a U.S. Government user, this Software is licensed with "restricted rights" as set forth in subparagraphs (a)-(d) of the Commercial Computer-Restricted Rights clause at FAR 52.227-19 or in subparagraphs (c)(1)(ii) of the Rights in Technical Data and Computer Software clause at DFARS 252.227-7013, and similar clauses, as applicable. Should you have any questions concerning this agreement or if you wish to contact the Company for any reason, please contact in writing: [Faculty Services, Prentice Hall, One Lake Street, Upper Saddle River, NJ 07458